NORTHLANDERS

BOOK TWO: THE CROSS + THE HAMMER

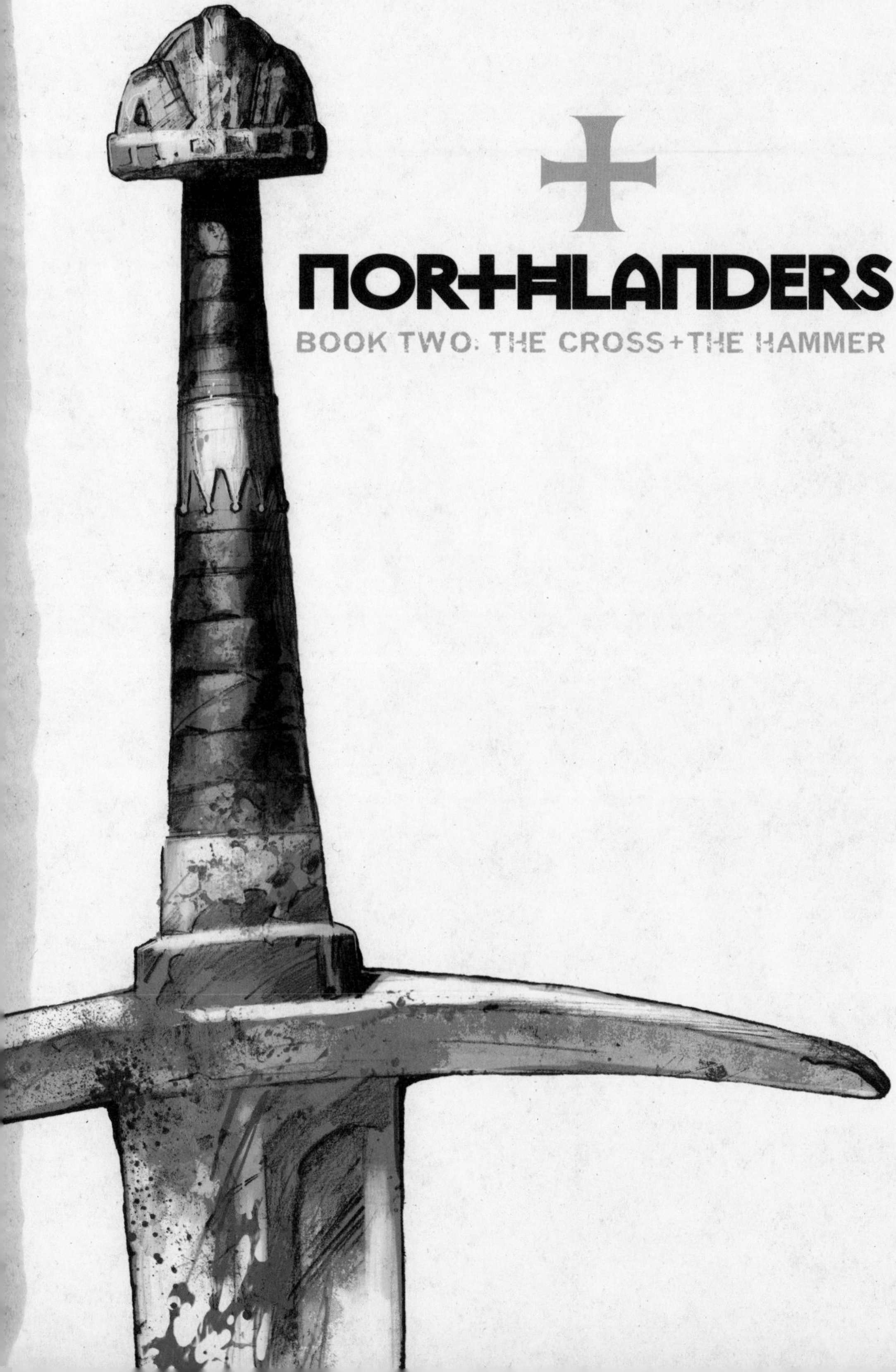

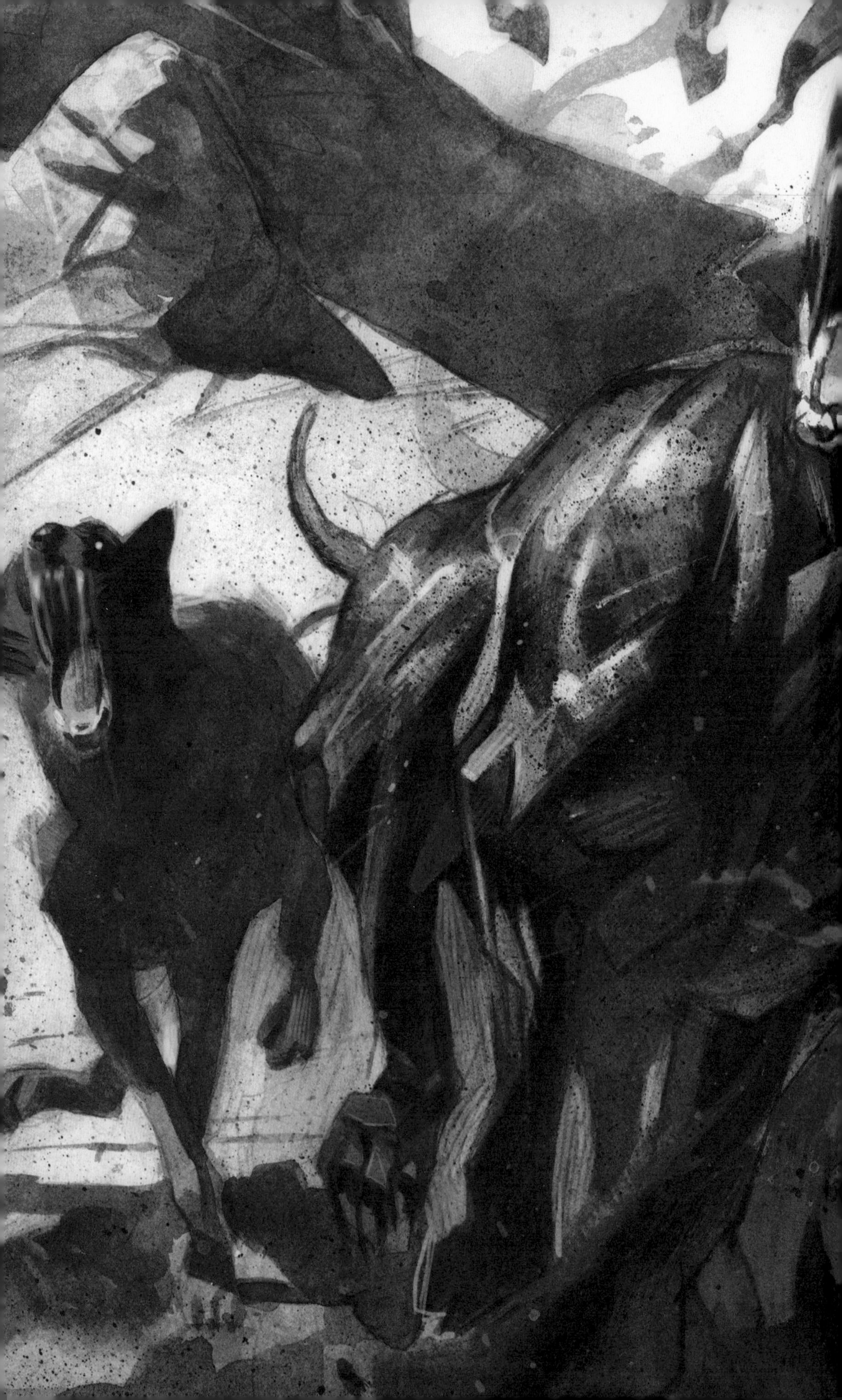

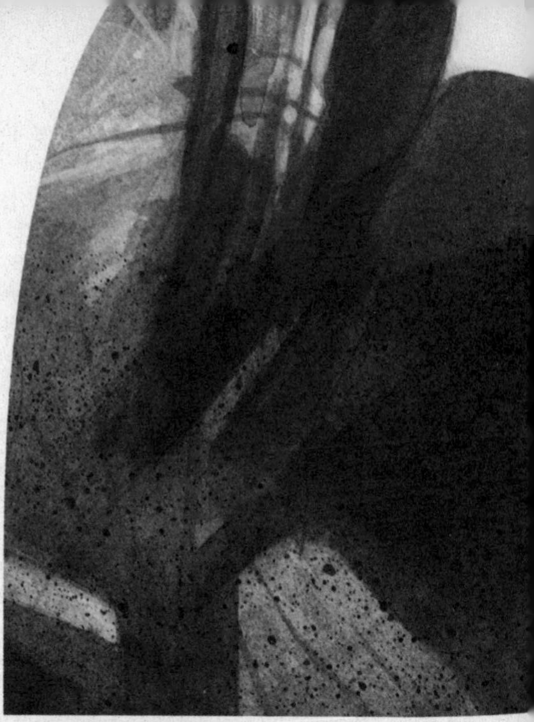

NORTHLANDERS

BOOK TWO: THE CROSS + THE HAMMER

Brian Wood Writer

Ryan Kelly Artist

Dave McCaig Colorist

Travis Lanham Letterer

Original series covers by

Massimo Carnevale

NORTHLANDERS created by

Brian Wood

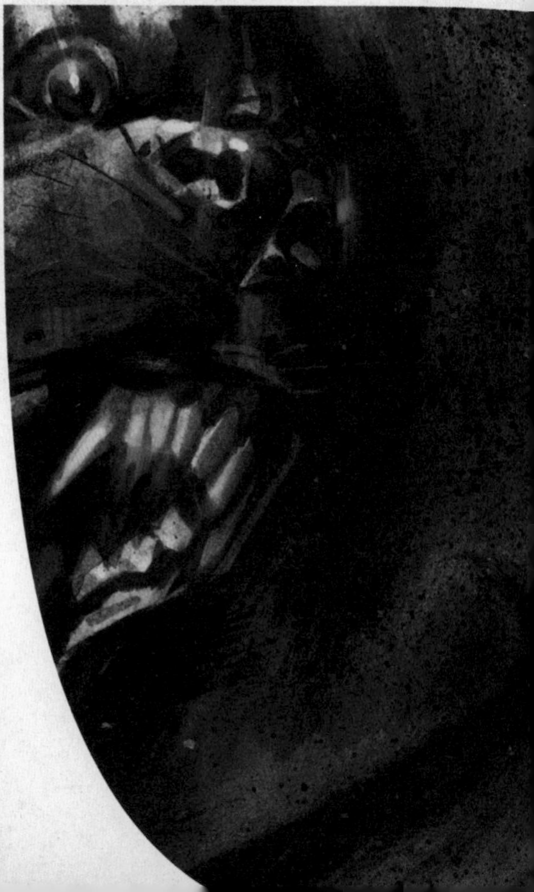

Karen Berger Senior VP-Executive Editor | **Will Dennis** Editor-original series | **Mark Doyle** Assistant Editor-original series

Bob Harras Editor-collected edition | **Robbin Brosterman** Senior Art Director | **Paul Levitz** President & Publisher

Georg Brewer VP-Design & DC Direct Creative | **Richard Bruning** Senior VP-Creative Director

Patrick Caldon Executive VP-Finance & Operations | **Chris Caramalis** VP-Finance

John Cunningham VP-Marketing | **Terri Cunningham** VP-Managing Editor

Amy Genkins Senior VP-Business & Legal Affairs | **Alison Gill** VP-Manufacturing | **David Hyde** VP-Publicity

Hank Kanalz VP-General Manager, WildStorm | **Jim Lee** Editorial Director-WildStorm

Gregory Noveck Senior VP-Creative Affairs | **Sue Pohja** VP-Book Trade Sales

Steve Rotterdam Senior VP-Sales & Marketing | **Cheryl Rubin** Senior VP-Brand Management

Alysse Soll VP-Advertising & Custom Publishing | **Jeff Trojan** VP-Business Development, DC Direct | **Bob Wayne** VP-Sales

Cover illustration by Massimo Carnevale and design by Brian Wood
Logo design by Jennifer Redding
Publication design by Amelia Grohman

NORTHLANDERS: THE CROSS+THE HAMMER

Published by DC Comics. Cover and compilation © 2009 DC Comics. All Rights Reserved.

Originally published in single magazine form as NORTHLANDERS 11-16.
Copyright © 2008, 2009 Brian Wood and DC Comics. All Rights Reserved.
VERTIGO and all characters, their distinctive likenesses and related elements featured in this publication are trademarks
of DC Comics. The stories, characters and incidents featured in this publication are entirely fictional.
DC Comics does not read or accept unsolicited submissions of ideas, stories or artwork.

DC Comics | 1700 Broadway, New York, NY 10019 | A Warner Bros. Entertainment Company
Printed in Canada | First Printing | ISBN: 978-1-4012-2296-3

1 A Rising Tide of Falling Blood

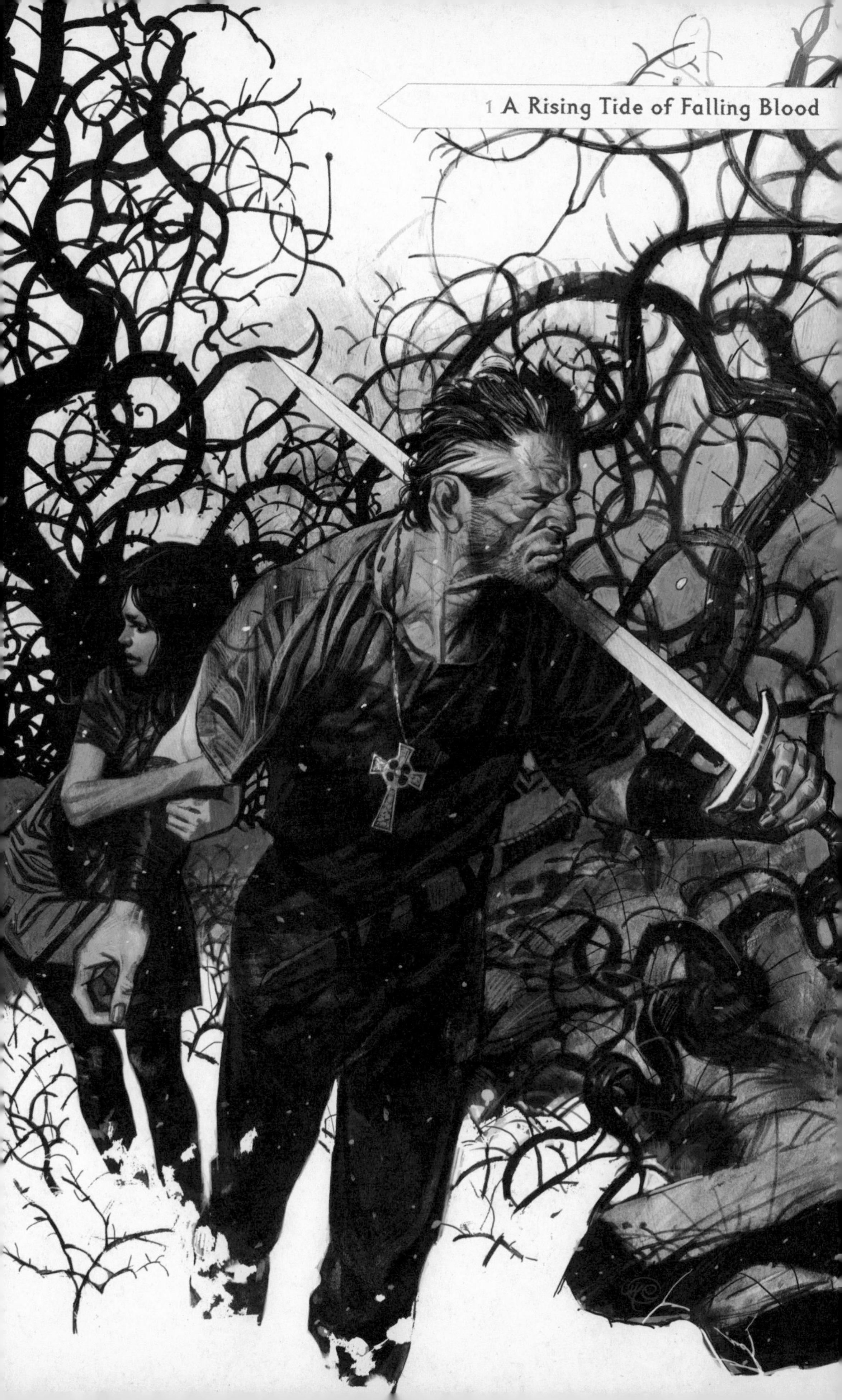

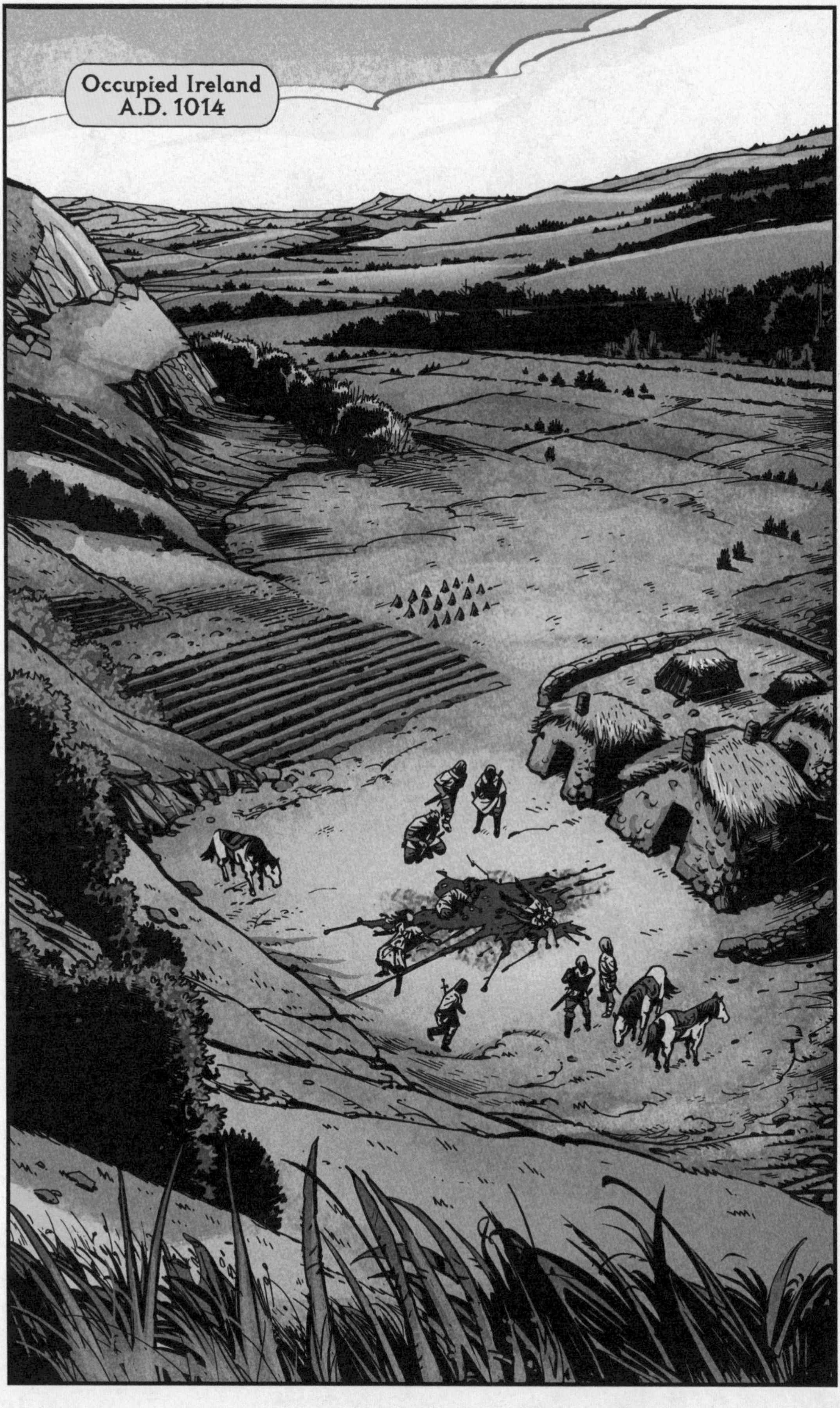
Occupied Ireland
A.D. 1014

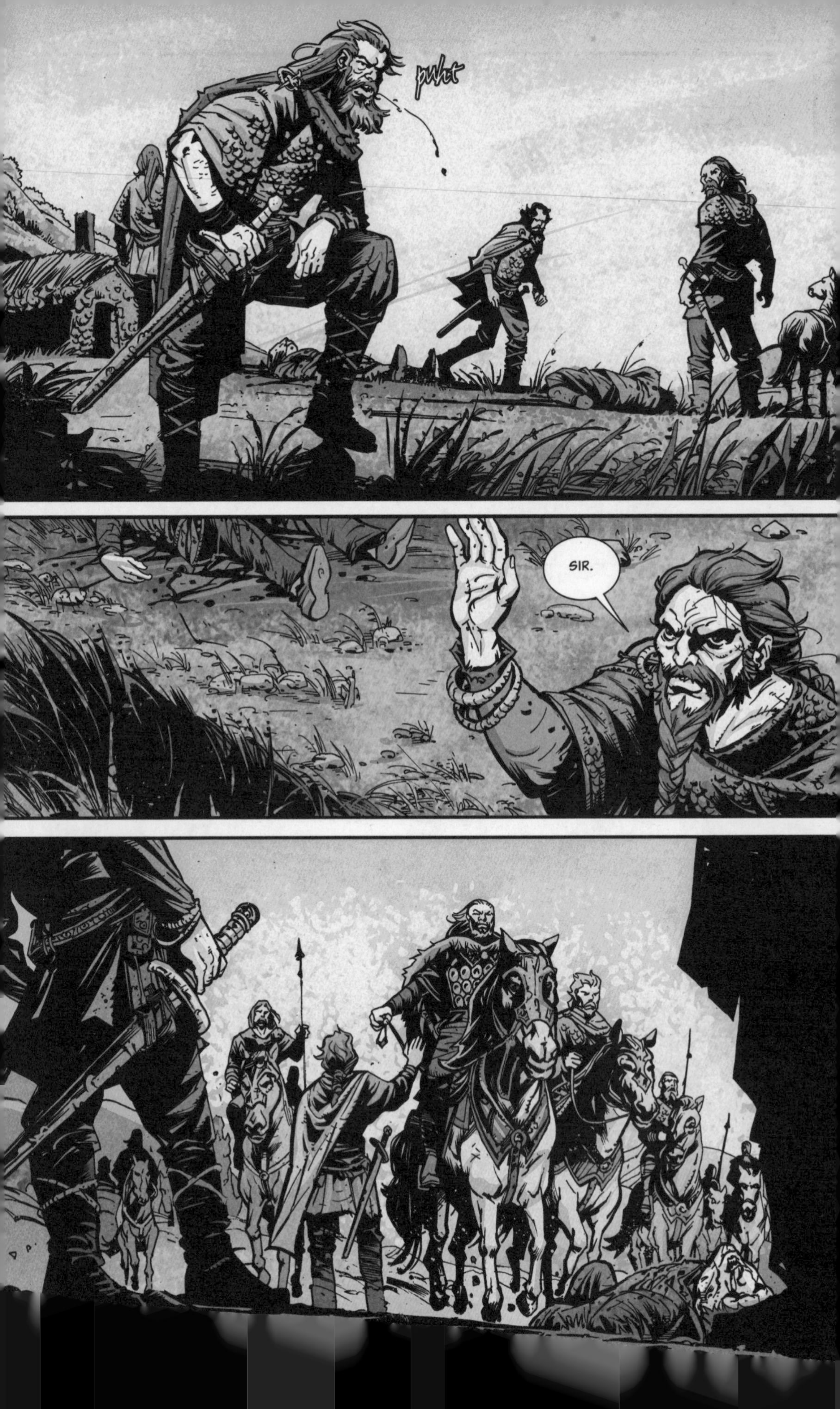
pwht
SIR.

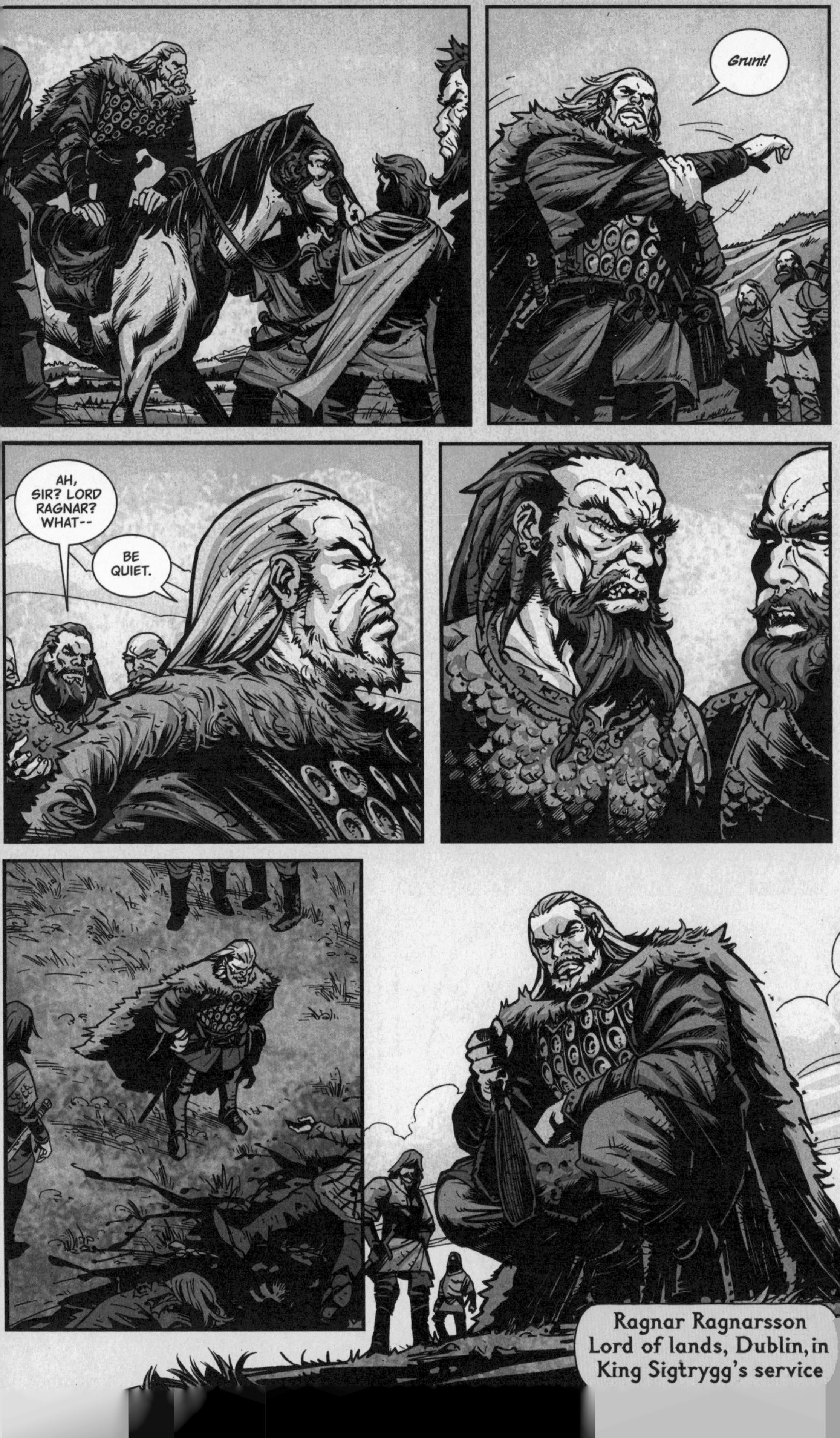
Grunt!
AH, SIR? LORD RAGNAR? WHAT--
BE QUIET.
Ragnar Ragnarsson
Lord of lands, Dublin, in
King Sigtrygg's service

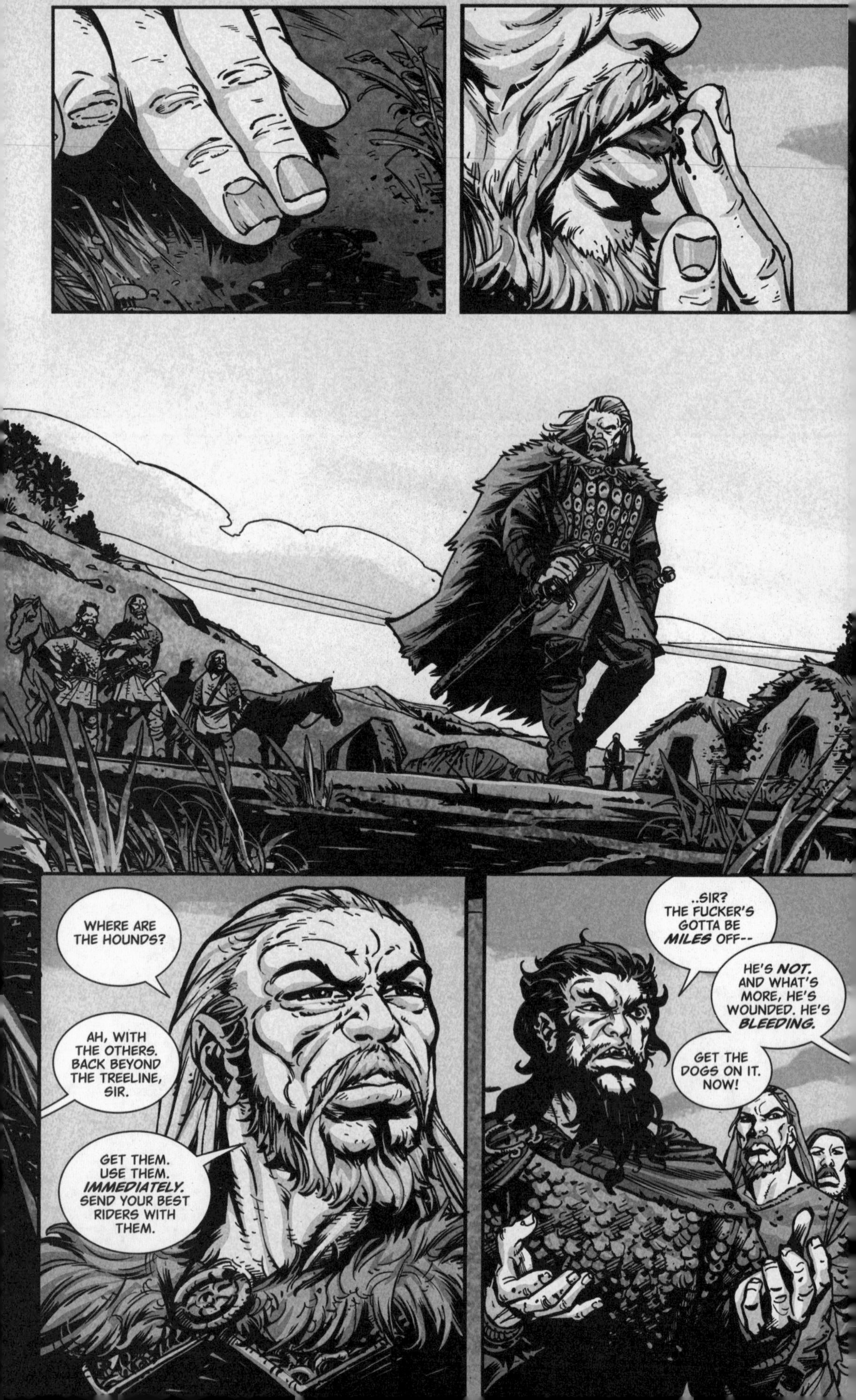
WHERE ARE THE HOUNDS?
AH, WITH THE OTHERS. BACK BEYOND THE TREELINE, SIR.
GET THEM. USE THEM. IMMEDIATELY. SEND YOUR BEST RIDERS WITH THEM.
..SIR? THE FUCKER'S GOTTA BE MILES OFF--
HE'S NOT. AND WHAT'S MORE, HE'S WOUNDED. HE'S BLEEDING.
GET THE DOGS ON IT. NOW!

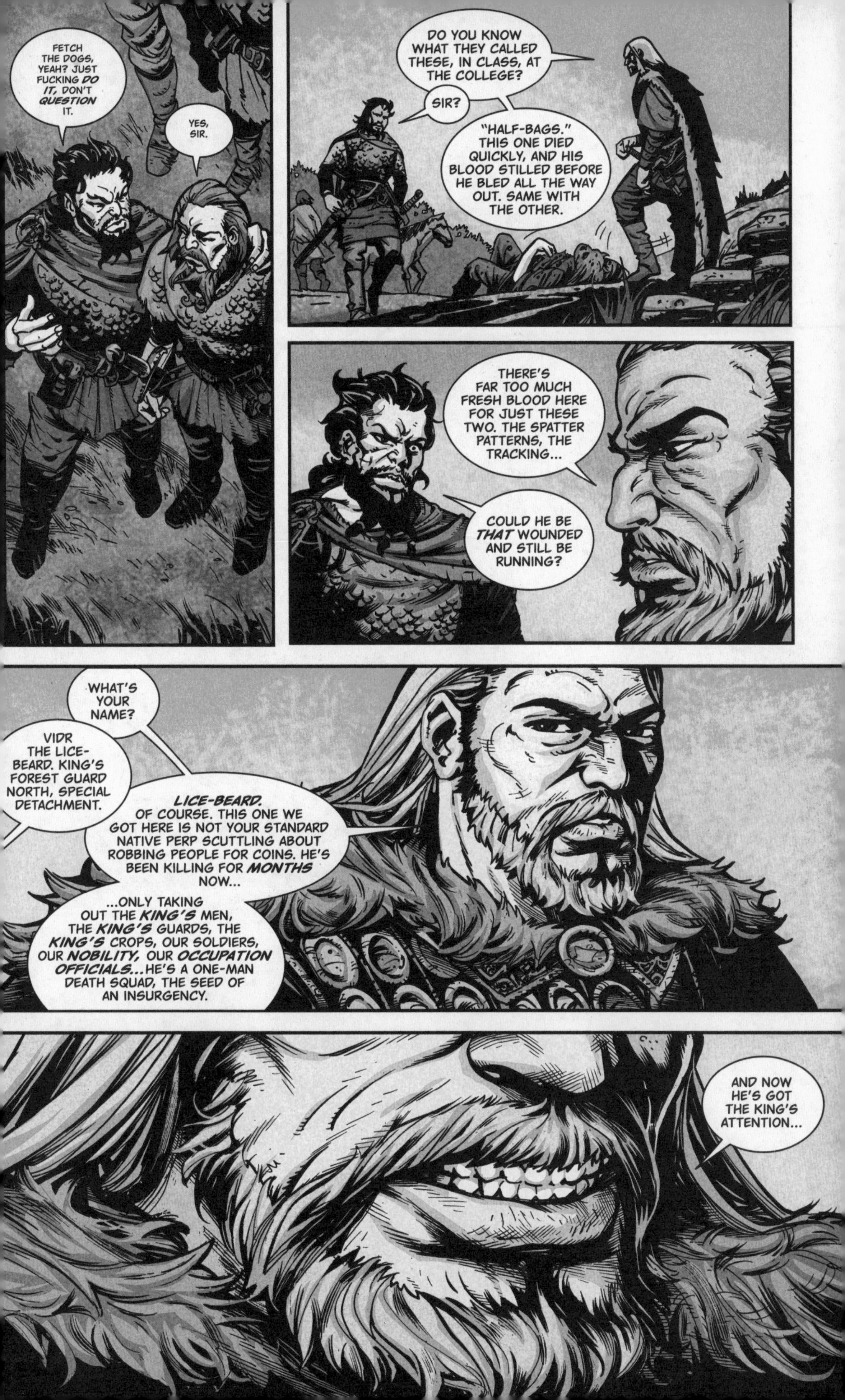
FETCH THE DOGS, YEAH? JUST FUCKING *DO IT,* DON'T *QUESTION* IT.
YES, SIR.
DO YOU KNOW WHAT THEY CALLED THESE, IN CLASS, AT THE COLLEGE?
SIR?
"HALF-BAGS." THIS ONE DIED QUICKLY, AND HIS BLOOD STILLED BEFORE HE BLED ALL THE WAY OUT. SAME WITH THE OTHER.
THERE'S FAR TOO MUCH FRESH BLOOD HERE FOR JUST THESE TWO. THE SPATTER PATTERNS, THE TRACKING...
COULD HE BE *THAT* WOUNDED AND STILL BE RUNNING?
WHAT'S YOUR NAME?
VIDR THE LICE-BEARD. KING'S FOREST GUARD NORTH, SPECIAL DETACHMENT.
LICE-BEARD. OF COURSE. THIS ONE WE GOT HERE IS NOT YOUR STANDARD NATIVE PERP SCUTTLING ABOUT ROBBING PEOPLE FOR COINS. HE'S BEEN KILLING FOR *MONTHS* NOW...
...ONLY TAKING OUT THE *KING'S* MEN, THE *KING'S* GUARDS, THE *KING'S* CROPS, OUR SOLDIERS, OUR *NOBILITY,* OUR *OCCUPATION OFFICIALS...* HE'S A ONE-MAN DEATH SQUAD, THE SEED OF AN INSURGENCY.
AND NOW HE'S GOT THE KING'S ATTENTION...

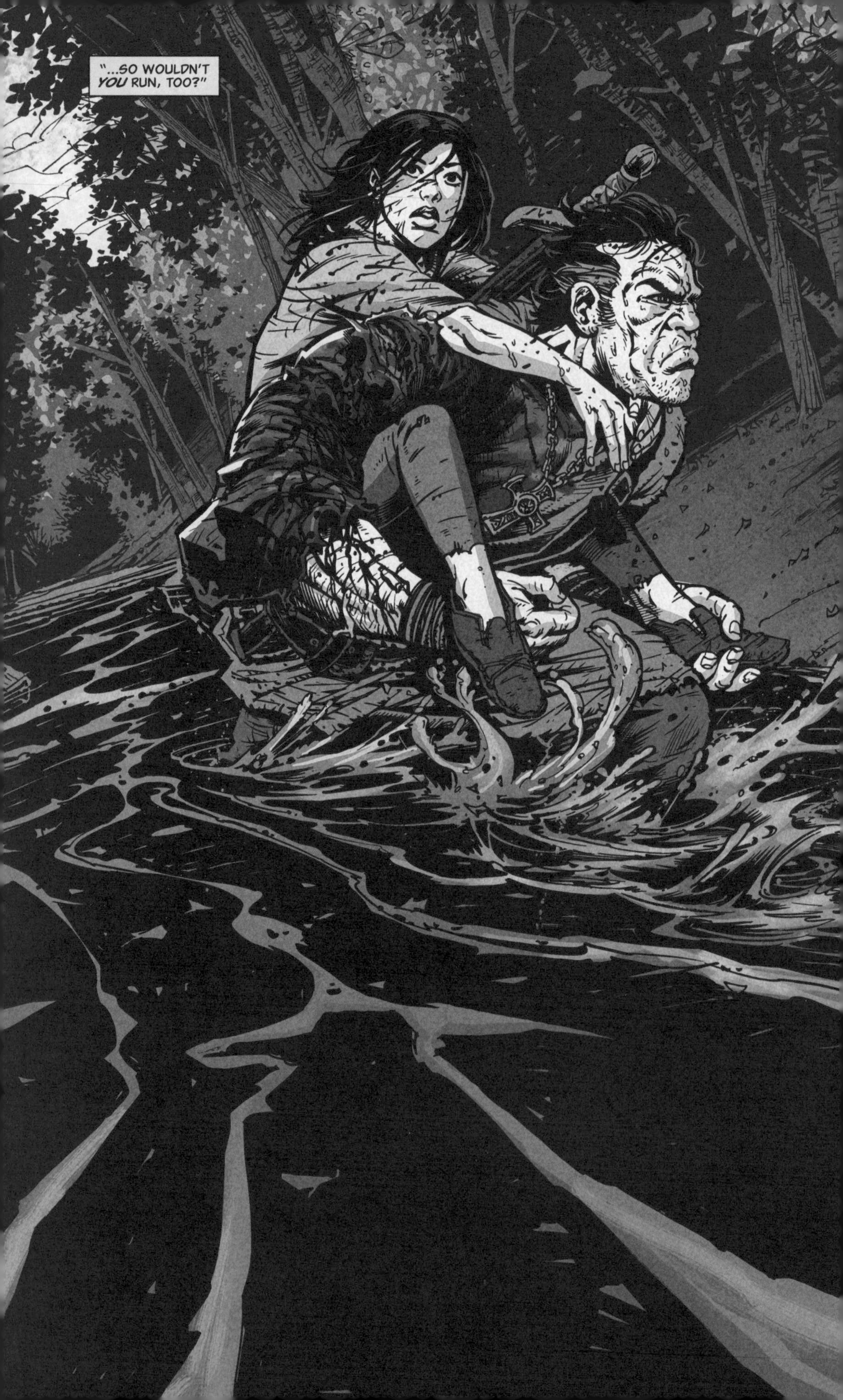
"...SO WOULDN'T YOU RUN, TOO?"

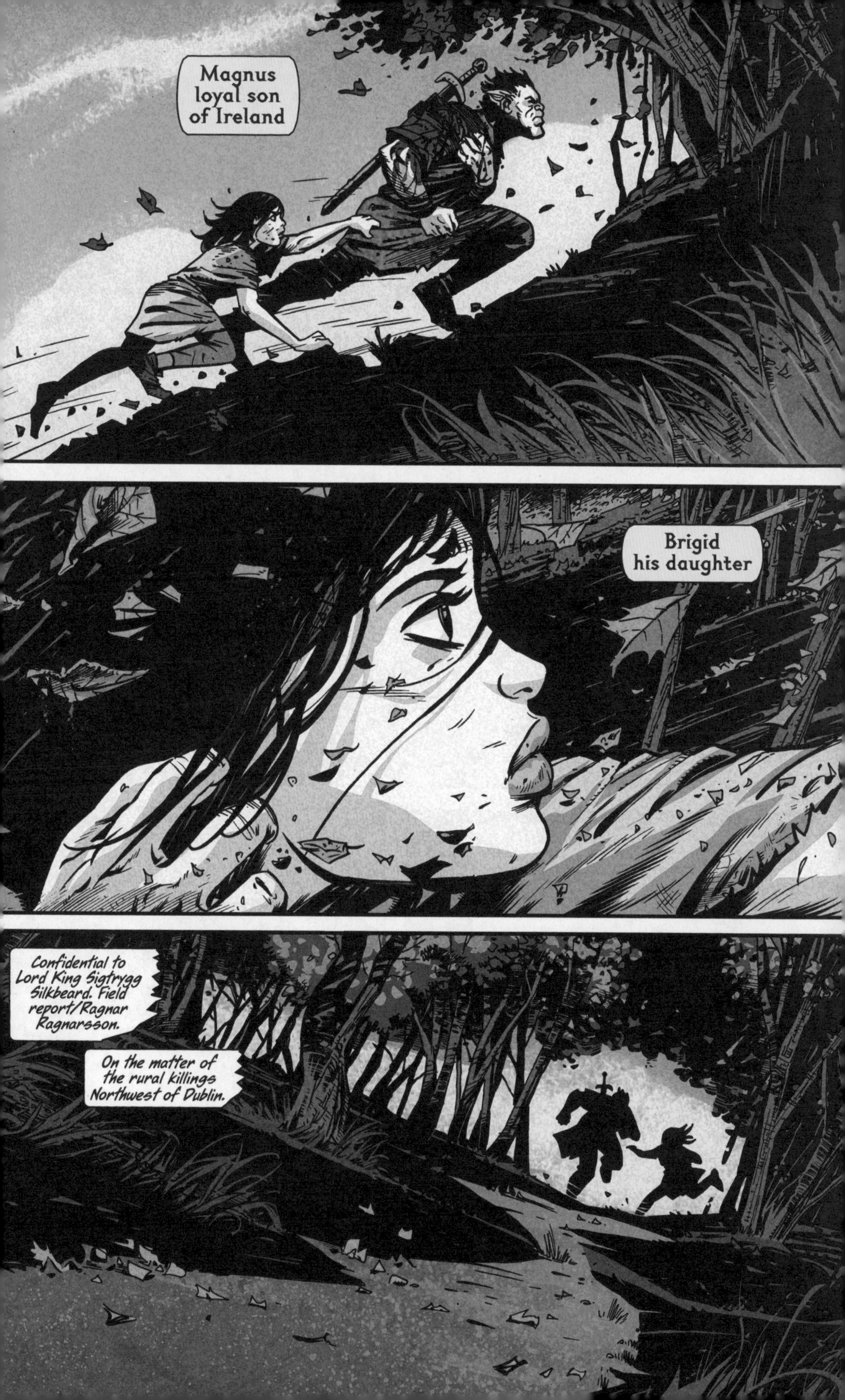
Magnus loyal son of Ireland
Brigid his daughter
Confidential to Lord King Sigtrygg Silkbeard. Field report/Ragnar Ragnarsson.
On the matter of the rural killings Northwest of Dublin.

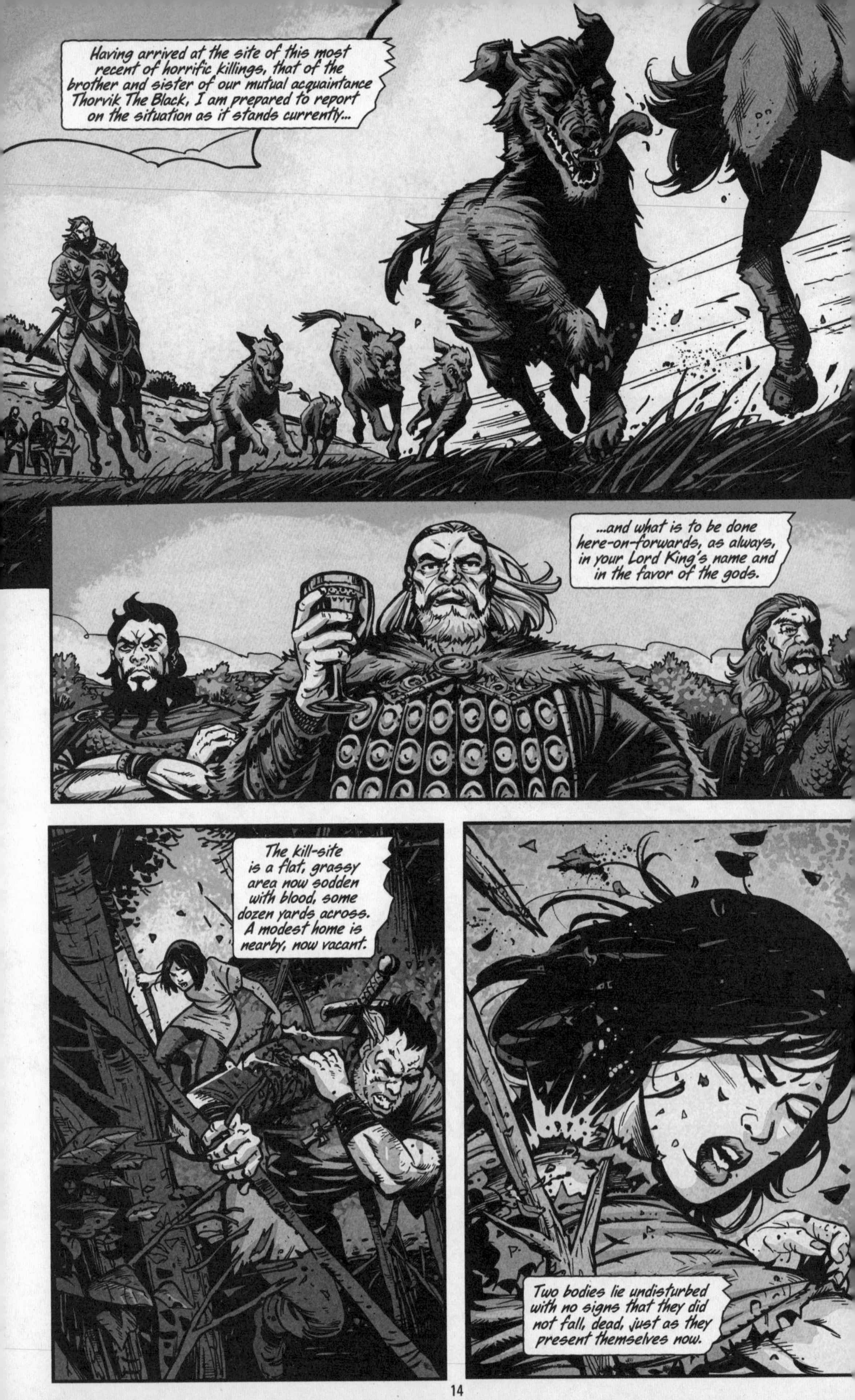
Having arrived at the site of this most recent of horrific killings, that of the brother and sister of our mutual acquaintance Thorvik The Black, I am prepared to report on the situation as it stands currently...
...and what is to be done here-on-forwards, as always, in your Lord King's name and in the favor of the gods.
The kill-site is a flat, grassy area now sodden with blood, some dozen yards across. A modest home is nearby, now vacant.
Two bodies lie undisturbed with no signs that they did not fall, dead, just as they present themselves now.

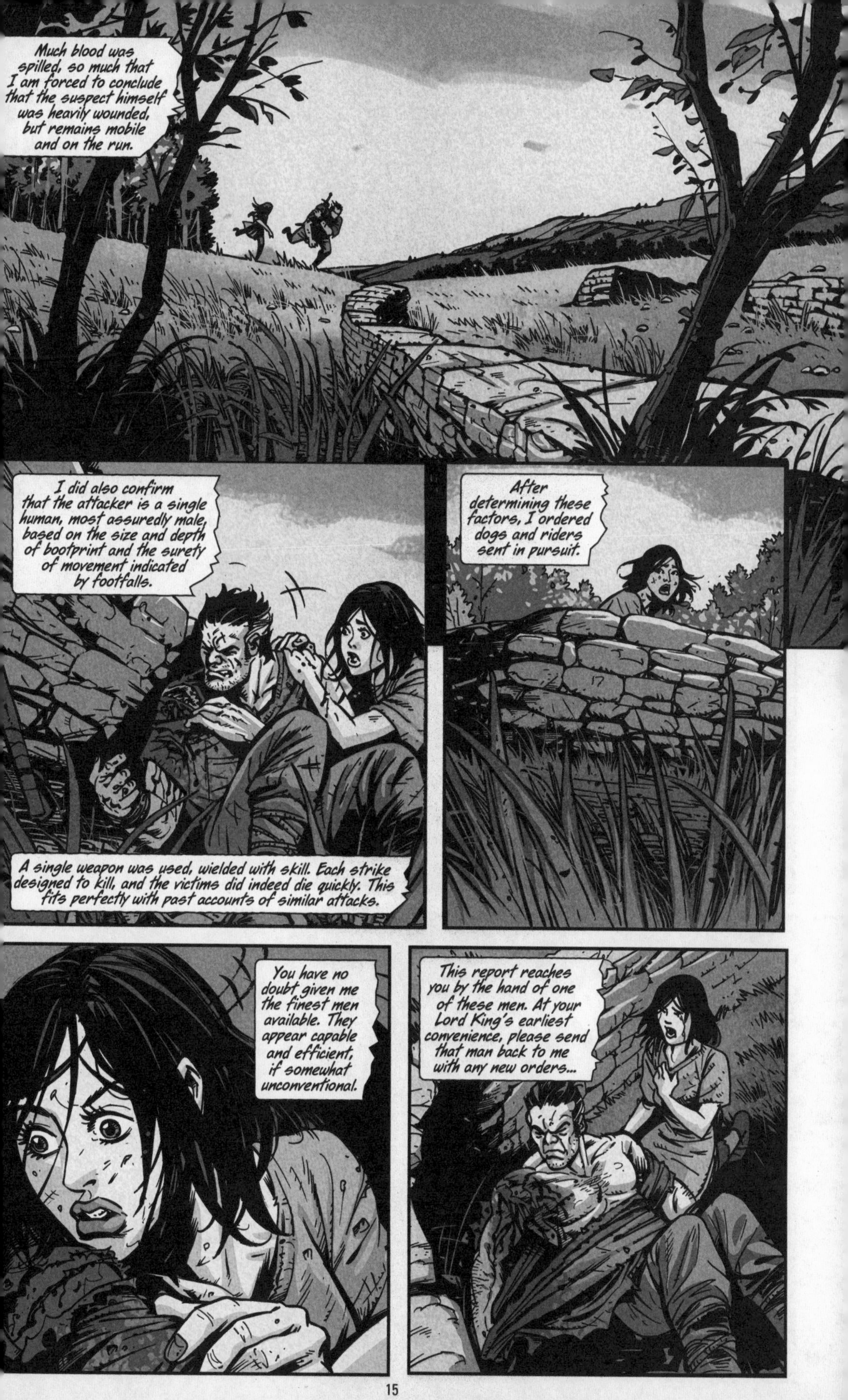

Much blood was spilled, so much that I am forced to conclude that the suspect himself was heavily wounded, but remains mobile and on the run.
I did also confirm that the attacker is a single human, most assuredly male, based on the size and depth of bootprint and the surety of movement indicated by footfalls.
A single weapon was used, wielded with skill. Each strike designed to kill, and the victims did indeed die quickly. This fits perfectly with past accounts of similar attacks.
After determining these factors, I ordered dogs and riders sent in pursuit.
You have no doubt given me the finest men available. They appear capable and efficient, if somewhat unconventional.
This report reaches you by the hand of one of these men. At your Lord King's earliest convenience, please send that man back to me with any new orders...

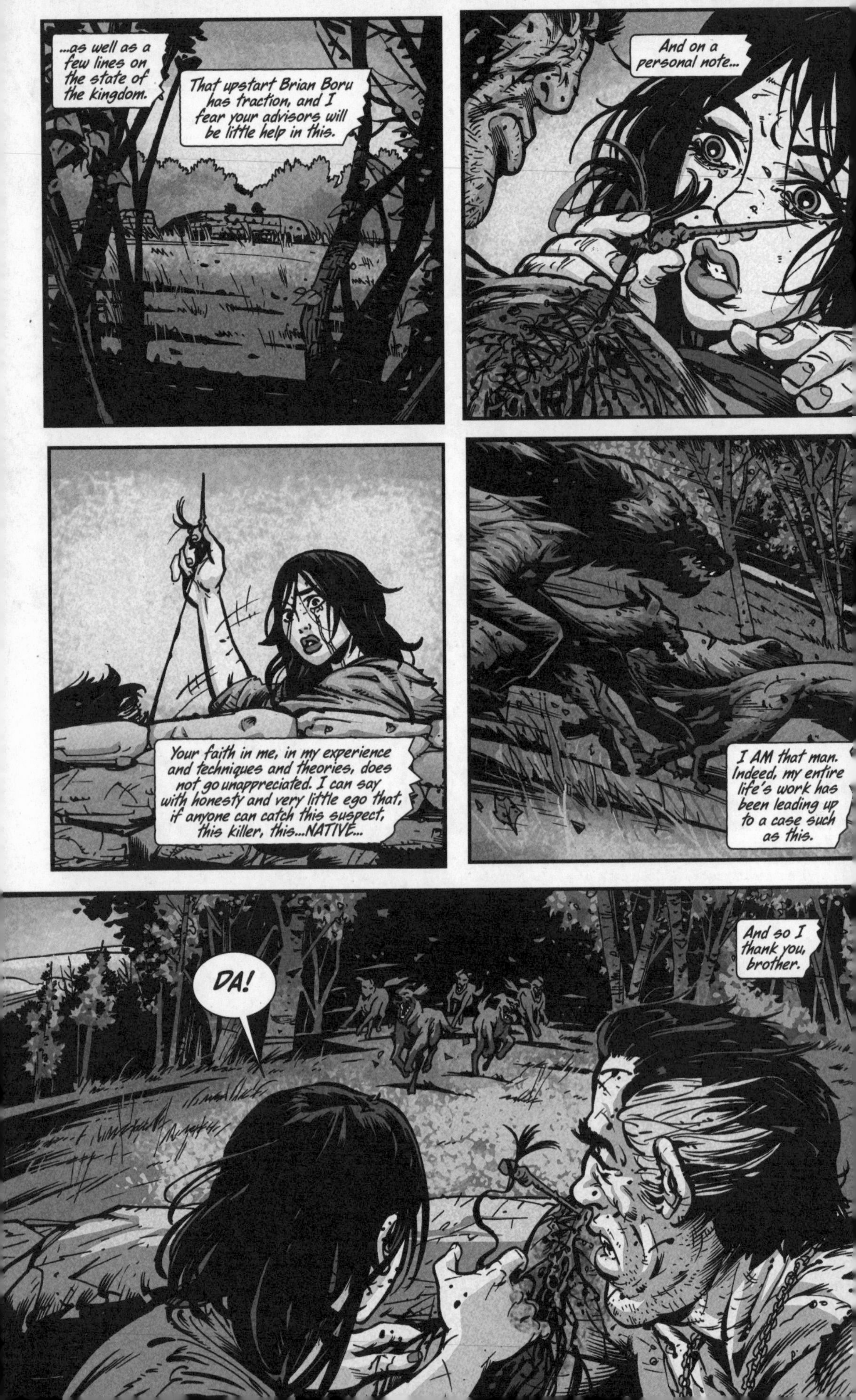
...as well as a few lines on the state of the kingdom.
That upstart Brian Boru has traction, and I fear your advisors will be little help in this.
And on a personal note...
Your faith in me, in my experience and techniques and theories, does not go unappreciated. I can say with honesty and very little ego that, if anyone can catch this suspect, this killer, this...NATIVE...
I AM that man. Indeed, my entire life's work has been leading up to a case such as this.
DA!
And so I thank you, brother.

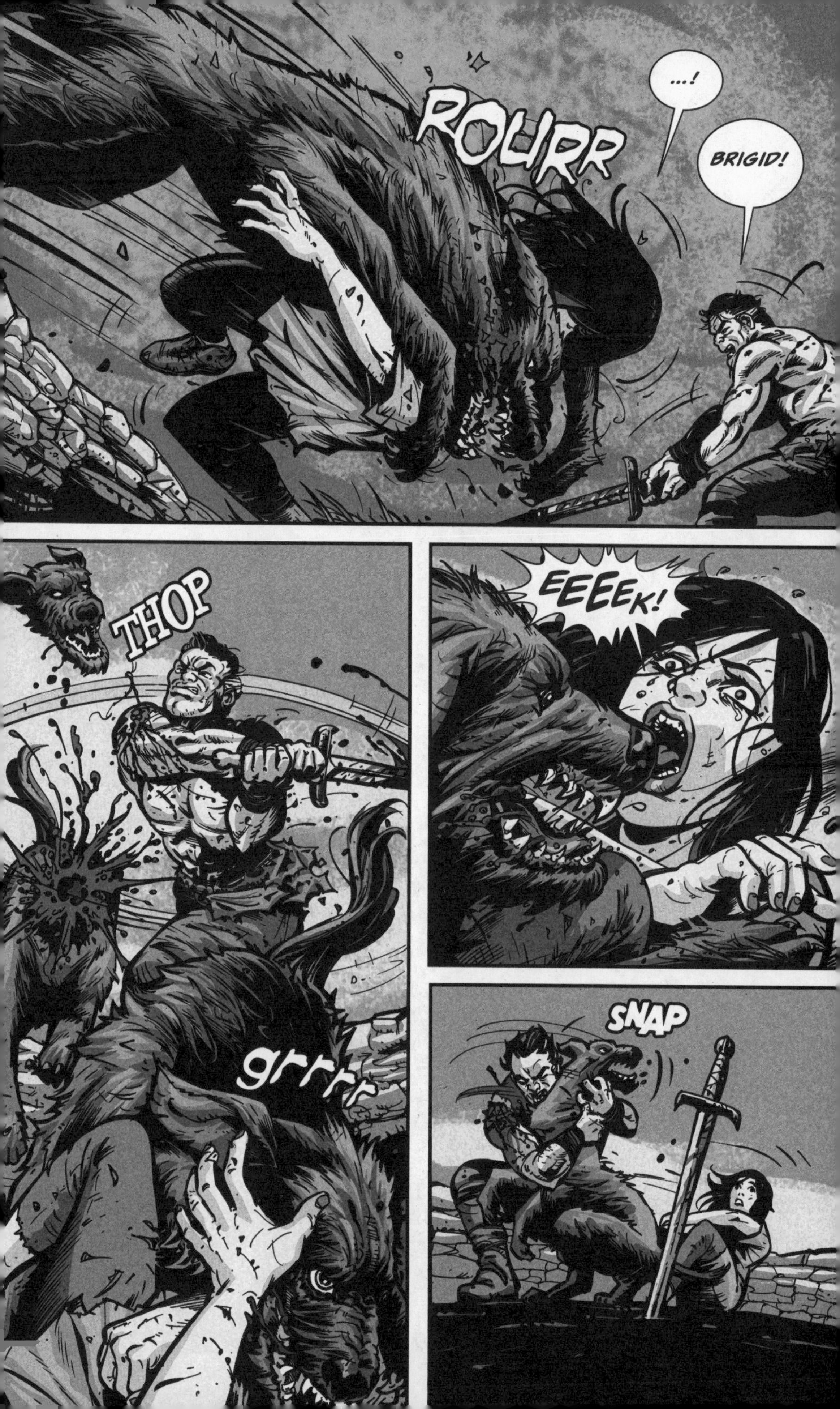
ROURR
...!
BRIGID!
THOP
grrrr
EEEEK!
SNAP

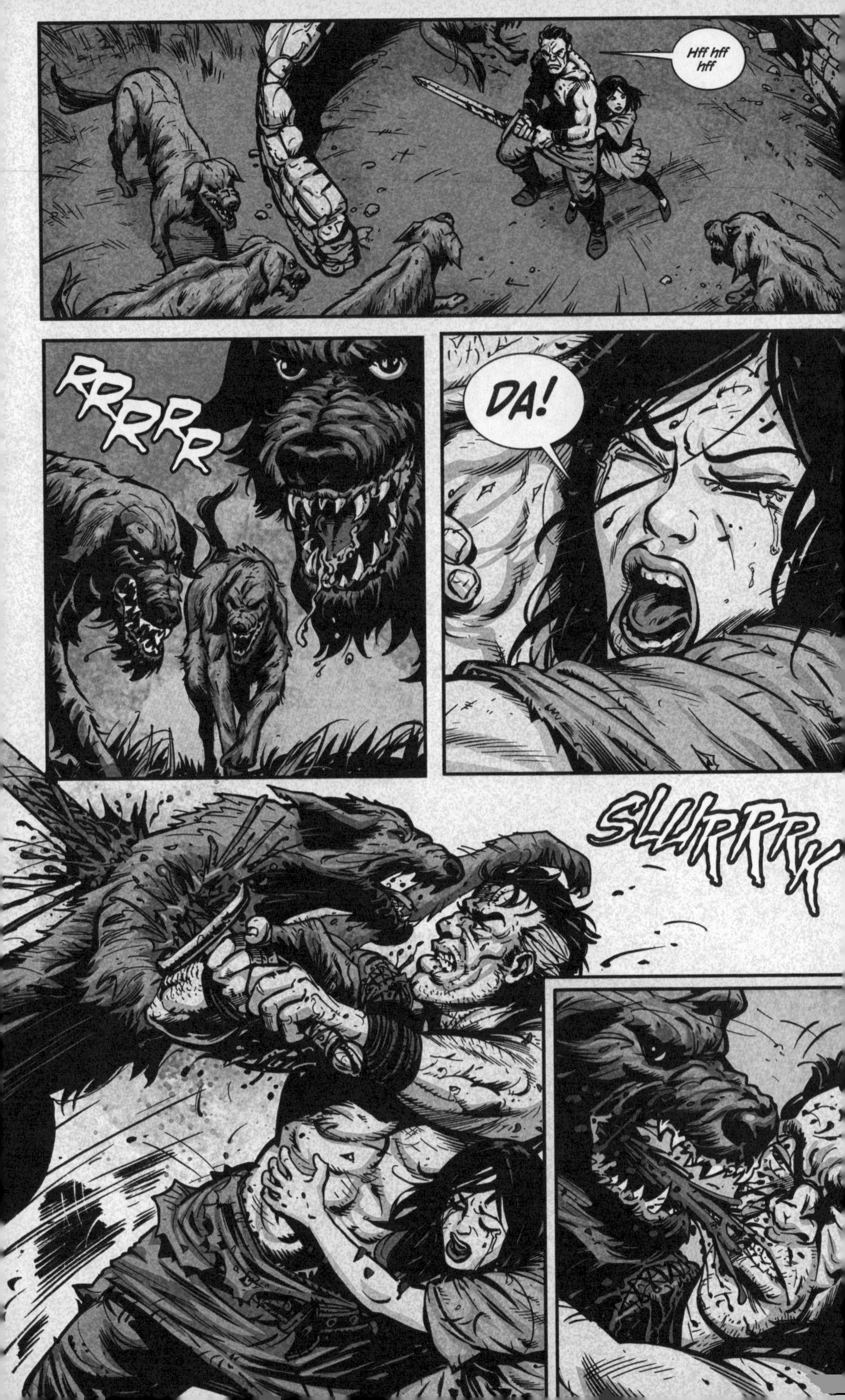

Hff hff
hff
RRRRR
DA!
SLLIRRRK

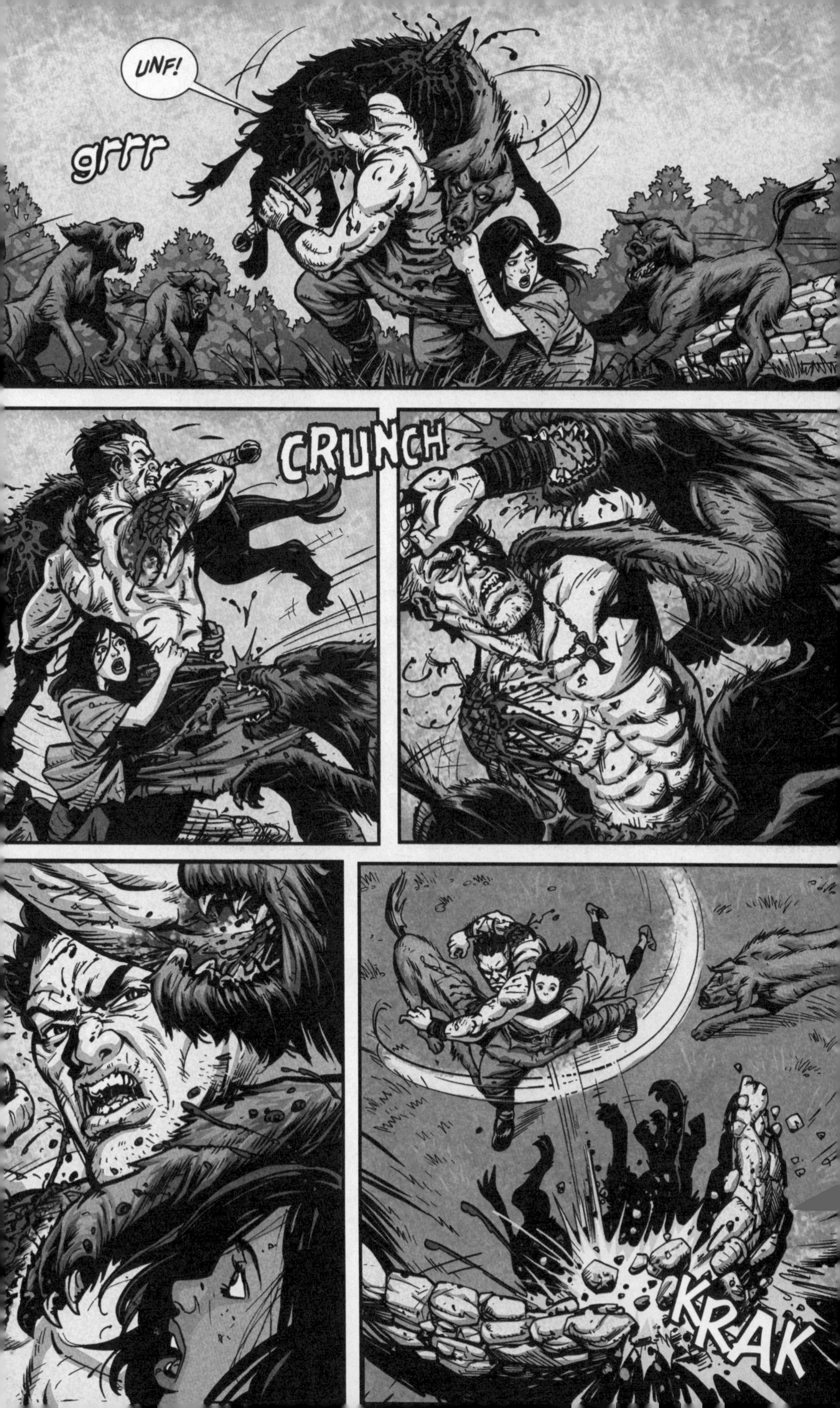
UNF!
grrr
CRUNCH
KRAK

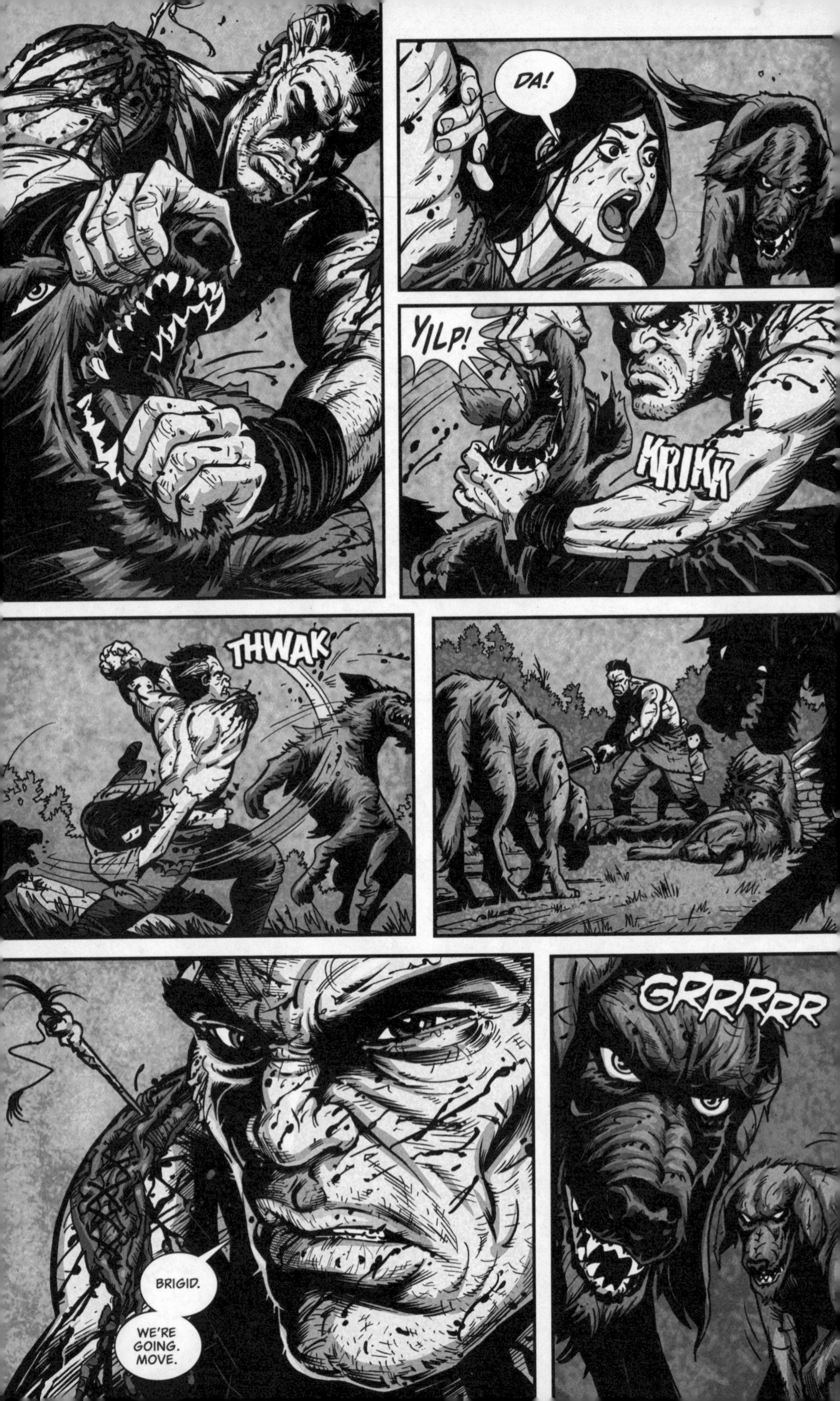
DA!
YILP!
KRIKK
THWAK
GRRRRR
BRIGID.
WE'RE GOING. MOVE.

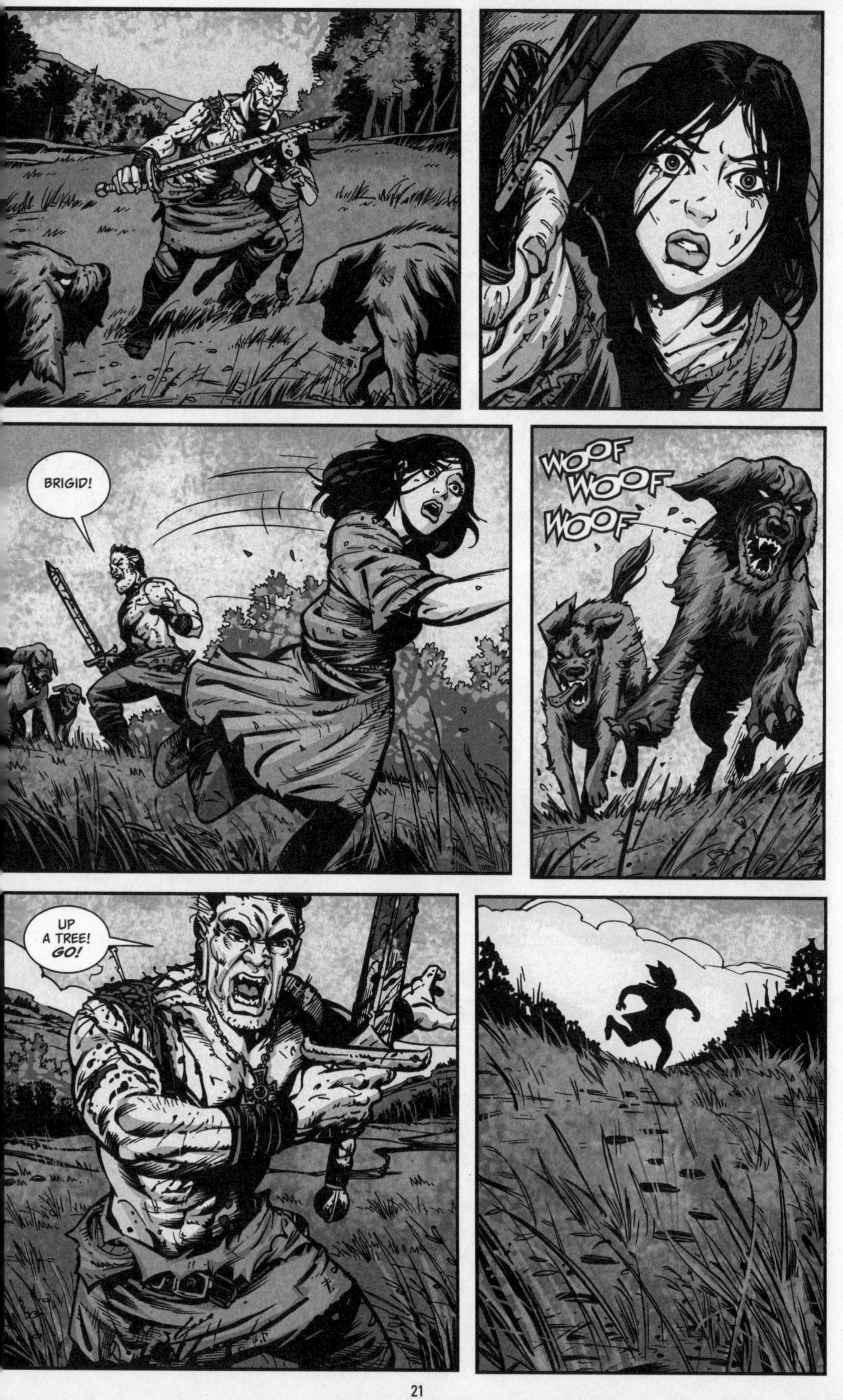
BRIGID!
WOOF
WOOF
WOOF
UP
A TREE!
GO!

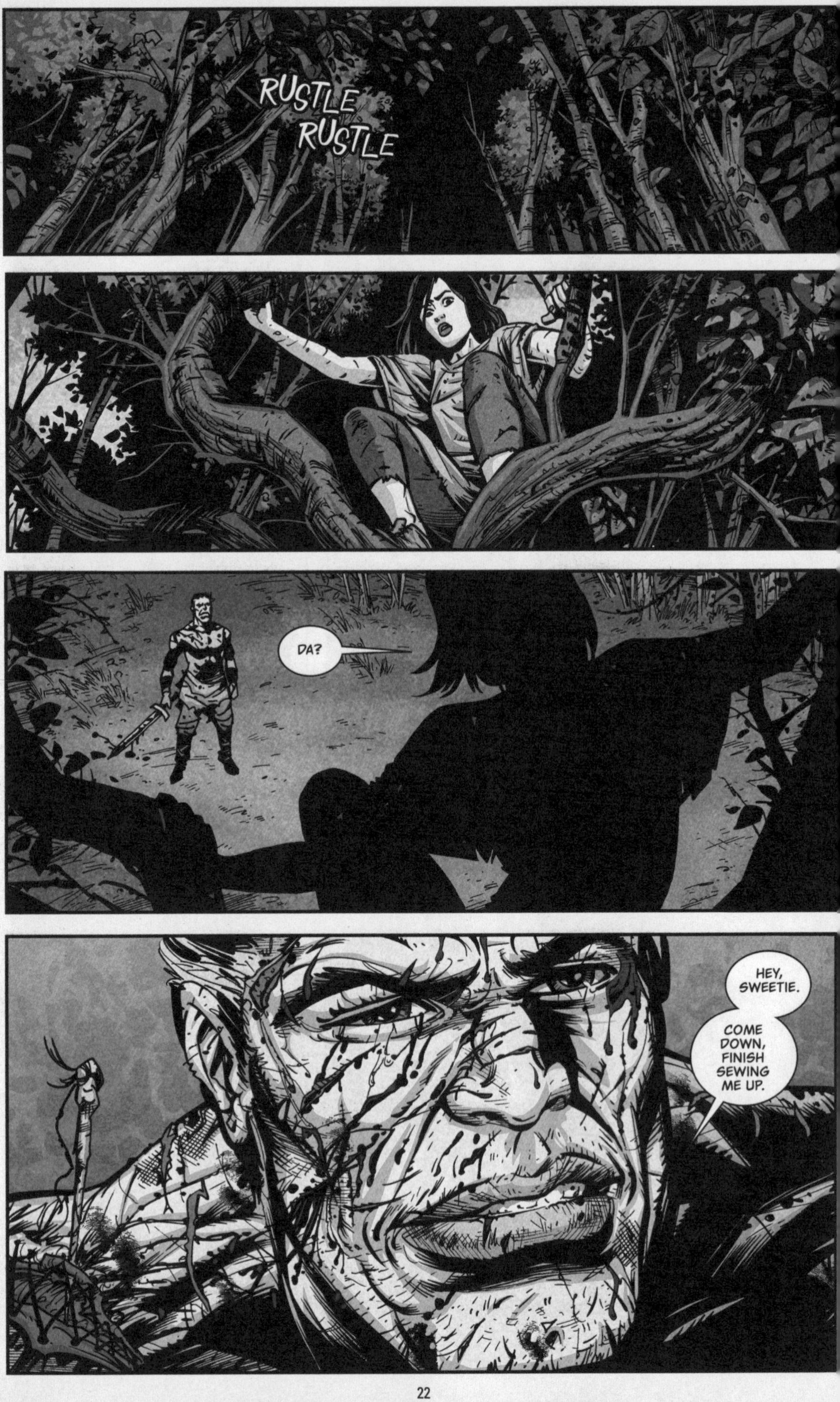
RUSTLE RUSTLE
DA?
HEY, SWEETIE.
COME DOWN, FINISH SEWING ME UP.

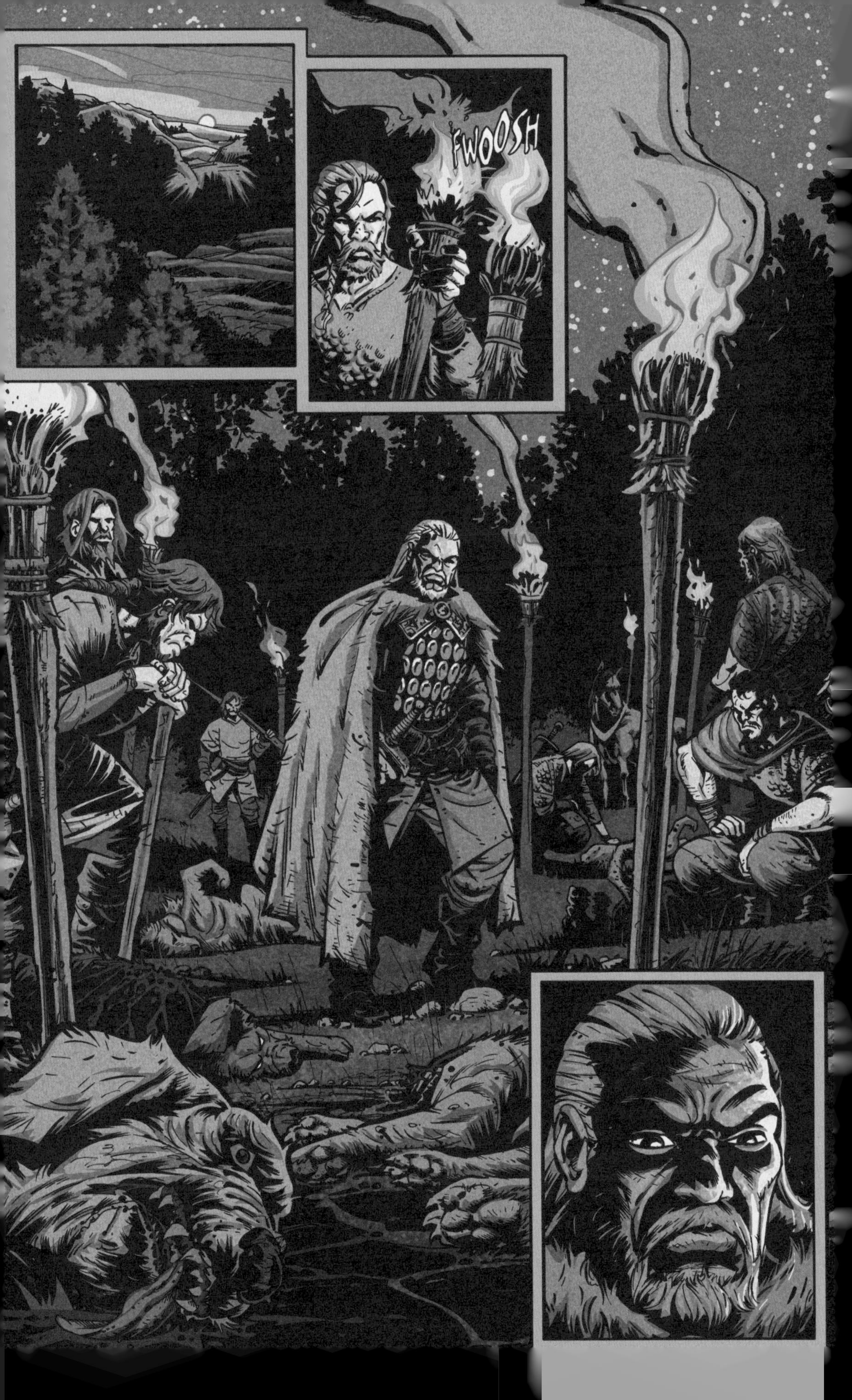
FWOOSH

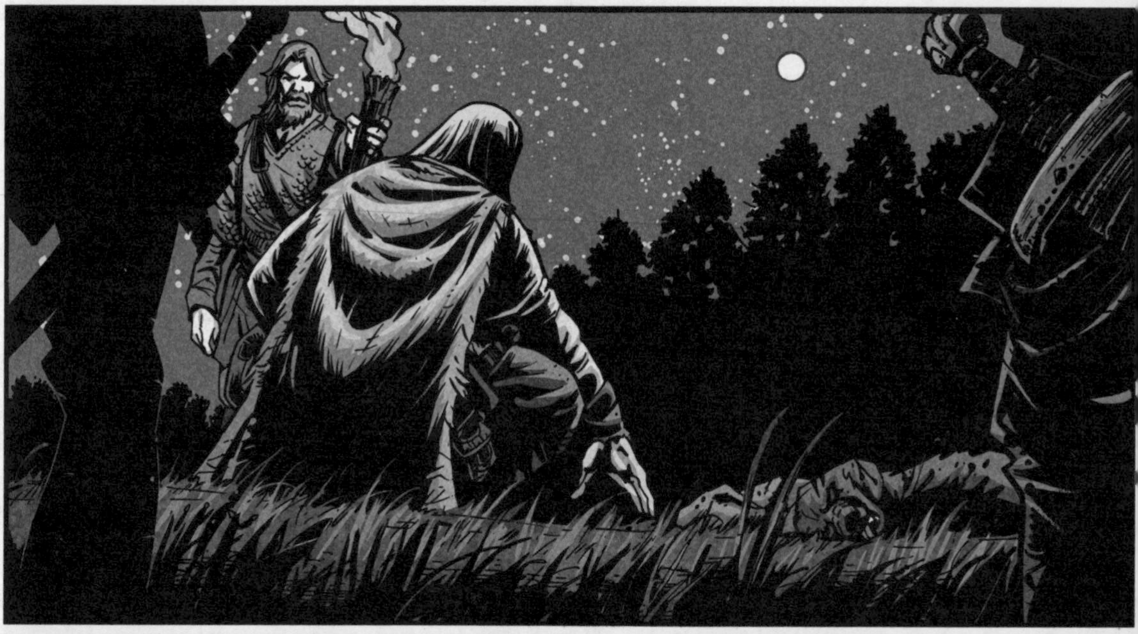

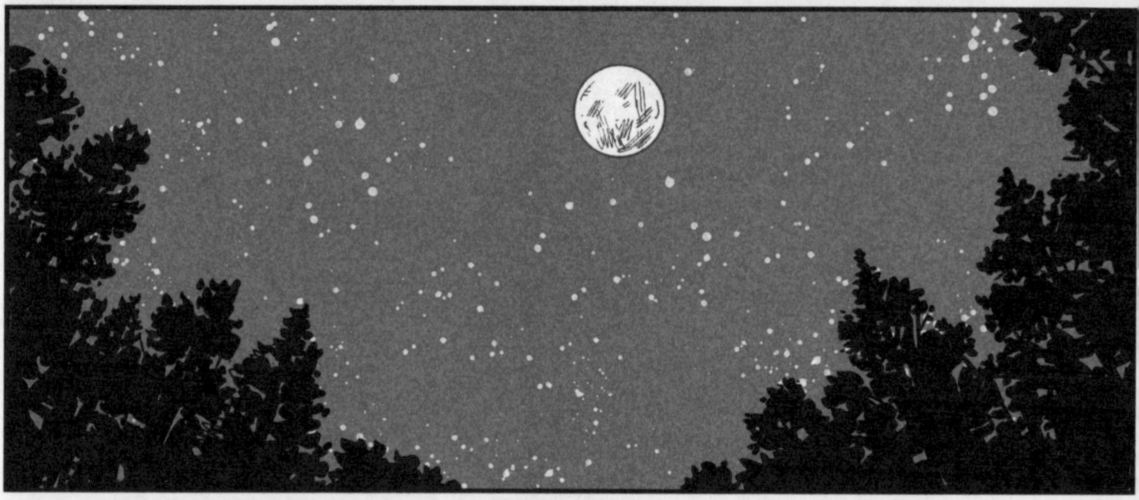

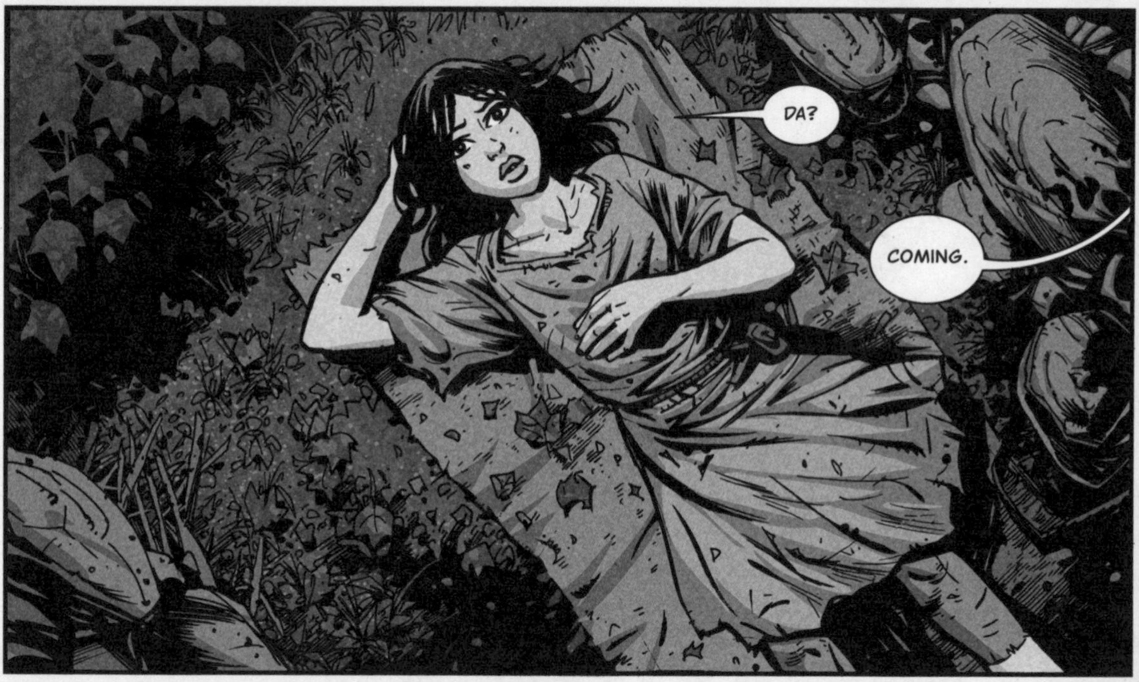
DA?
COMING.

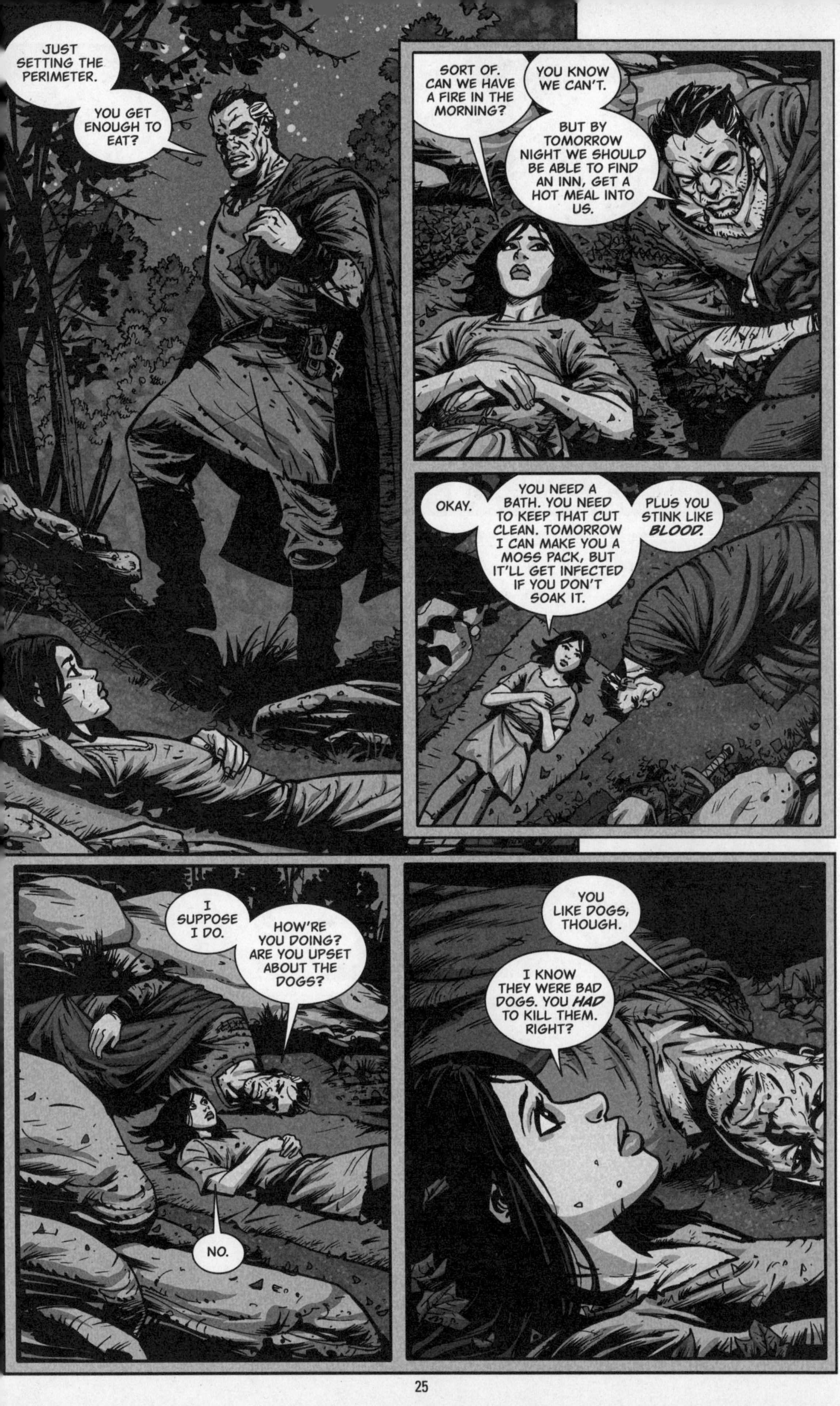
JUST SETTING THE PERIMETER.
YOU GET ENOUGH TO EAT?
SORT OF. CAN WE HAVE A FIRE IN THE MORNING?
YOU KNOW WE CAN'T.
BUT BY TOMORROW NIGHT WE SHOULD BE ABLE TO FIND AN INN, GET A HOT MEAL INTO US.
OKAY.
YOU NEED A BATH. YOU NEED TO KEEP THAT CUT CLEAN. TOMORROW I CAN MAKE YOU A MOSS PACK, BUT IT'LL GET INFECTED IF YOU DON'T SOAK IT.
PLUS YOU STINK LIKE *BLOOD.*
I SUPPOSE I DO.
HOW'RE YOU DOING? ARE YOU UPSET ABOUT THE DOGS?
NO.
YOU LIKE DOGS, THOUGH.
I KNOW THEY WERE BAD DOGS. YOU *HAD* TO KILL THEM. RIGHT?

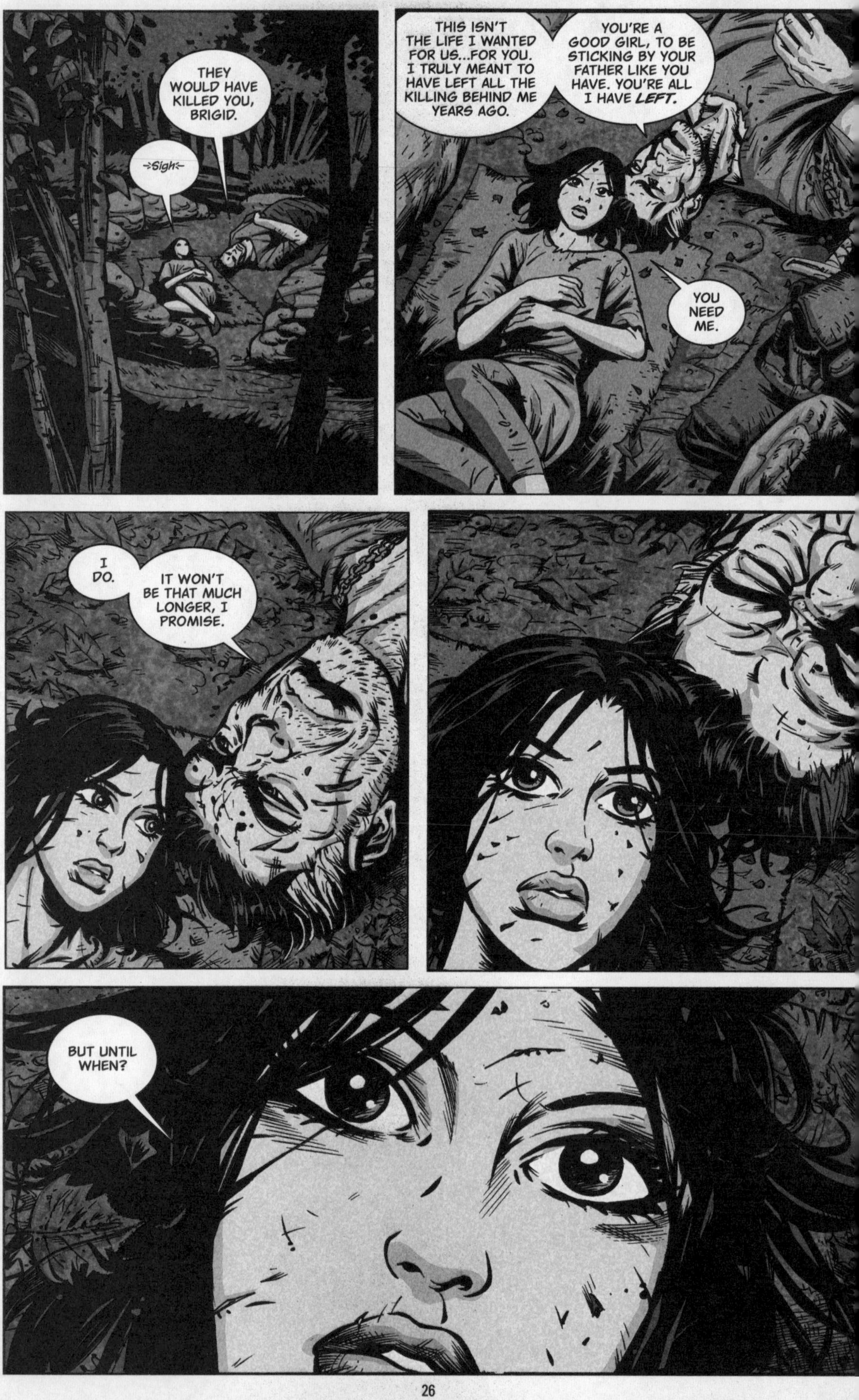
THEY WOULD HAVE KILLED YOU, BRIGID.
Sigh
THIS ISN'T THE LIFE I WANTED FOR US...FOR YOU. I TRULY MEANT TO HAVE LEFT ALL THE KILLING BEHIND ME YEARS AGO.
YOU'RE A GOOD GIRL, TO BE STICKING BY YOUR FATHER LIKE YOU HAVE. YOU'RE ALL I HAVE *LEFT.*
YOU NEED ME.
I DO.
IT WON'T BE THAT MUCH LONGER, I PROMISE.
BUT UNTIL WHEN?

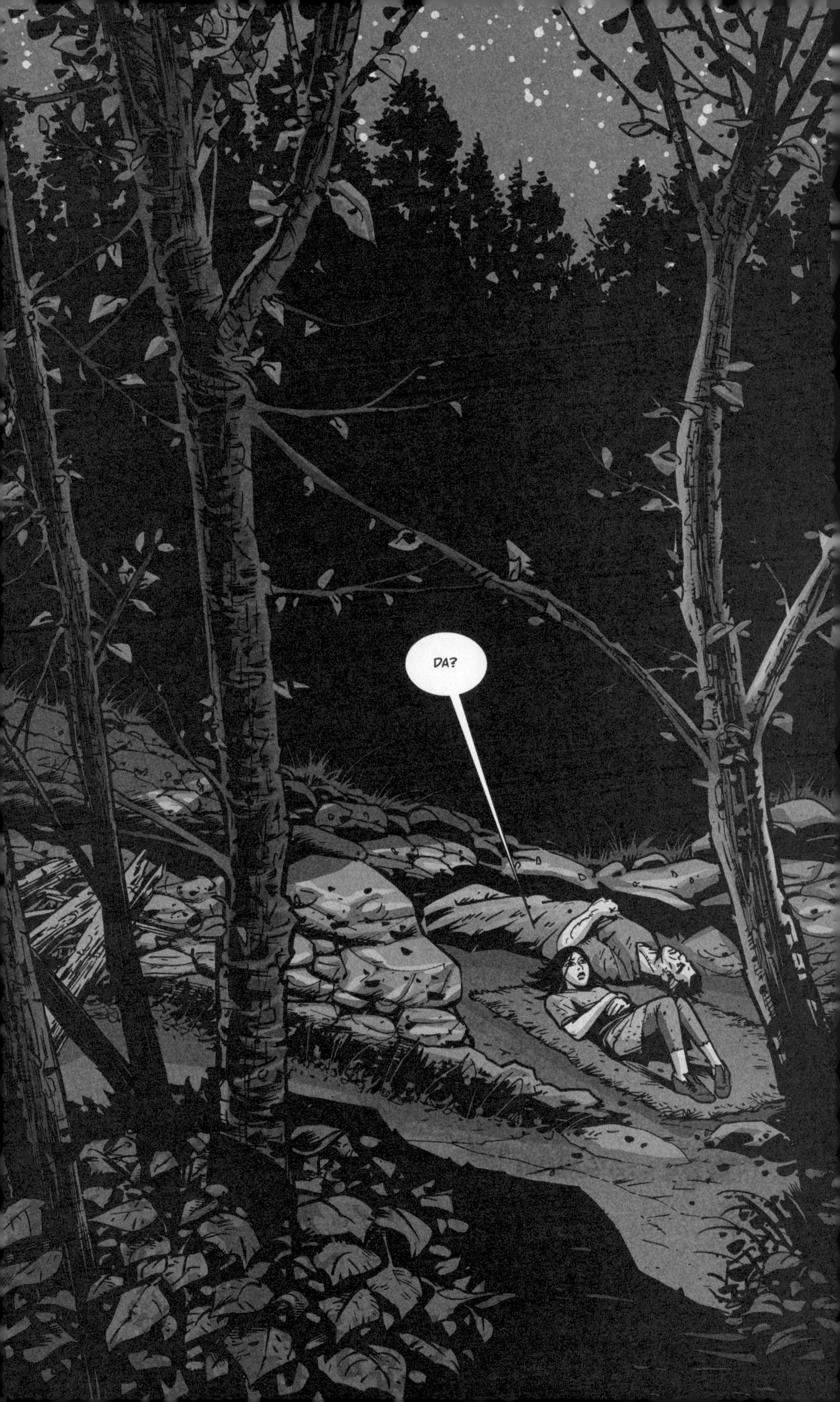
DA?

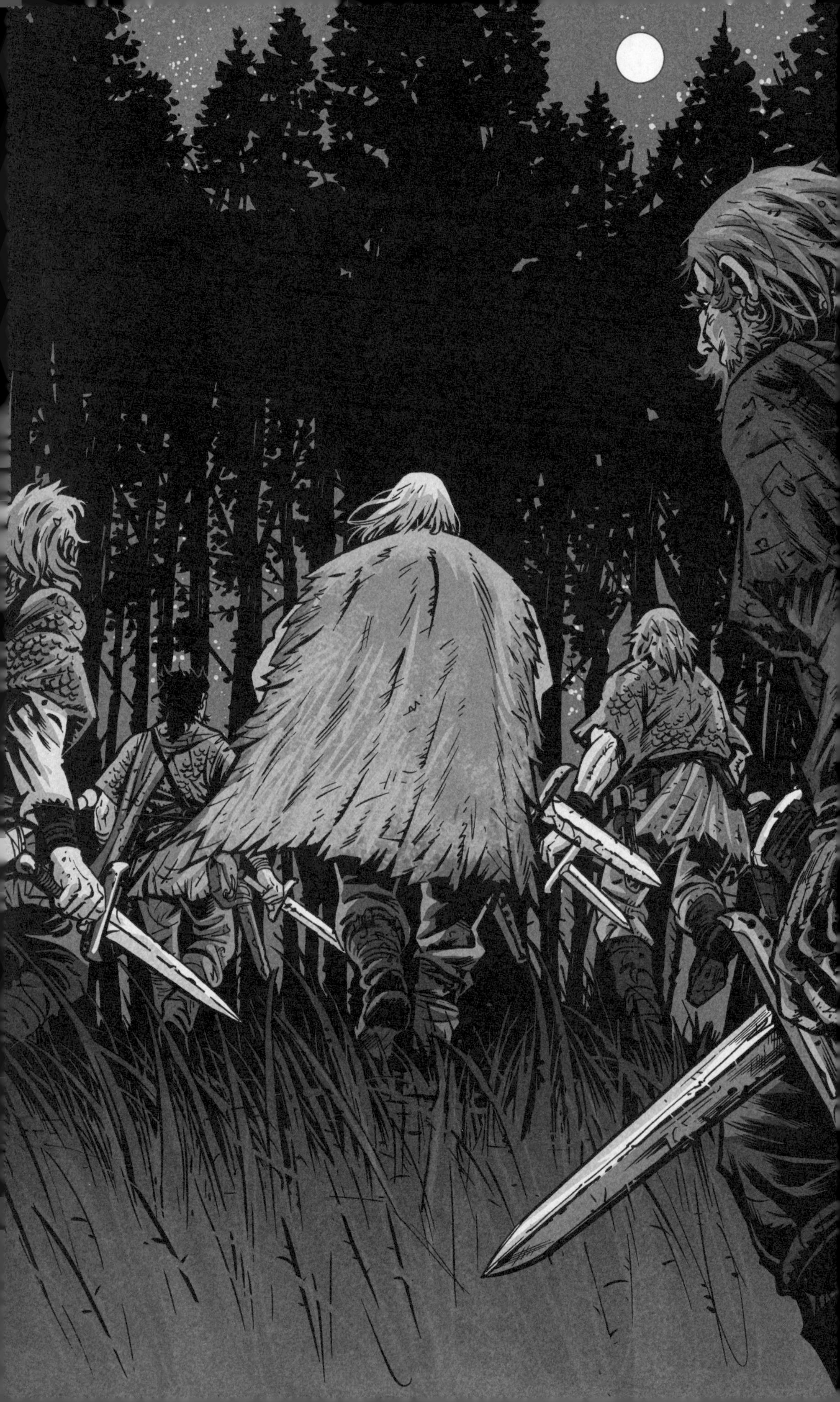

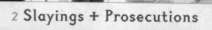

2 Slayings + Prosecutions

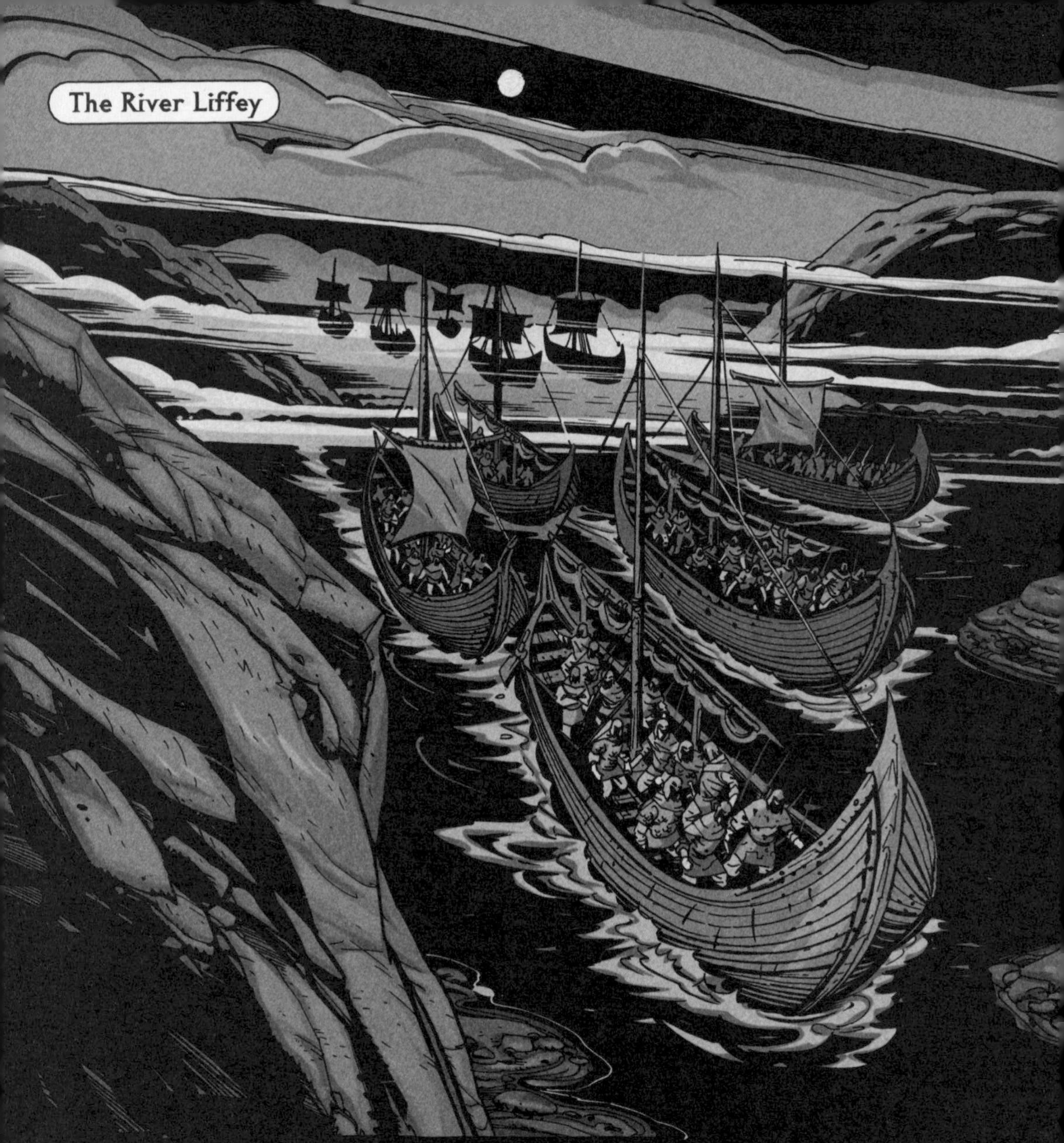
The River Liffey

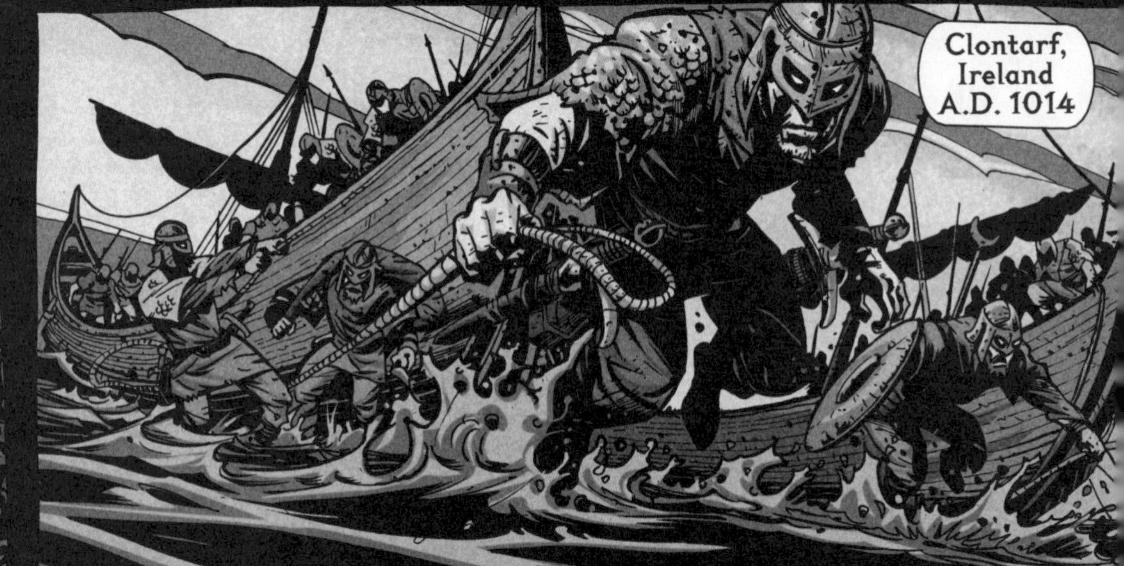
Clontarf,
Ireland
A.D. 1014

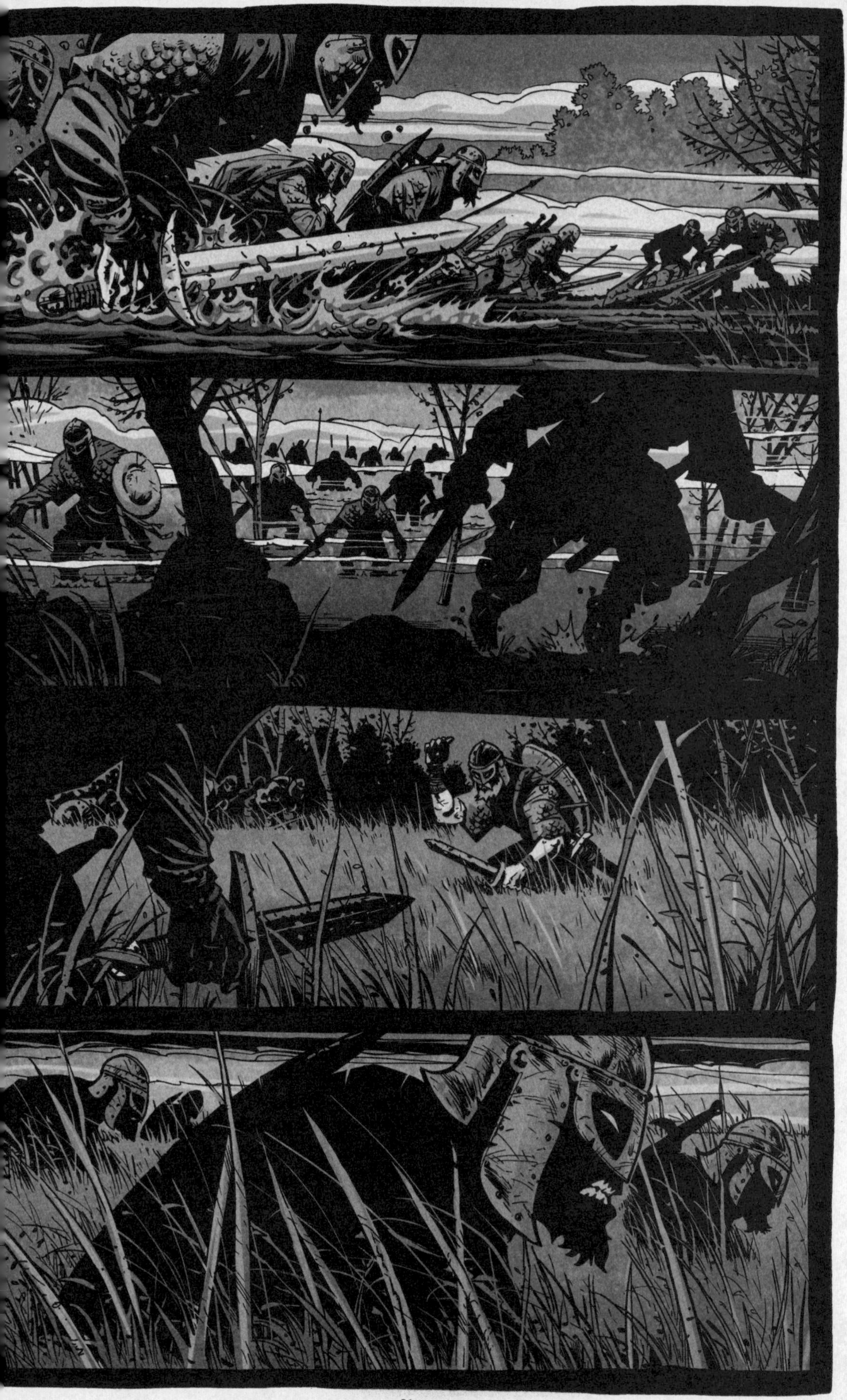

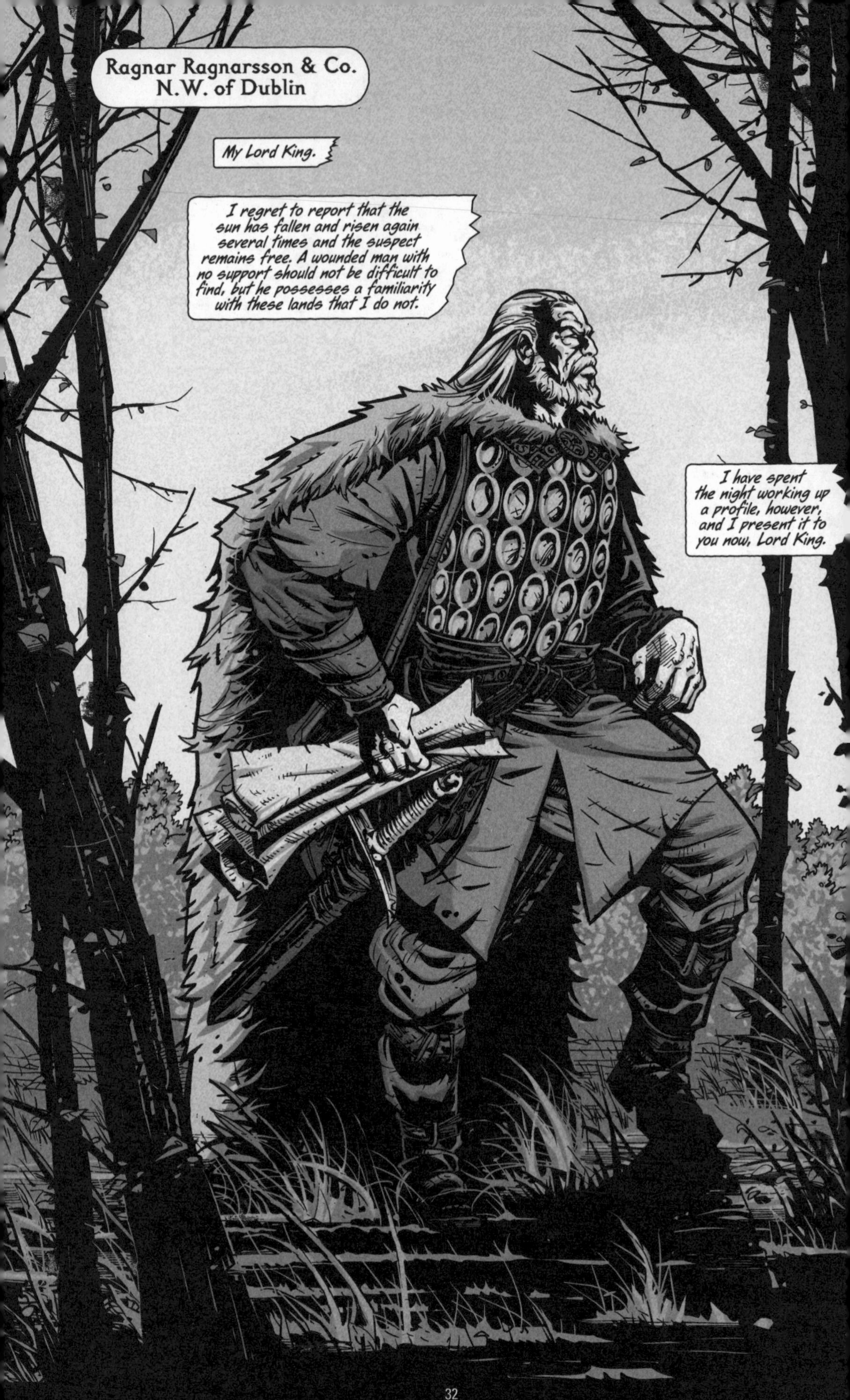
Ragnar Ragnarsson & Co.
N.W. of Dublin
My Lord King.
I regret to report that the sun has fallen and risen again several times and the suspect remains free. A wounded man with no support should not be difficult to find, but he possesses a familiarity with these lands that I do not.
I have spent the night working up a profile, however, and I present it to you now, Lord King.

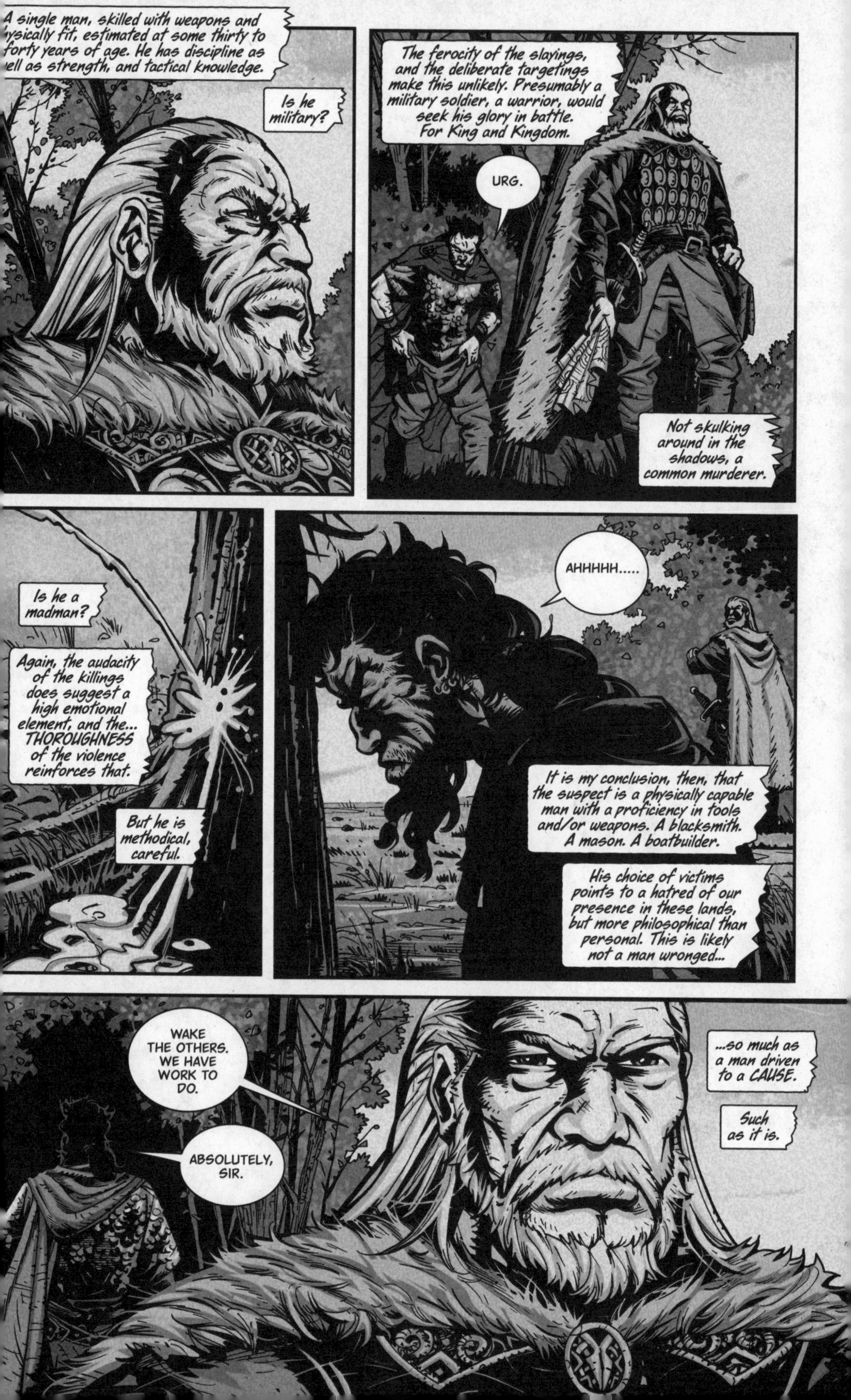
A single man, skilled with weapons and
ysically fit, estimated at some thirty to
forty years of age. He has discipline as
ell as strength, and tactical knowledge.
Is he military?
The ferocity of the slayings, and the deliberate targetings make this unlikely. Presumably a military soldier, a warrior, would seek his glory in battle. For King and Kingdom.
URG.
Not skulking around in the shadows, a common murderer.
Is he a madman?
Again, the audacity of the killings does suggest a high emotional element, and the... THOROUGHNESS of the violence reinforces that.
But he is methodical, careful.
AHHHHH.....
It is my conclusion, then, that the suspect is a physically capable man with a proficiency in tools and/or weapons. A blacksmith. A mason. A boatbuilder.
His choice of victims points to a hatred of our presence in these lands, but more philosophical than personal. This is likely not a man wronged...
...so much as a man driven to a CAUSE.
Such as it is.
WAKE THE OTHERS. WE HAVE WORK TO DO.
ABSOLUTELY, SIR.

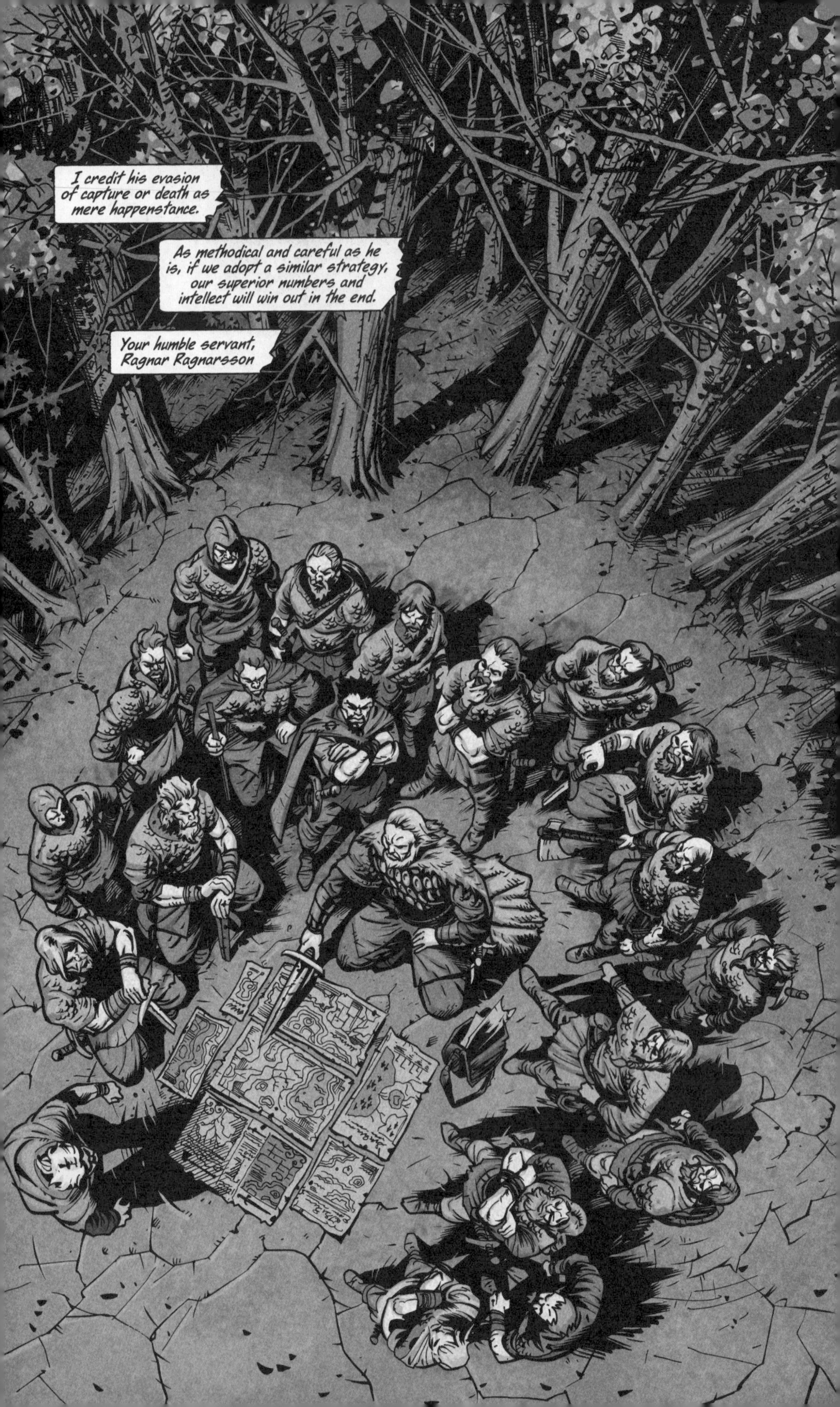
I credit his evasion of capture or death as mere happenstance.
As methodical and careful as he is, if we adopt a similar strategy, our superior numbers and intellect will win out in the end.
Your humble servant, Ragnar Ragnarsson

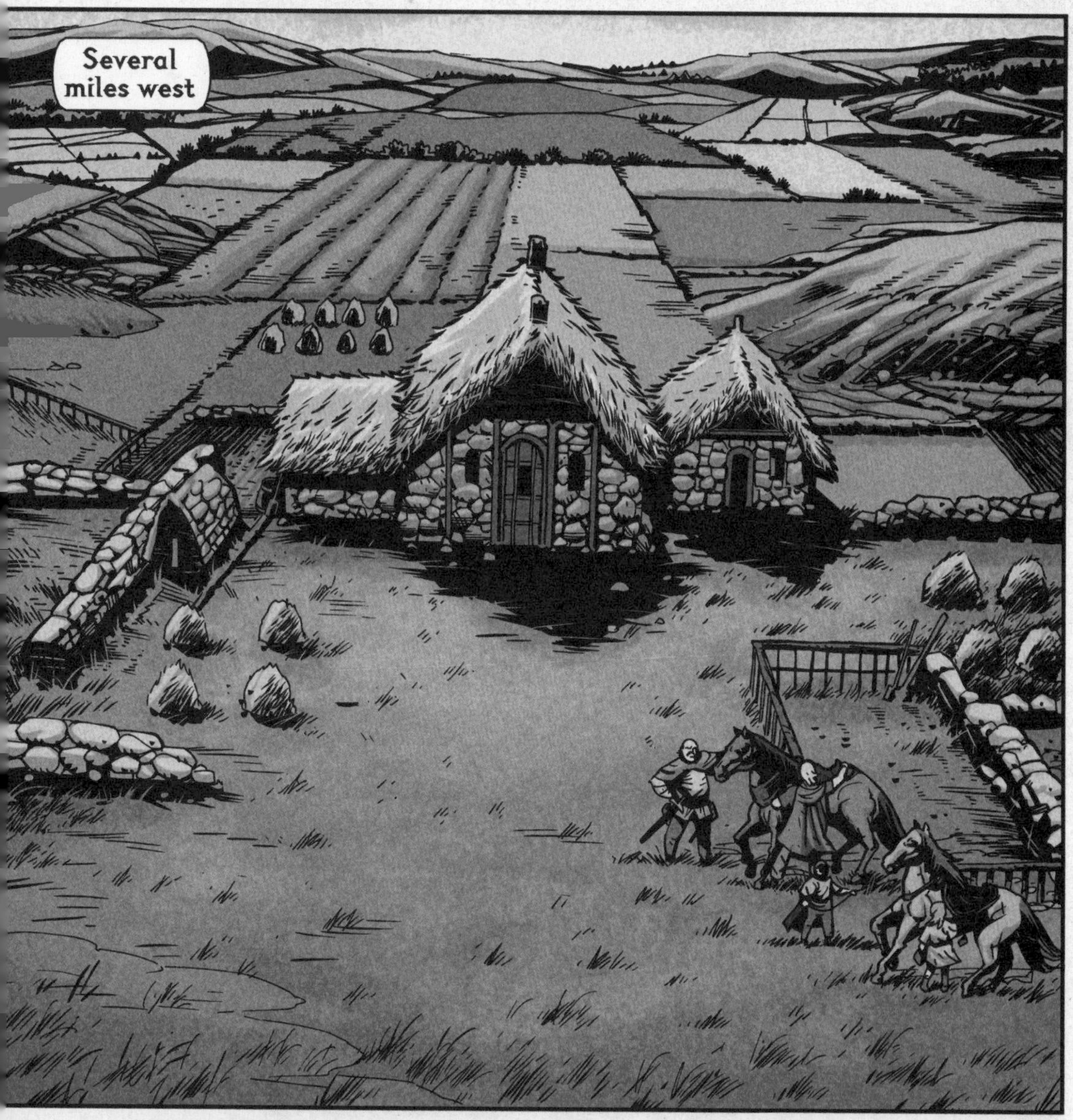
Several miles west

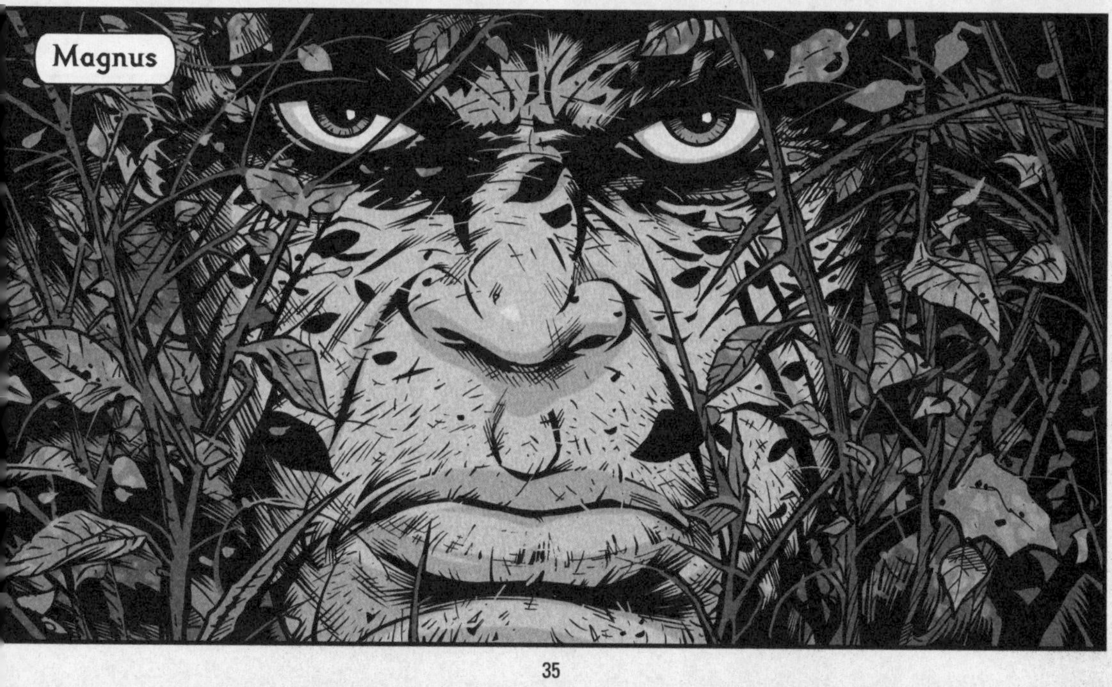
Magnus

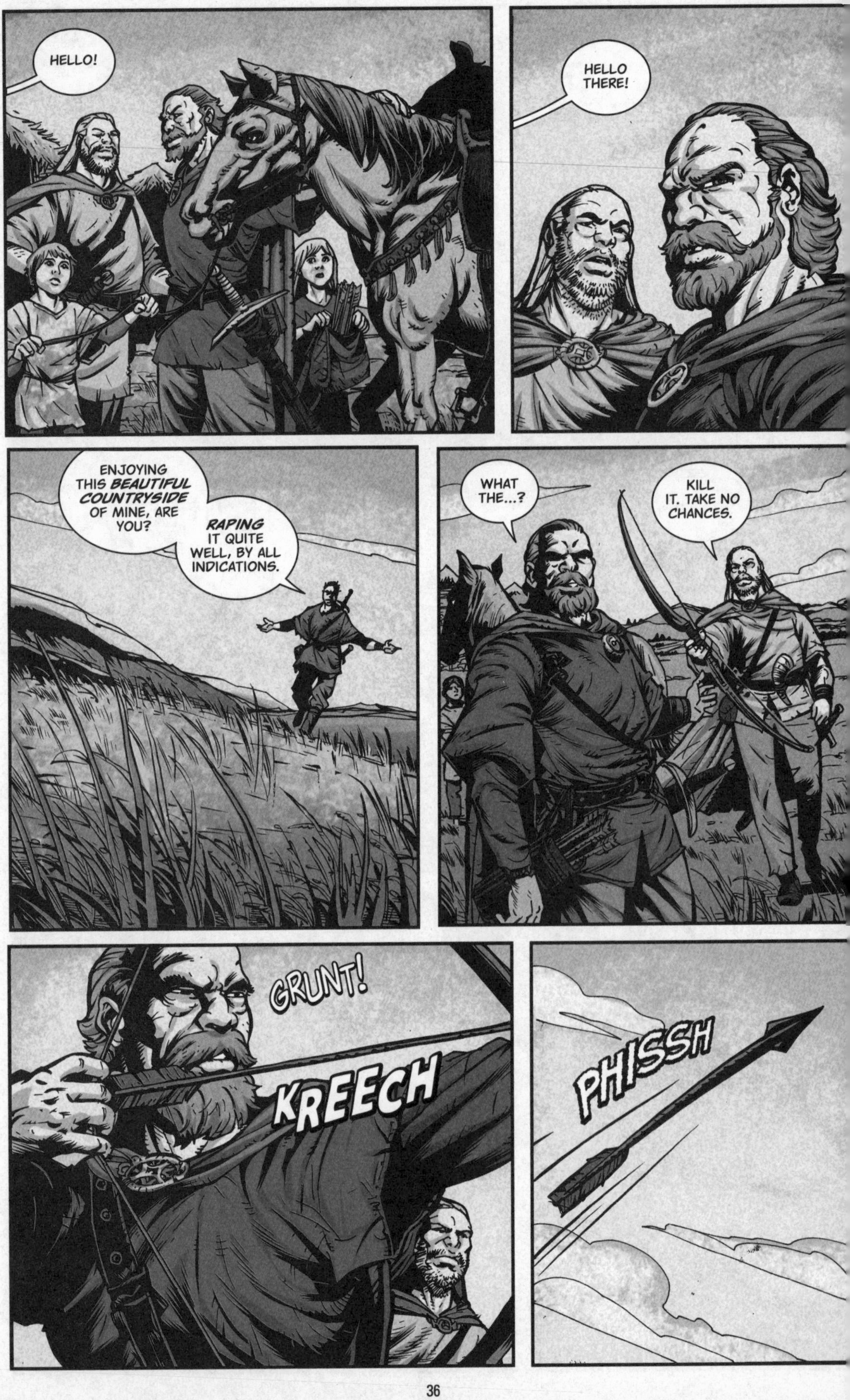
HELLO!
HELLO THERE!
ENJOYING THIS *BEAUTIFUL COUNTRYSIDE* OF MINE, ARE YOU?
RAPING IT QUITE WELL, BY ALL INDICATIONS.
WHAT THE...?
KILL IT. TAKE NO CHANCES.
GRUNT!
KREECH
PHISSH

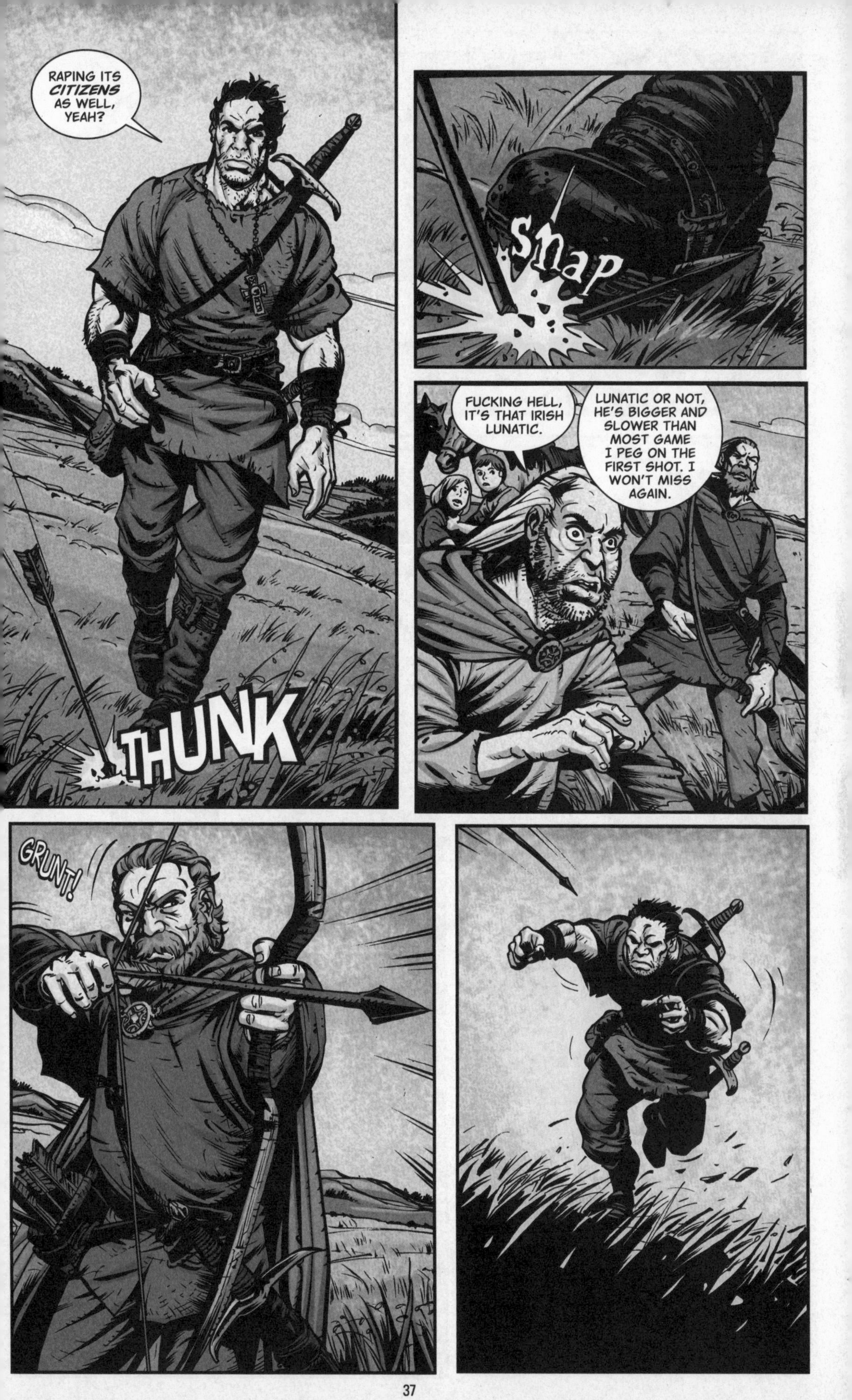

RAPING ITS CITIZENS AS WELL, YEAH?
THUNK
SNAP
FUCKING HELL, IT'S THAT IRISH LUNATIC.
LUNATIC OR NOT, HE'S BIGGER AND SLOWER THAN MOST GAME I PEG ON THE FIRST SHOT. I WON'T MISS AGAIN.
GRUNT!

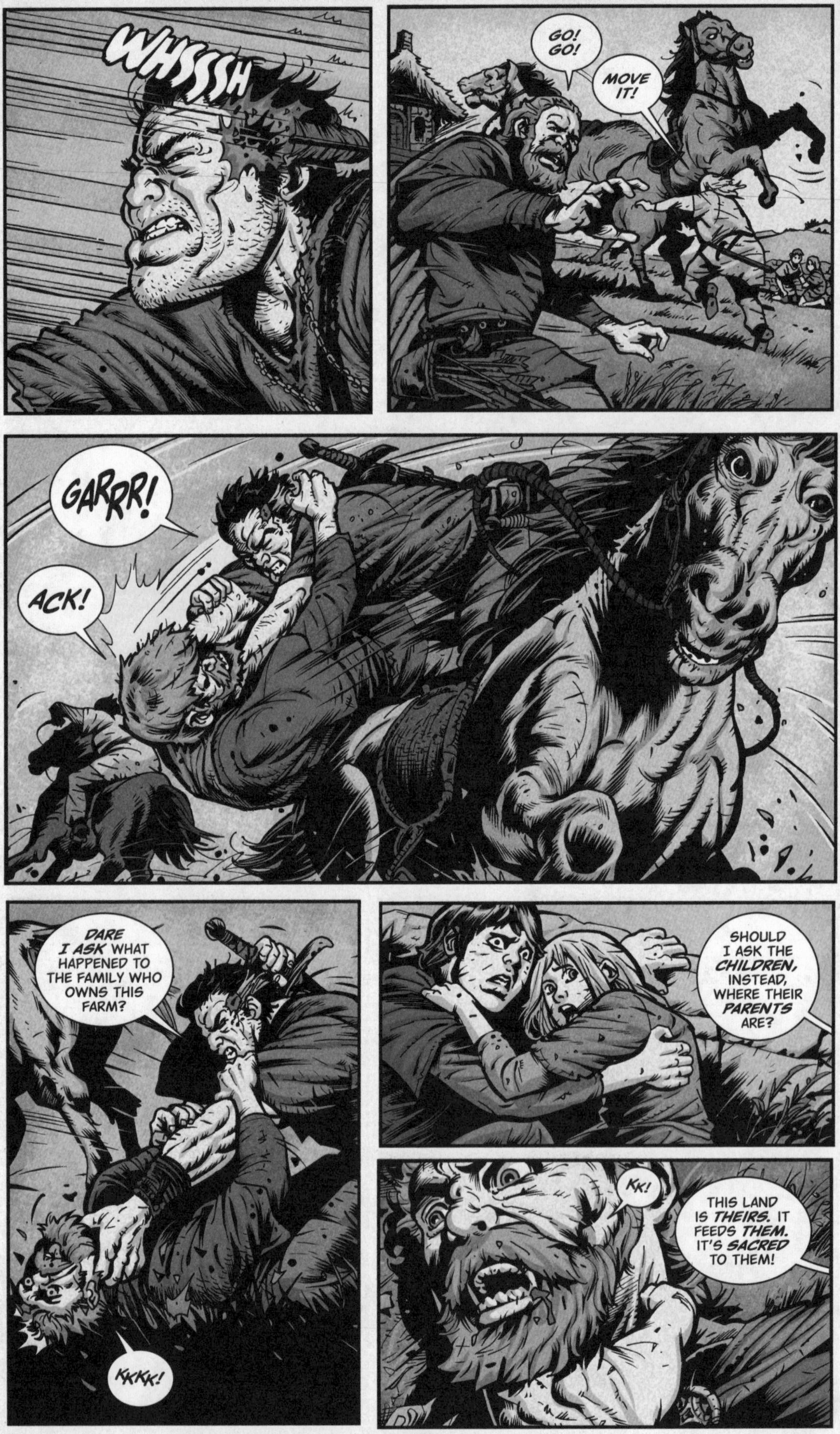
WHSSSH
GO! GO!
MOVE IT!
GARRR!
ACK!
DARE I ASK WHAT HAPPENED TO THE FAMILY WHO OWNS THIS FARM?
KKKK!
SHOULD I ASK THE CHILDREN, INSTEAD, WHERE THEIR PARENTS ARE?
KK!
THIS LAND IS THEIRS. IT FEEDS THEM. IT'S SACRED TO THEM!

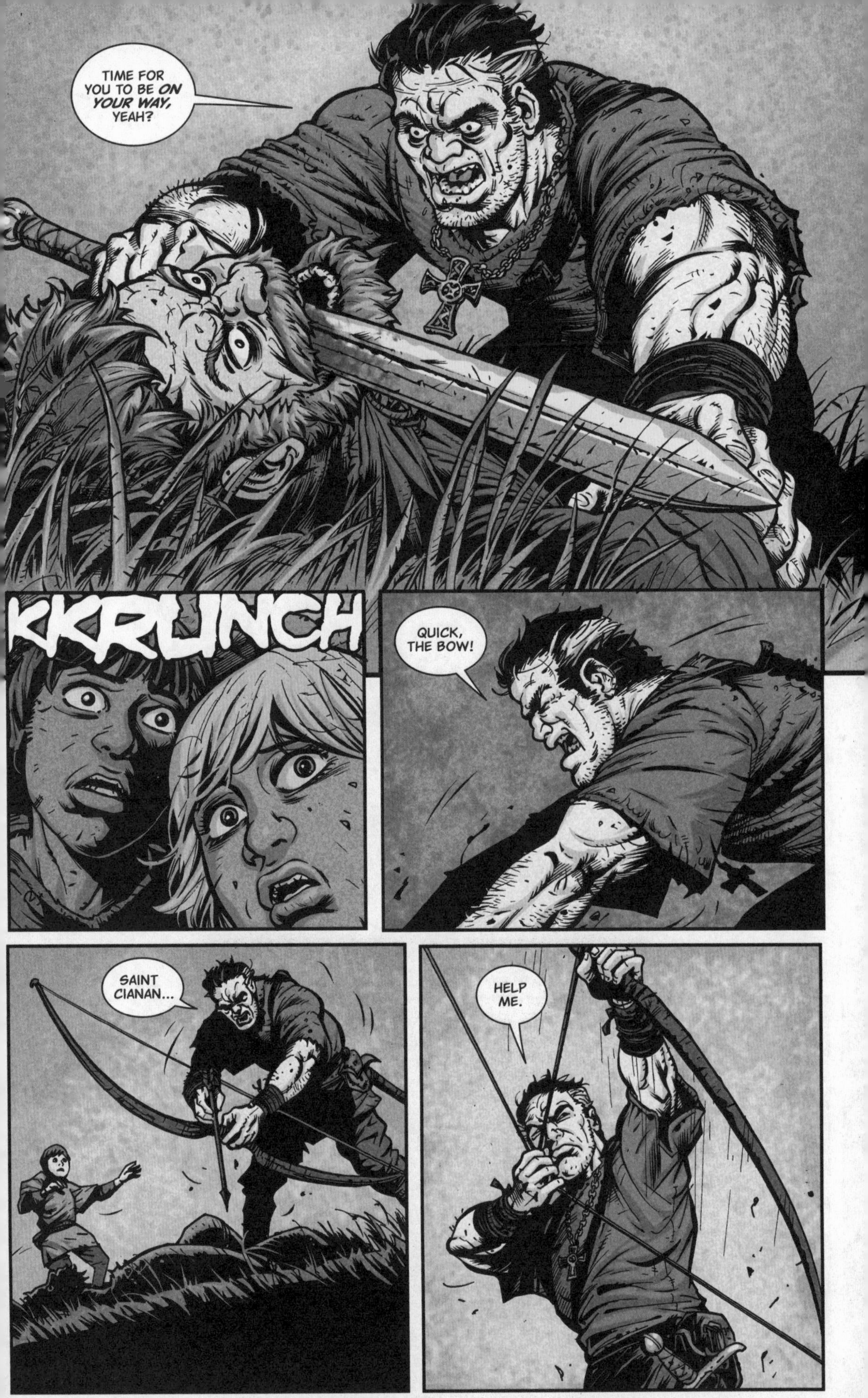
TIME FOR YOU TO BE ON YOUR WAY, YEAH?
KKRUNCH
QUICK, THE BOW!
SAINT CIANAN...
HELP ME.

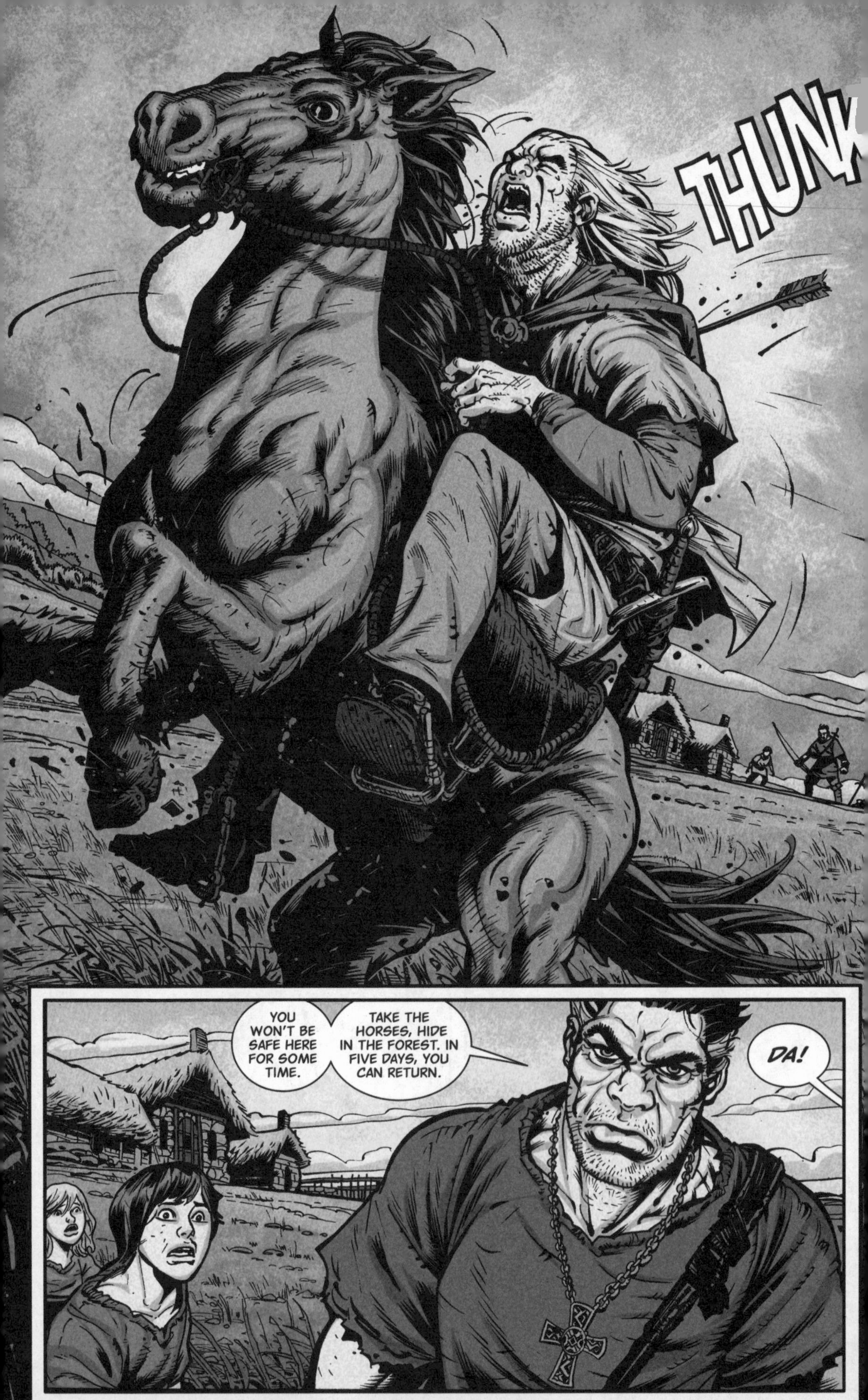
THUNK
YOU WON'T BE SAFE HERE FOR SOME TIME.
TAKE THE HORSES, HIDE IN THE FOREST. IN FIVE DAYS, YOU CAN RETURN.
DA!

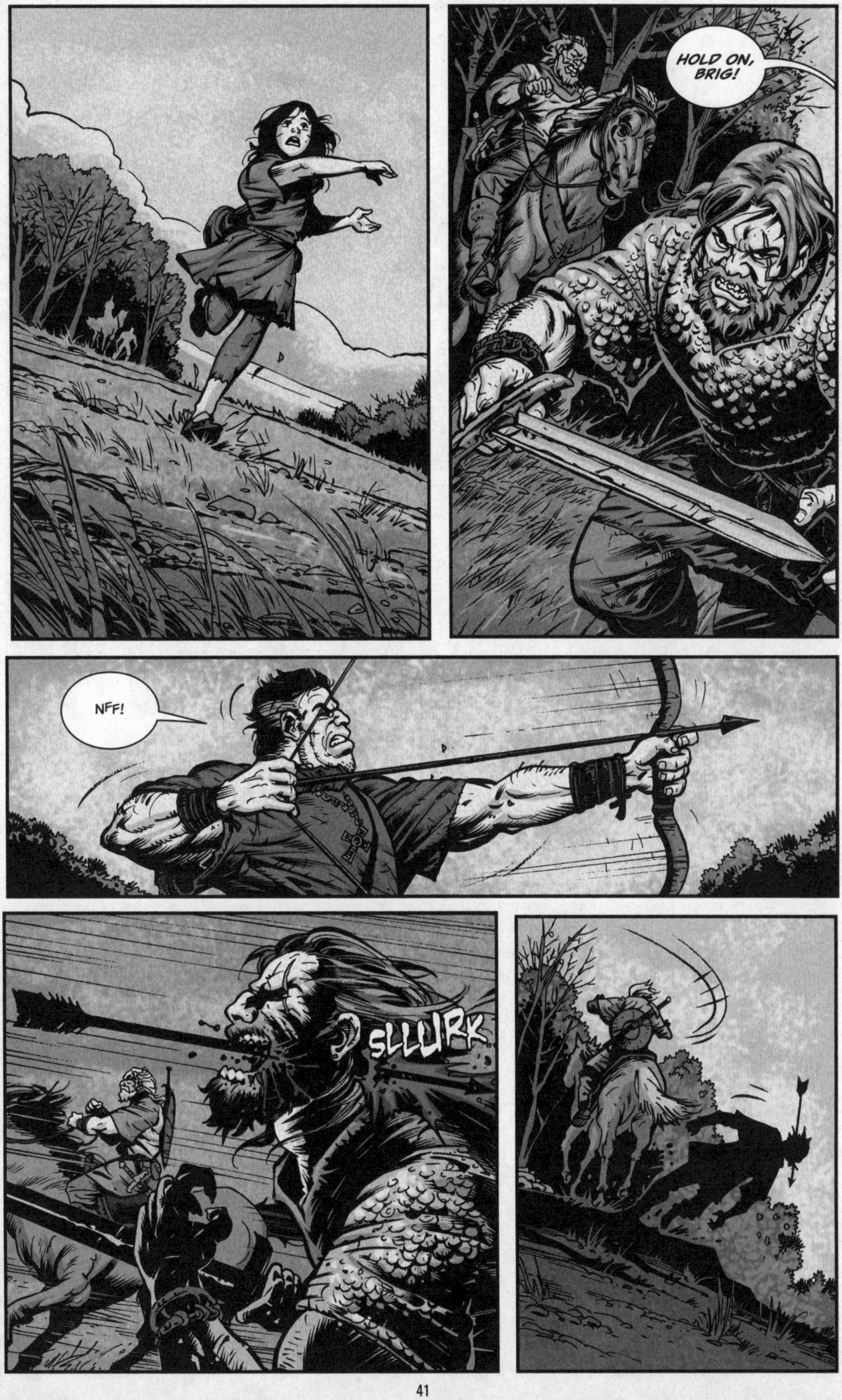
HOLD ON, BRIG!
NFF!
SLLURK

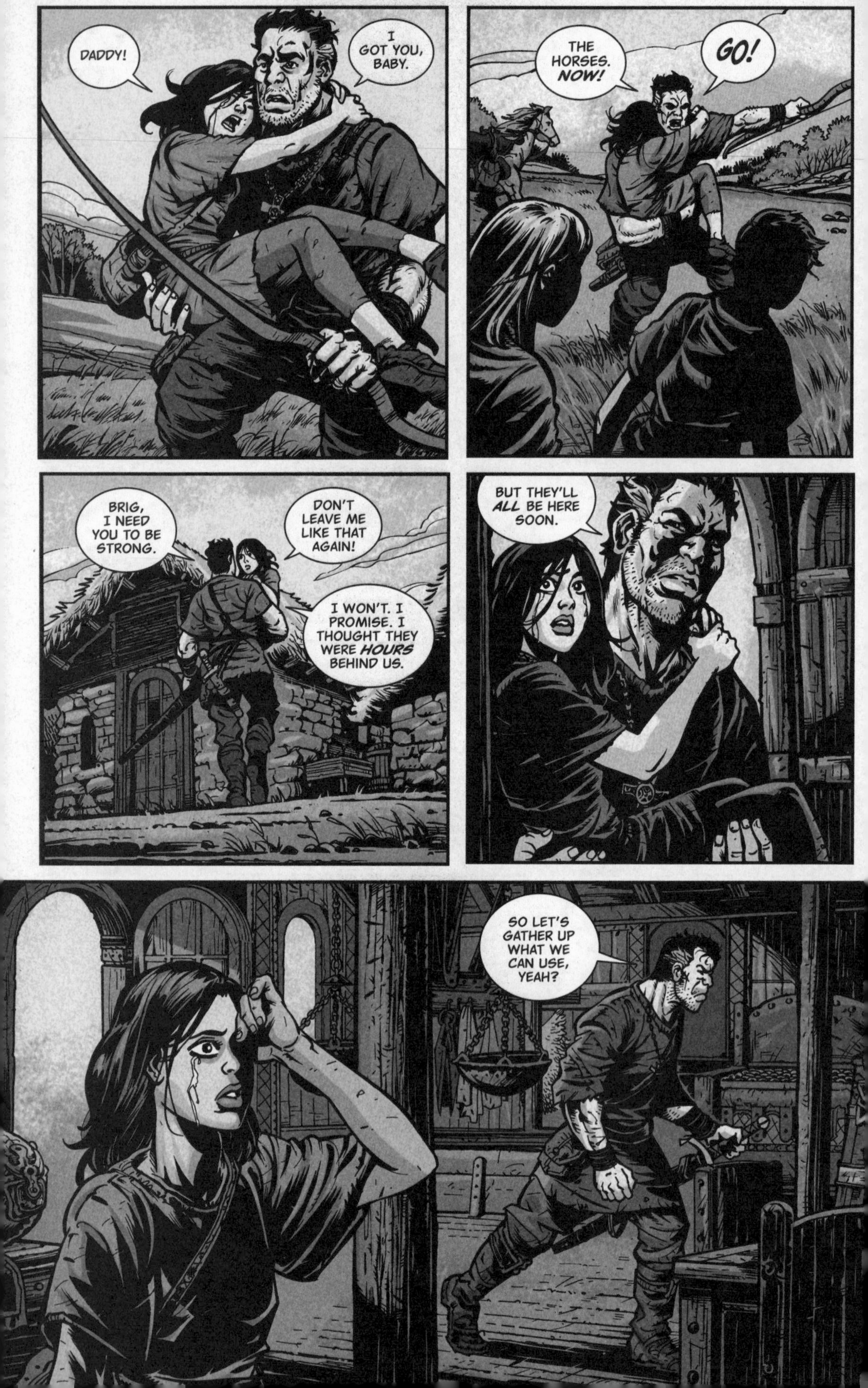
DADDY!
I GOT YOU, BABY.
THE HORSES. NOW!
GO!
BRIG, I NEED YOU TO BE STRONG.
DON'T LEAVE ME LIKE THAT AGAIN!
I WON'T. I PROMISE. I THOUGHT THEY WERE HOURS BEHIND US.
BUT THEY'LL ALL BE HERE SOON.
SO LET'S GATHER UP WHAT WE CAN USE, YEAH?

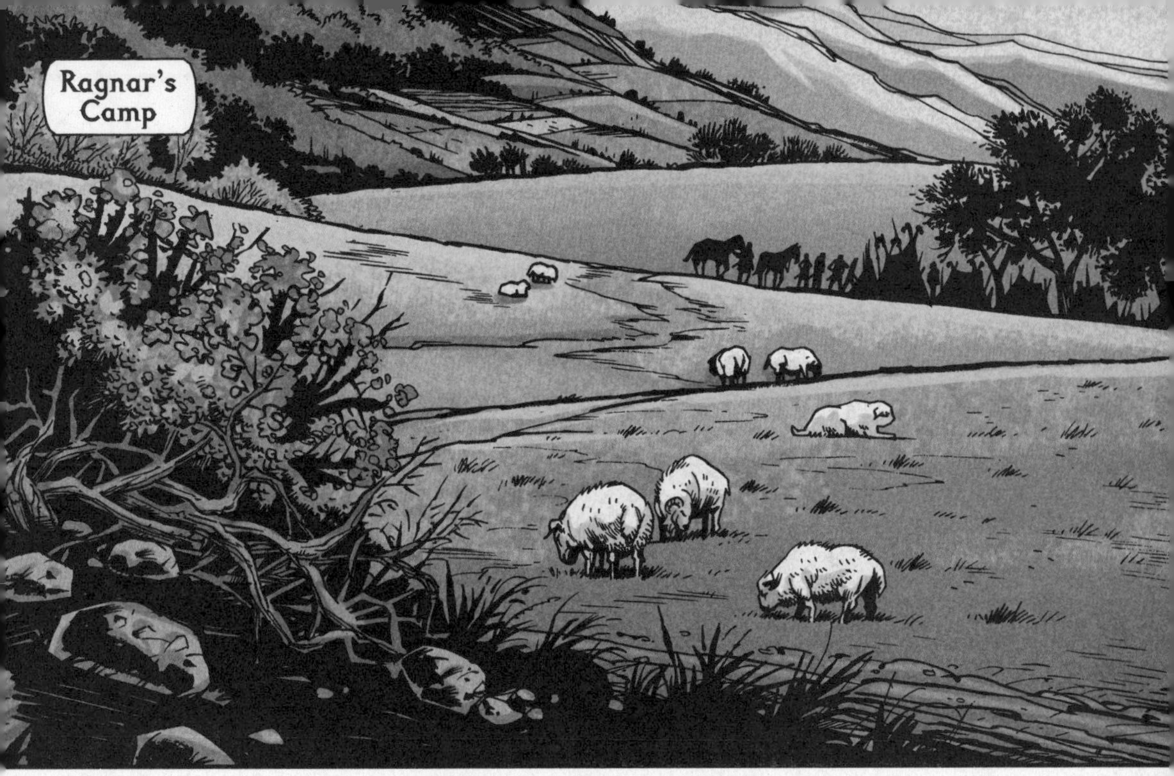
Ragnar's Camp

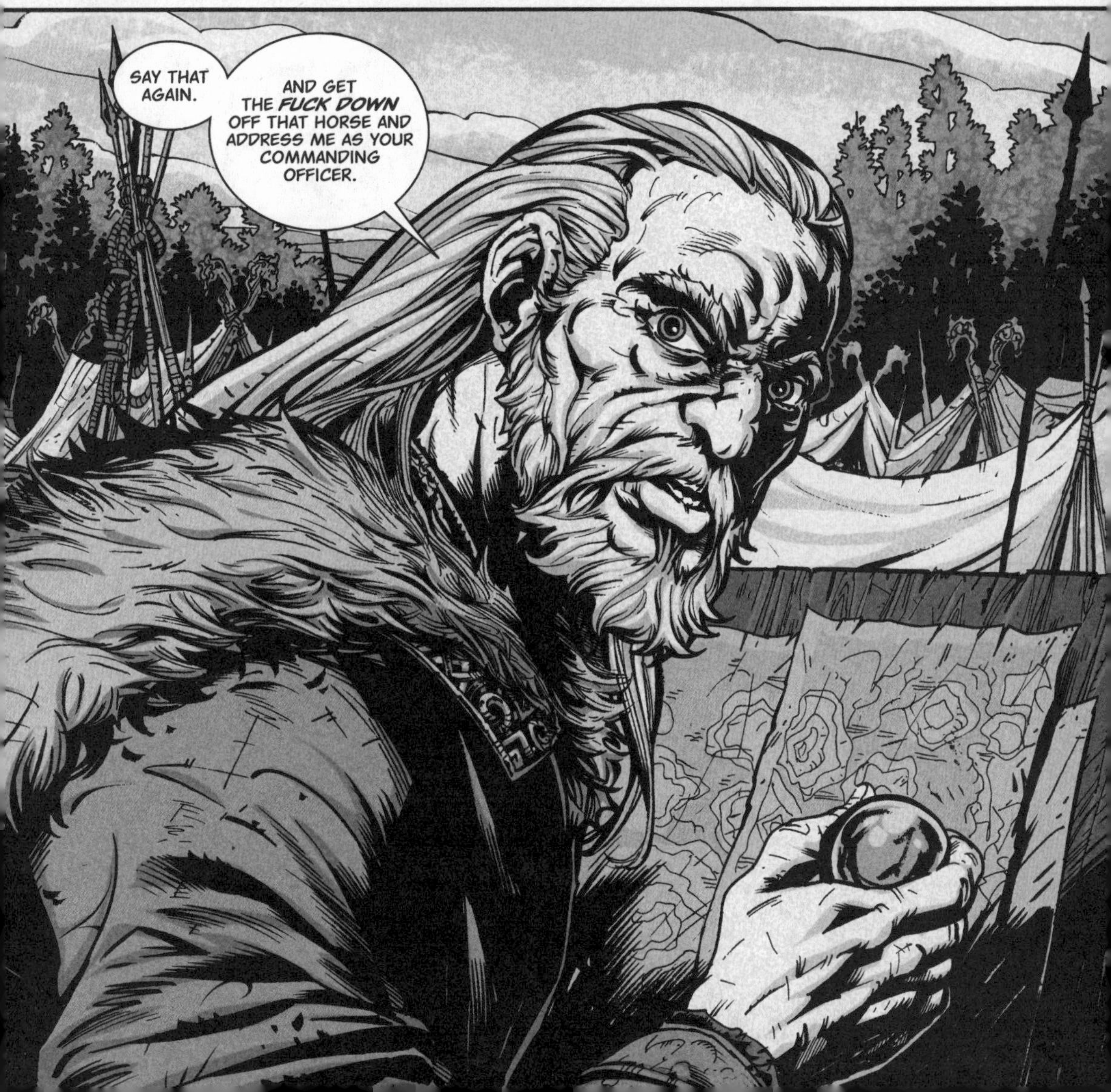
SAY THAT AGAIN.
AND GET THE *FUCK DOWN* OFF THAT HORSE AND ADDRESS ME AS YOUR COMMANDING OFFICER.

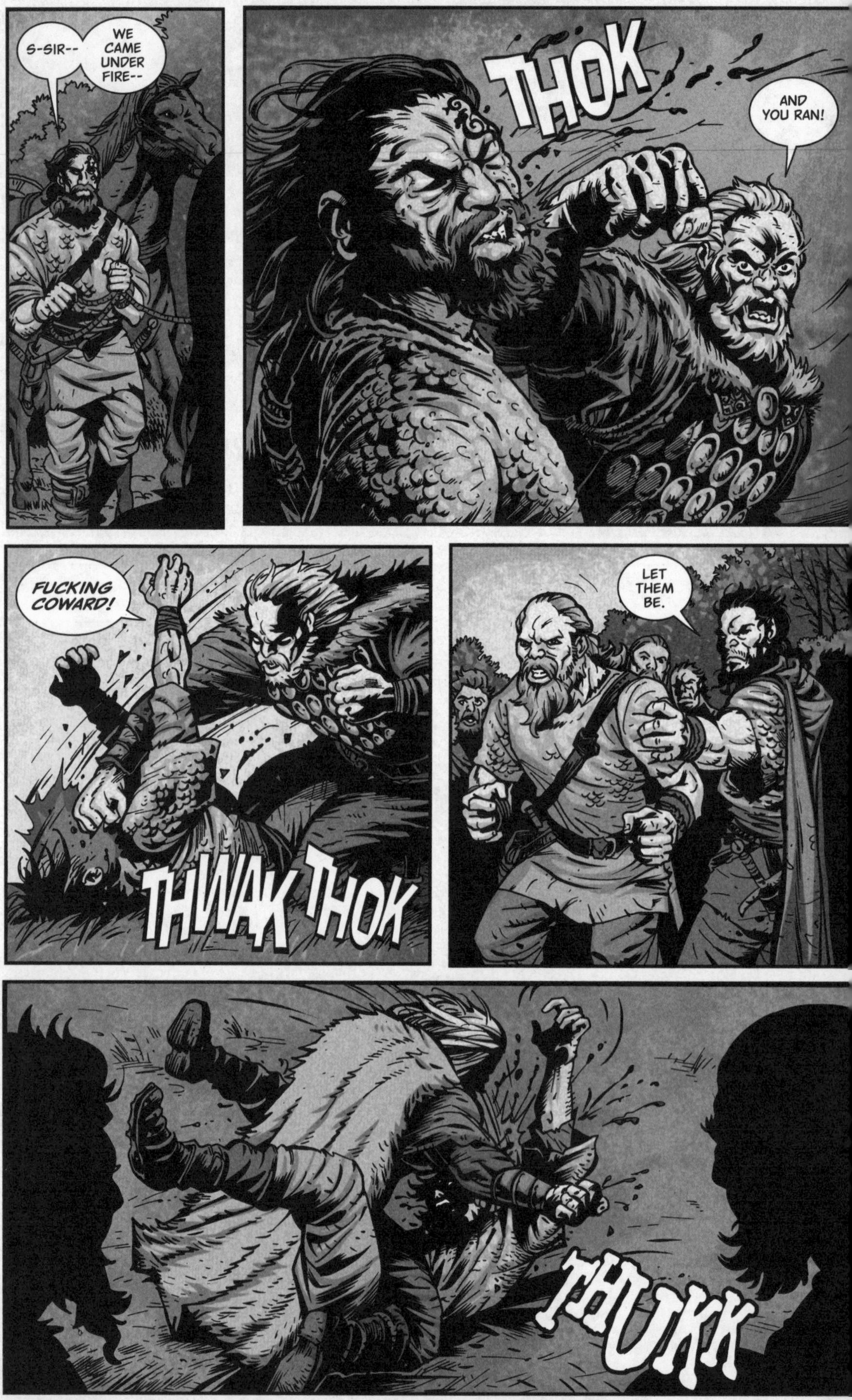
S-SIR--
WE CAME UNDER FIRE--
THOK
AND YOU RAN!
FUCKING COWARD!
THWAK THOK
LET THEM BE.
THUKK

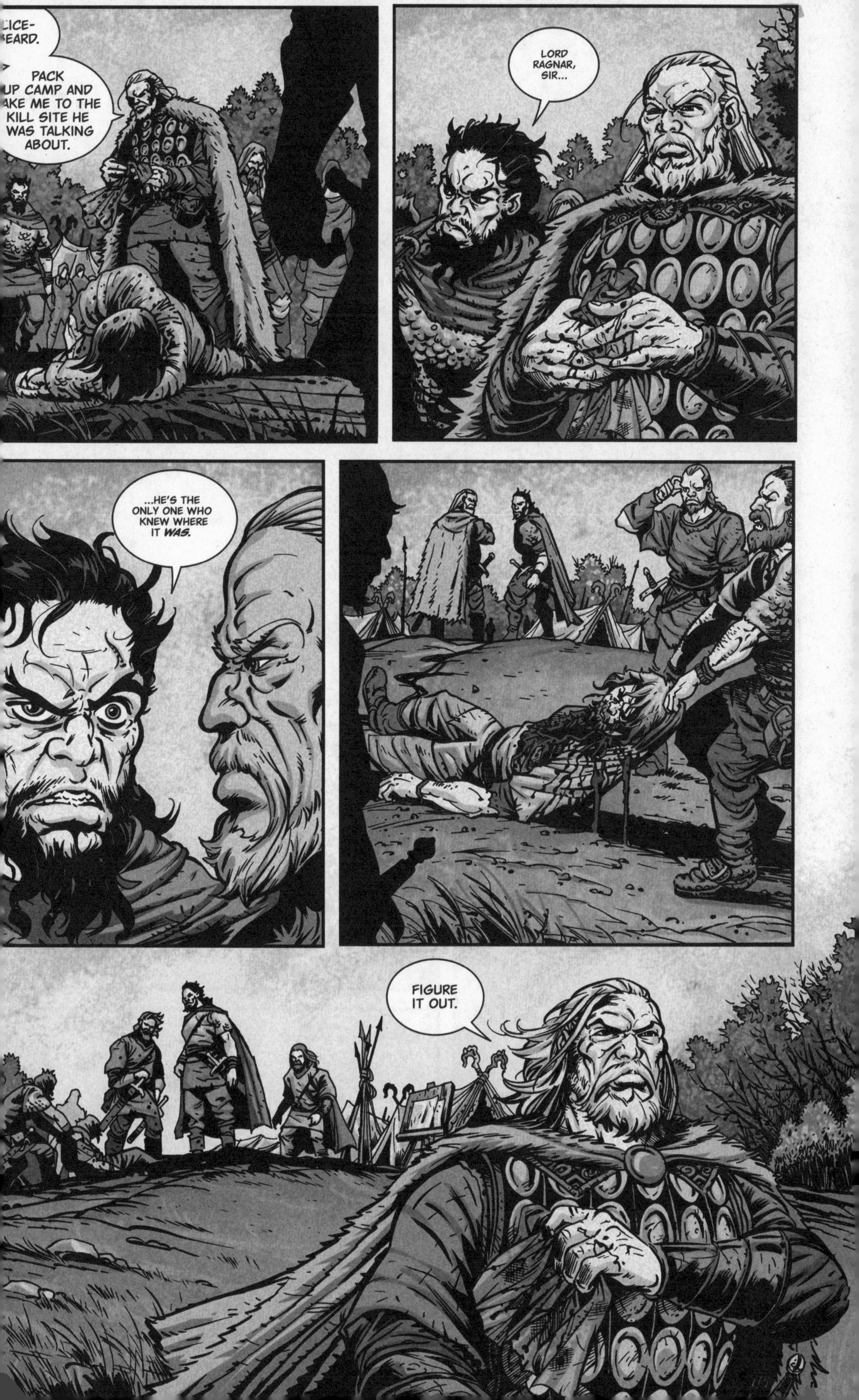

LICE-
BEARD.
PACK
UP CAMP AND
TAKE ME TO THE
KILL SITE HE
WAS TALKING
ABOUT.
LORD
RAGNAR,
SIR...
...HE'S THE
ONLY ONE WHO
KNEW WHERE
IT WAS.
FIGURE
IT OUT.

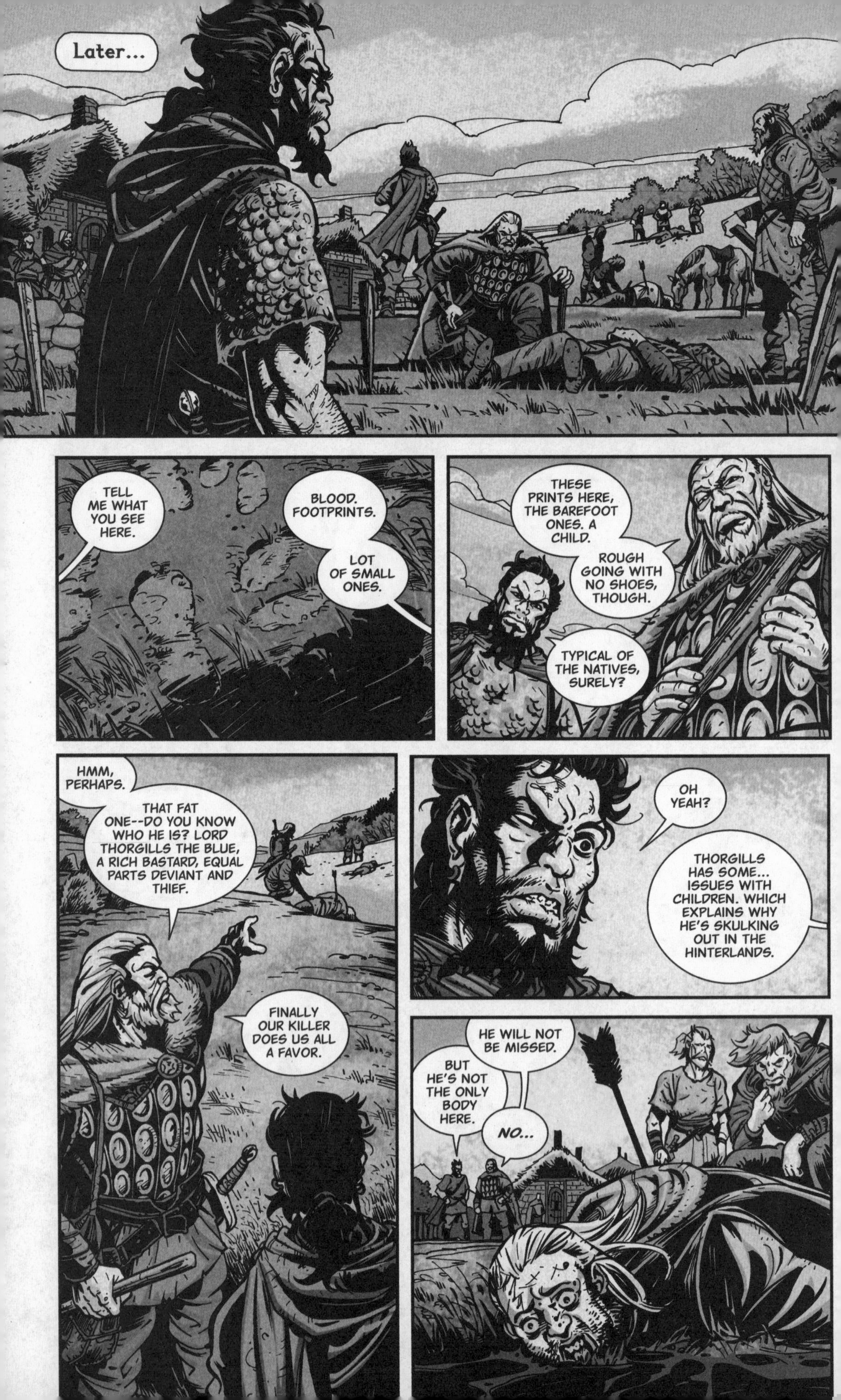

Later...
TELL ME WHAT YOU SEE HERE.
BLOOD. FOOTPRINTS.
LOT OF SMALL ONES.
THESE PRINTS HERE, THE BAREFOOT ONES. A CHILD.
ROUGH GOING WITH NO SHOES, THOUGH.
TYPICAL OF THE NATIVES, SURELY?
HMM, PERHAPS.
THAT FAT ONE--DO YOU KNOW WHO HE IS? LORD THORGILLS THE BLUE, A RICH BASTARD, EQUAL PARTS DEVIANT AND THIEF.
FINALLY OUR KILLER DOES US ALL A FAVOR.
OH YEAH?
THORGILLS HAS SOME... ISSUES WITH CHILDREN. WHICH EXPLAINS WHY HE'S SKULKING OUT IN THE HINTERLANDS.
HE WILL NOT BE MISSED.
BUT HE'S NOT THE ONLY BODY HERE.
NO...

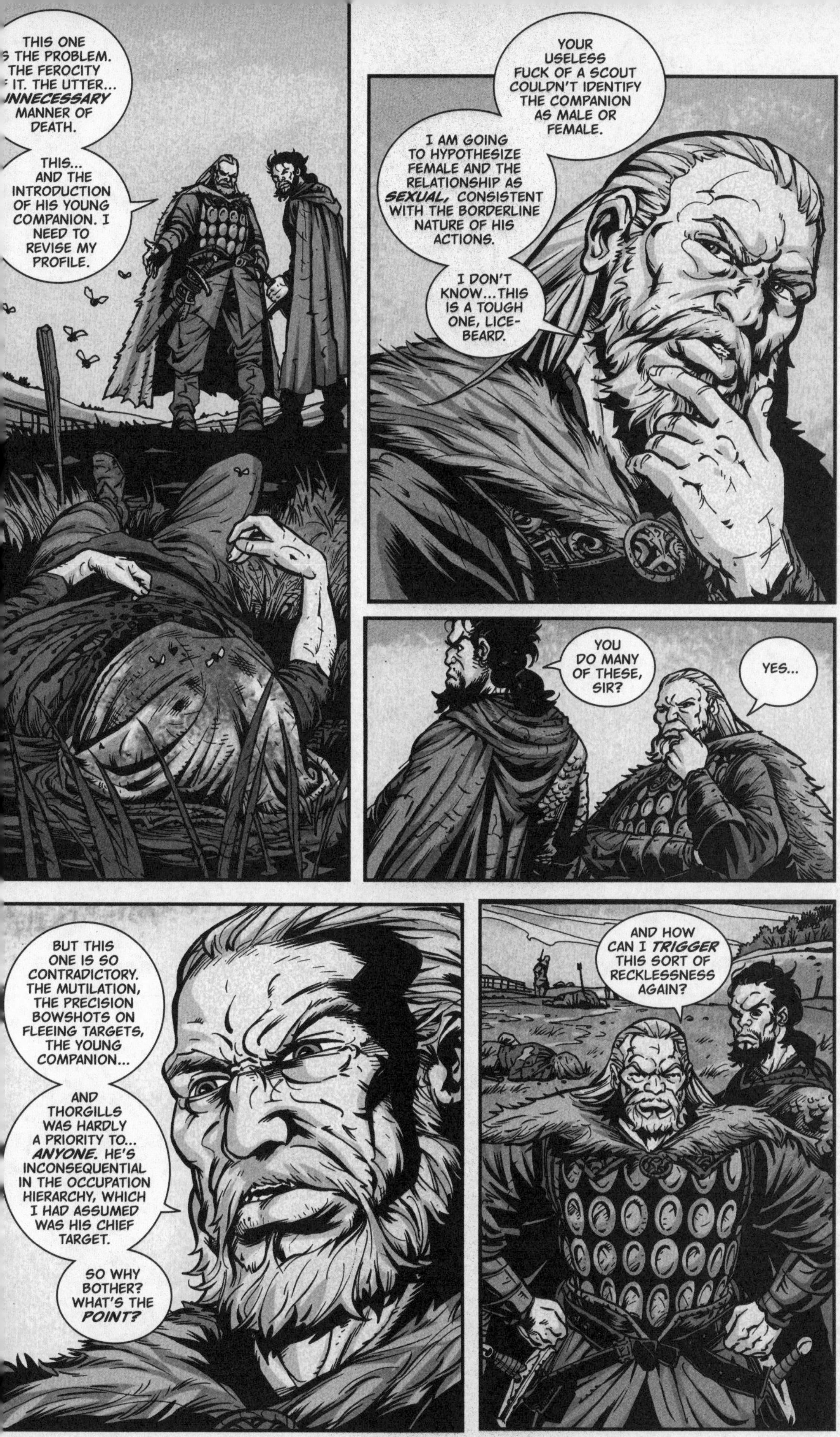
THIS ONE S THE PROBLEM. THE FEROCITY F IT. THE UTTER... INNECESSARY MANNER OF DEATH.
THIS... AND THE INTRODUCTION OF HIS YOUNG COMPANION. I NEED TO REVISE MY PROFILE.
YOUR USELESS FUCK OF A SCOUT COULDN'T IDENTIFY THE COMPANION AS MALE OR FEMALE.
I AM GOING TO HYPOTHESIZE FEMALE AND THE RELATIONSHIP AS SEXUAL, CONSISTENT WITH THE BORDERLINE NATURE OF HIS ACTIONS.
I DON'T KNOW...THIS IS A TOUGH ONE, LICE-BEARD.
YOU DO MANY OF THESE, SIR?
YES...
BUT THIS ONE IS SO CONTRADICTORY. THE MUTILATION, THE PRECISION BOWSHOTS ON FLEEING TARGETS, THE YOUNG COMPANION...
AND THORGILLS WAS HARDLY A PRIORITY TO... ANYONE. HE'S INCONSEQUENTIAL IN THE OCCUPATION HIERARCHY, WHICH I HAD ASSUMED WAS HIS CHIEF TARGET.
SO WHY BOTHER? WHAT'S THE POINT?
AND HOW CAN I TRIGGER THIS SORT OF RECKLESSNESS AGAIN?

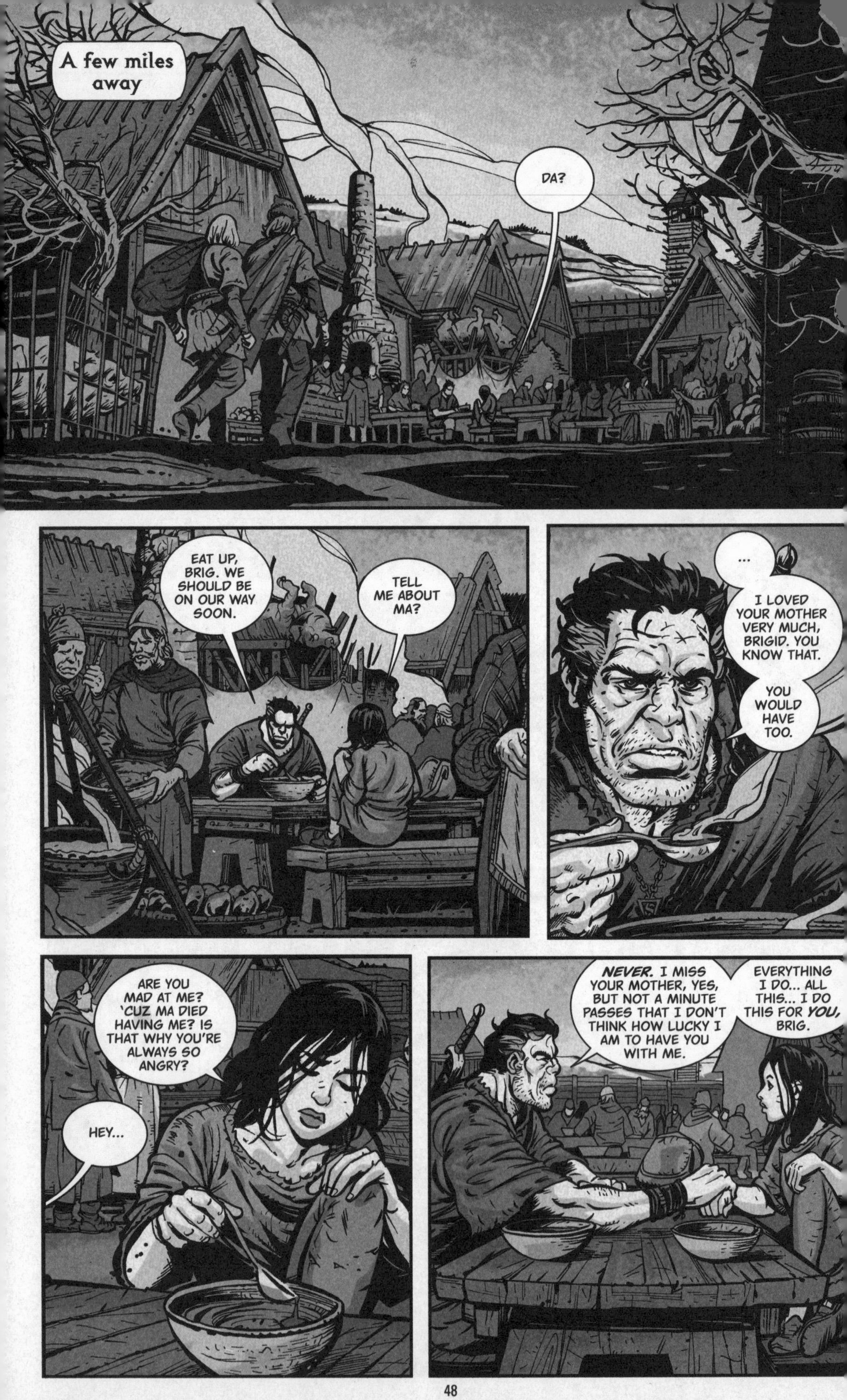
A few miles away
DA?
EAT UP, BRIG. WE SHOULD BE ON OUR WAY SOON.
TELL ME ABOUT MA?
...
I LOVED YOUR MOTHER VERY MUCH, BRIGID. YOU KNOW THAT.
YOU WOULD HAVE TOO.
ARE YOU MAD AT ME? 'CUZ MA DIED HAVING ME? IS THAT WHY YOU'RE ALWAYS SO ANGRY?
HEY...
NEVER. I MISS YOUR MOTHER, YES, BUT NOT A MINUTE PASSES THAT I DON'T THINK HOW LUCKY I AM TO HAVE YOU WITH ME.
EVERYTHING I DO... ALL THIS... I DO THIS FOR YOU, BRIG.

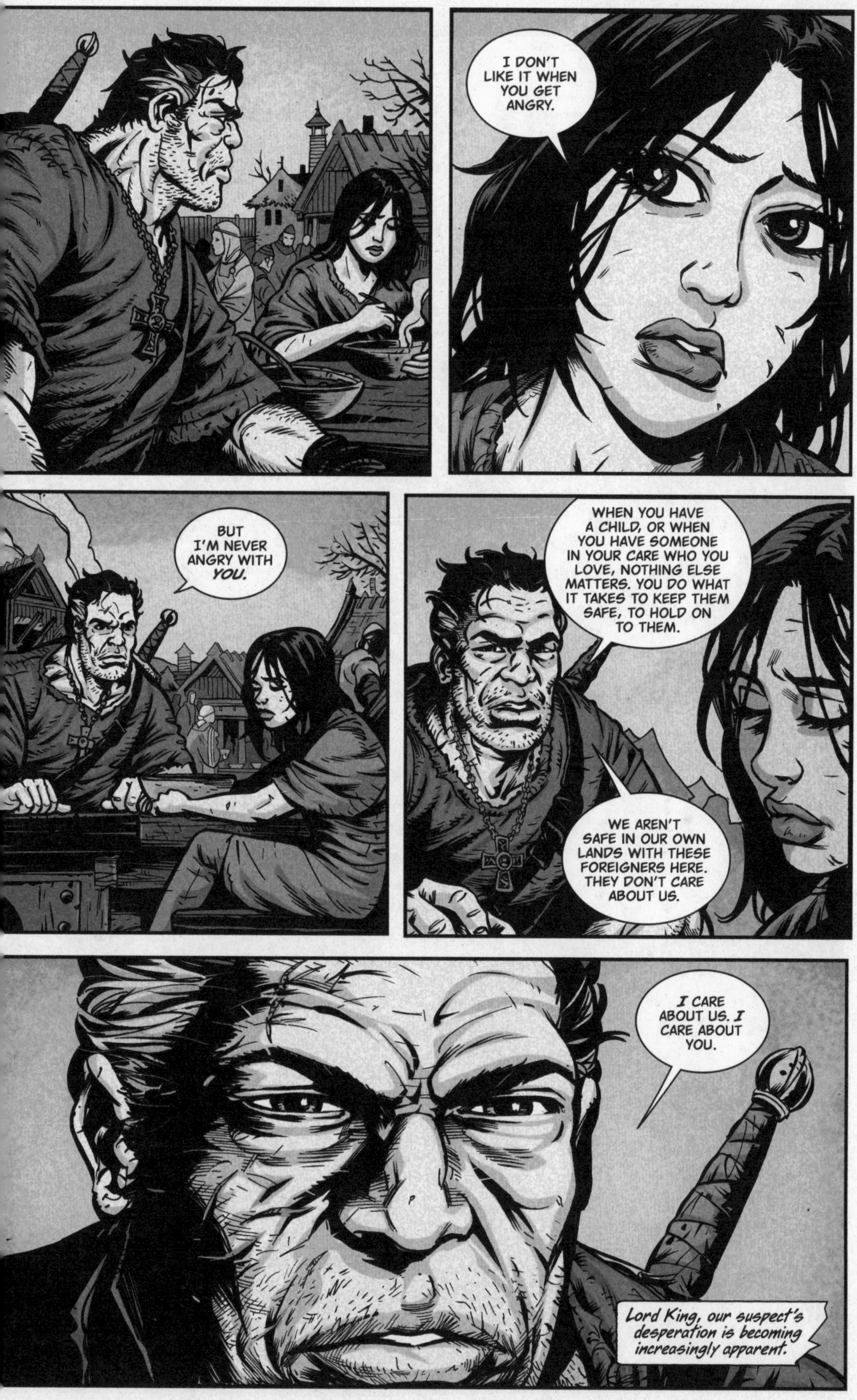
I DON'T LIKE IT WHEN YOU GET ANGRY.
BUT I'M NEVER ANGRY WITH *YOU.*
WHEN YOU HAVE A CHILD, OR WHEN YOU HAVE SOMEONE IN YOUR CARE WHO YOU LOVE, NOTHING ELSE MATTERS. YOU DO WHAT IT TAKES TO KEEP THEM SAFE, TO HOLD ON TO THEM.
WE AREN'T SAFE IN OUR OWN LANDS WITH THESE FOREIGNERS HERE. THEY DON'T CARE ABOUT US.
I CARE ABOUT US. *I* CARE ABOUT YOU.
Lord King, our suspect's desperation is becoming increasingly apparent.

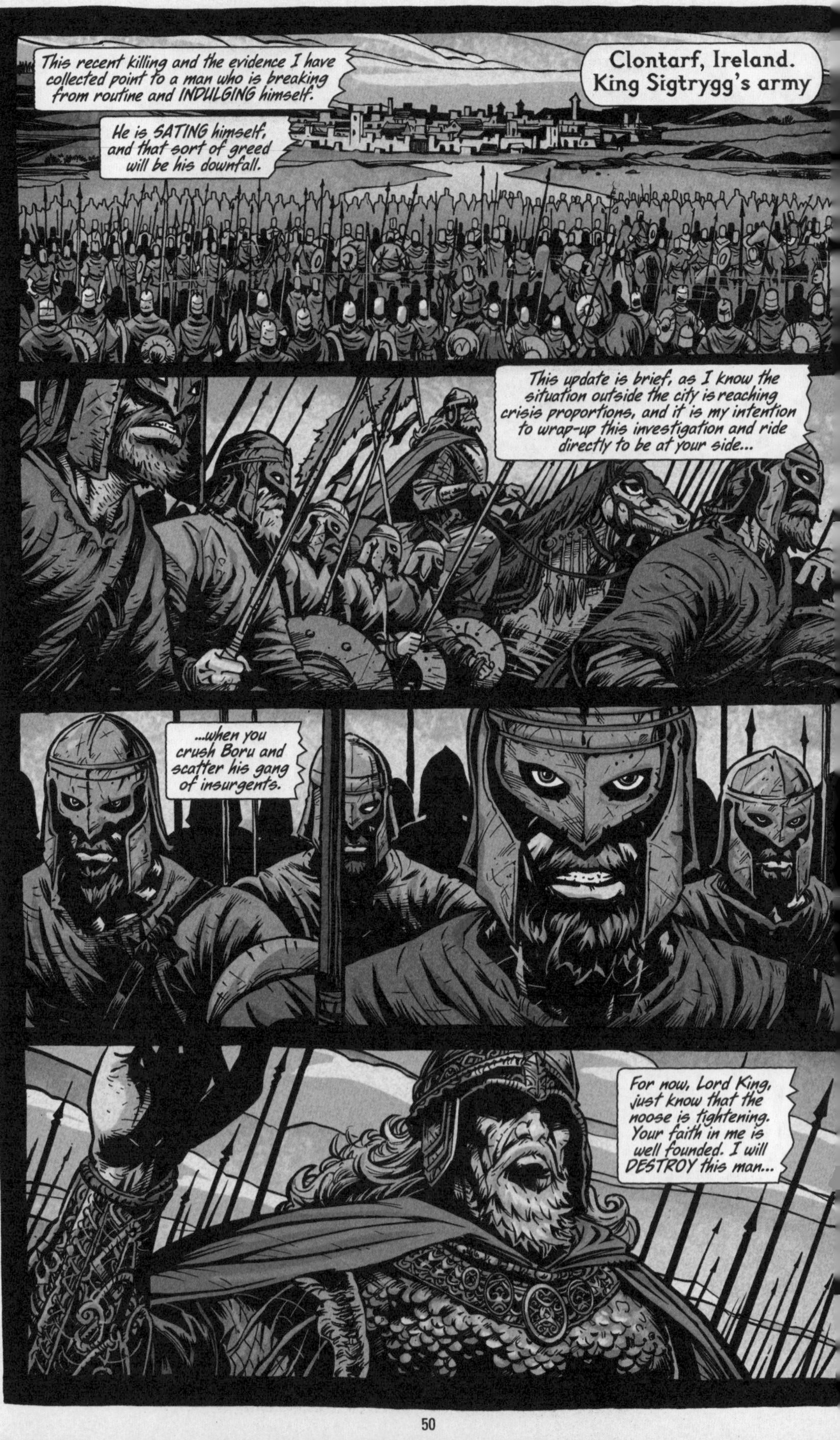
Clontarf, Ireland. King Sigtrygg's army
This recent killing and the evidence I have collected point to a man who is breaking from routine and INDULGING himself.
He is SATING himself, and that sort of greed will be his downfall.
This update is brief, as I know the situation outside the city is reaching crisis proportions, and it is my intention to wrap-up this investigation and ride directly to be at your side...
...when you crush Boru and scatter his gang of insurgents.
For now, Lord King, just know that the noose is tightening. Your faith in me is well founded. I will DESTROY this man...

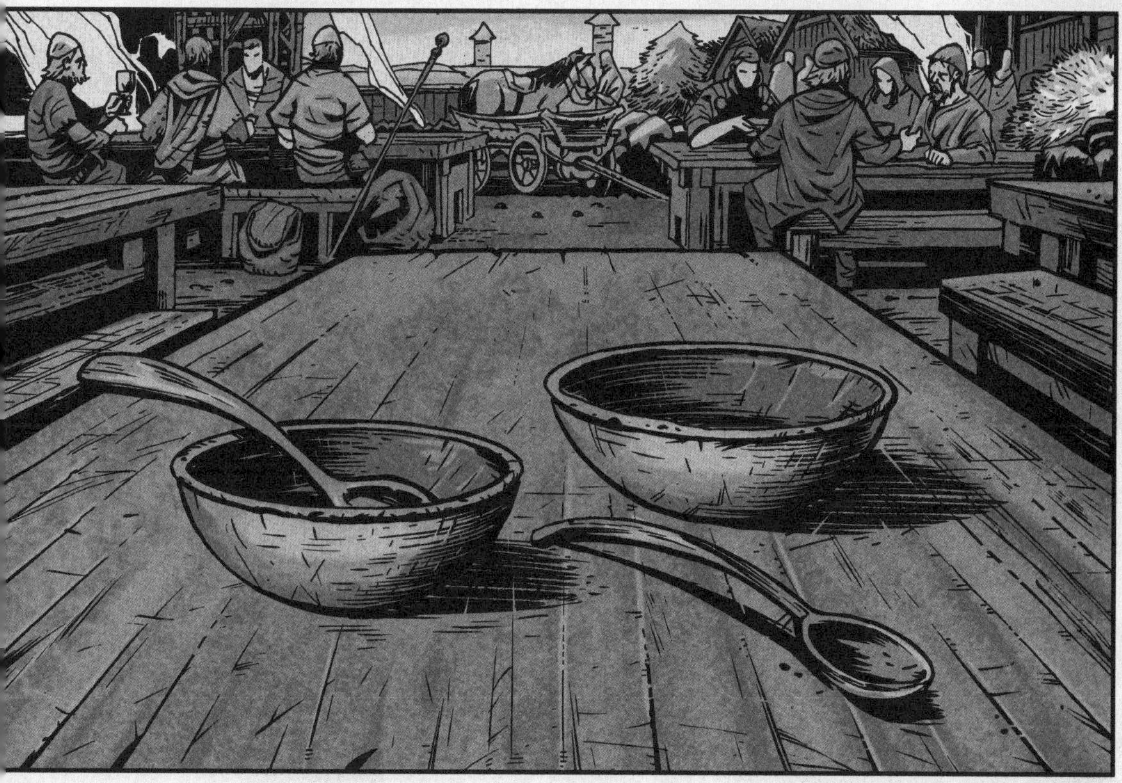

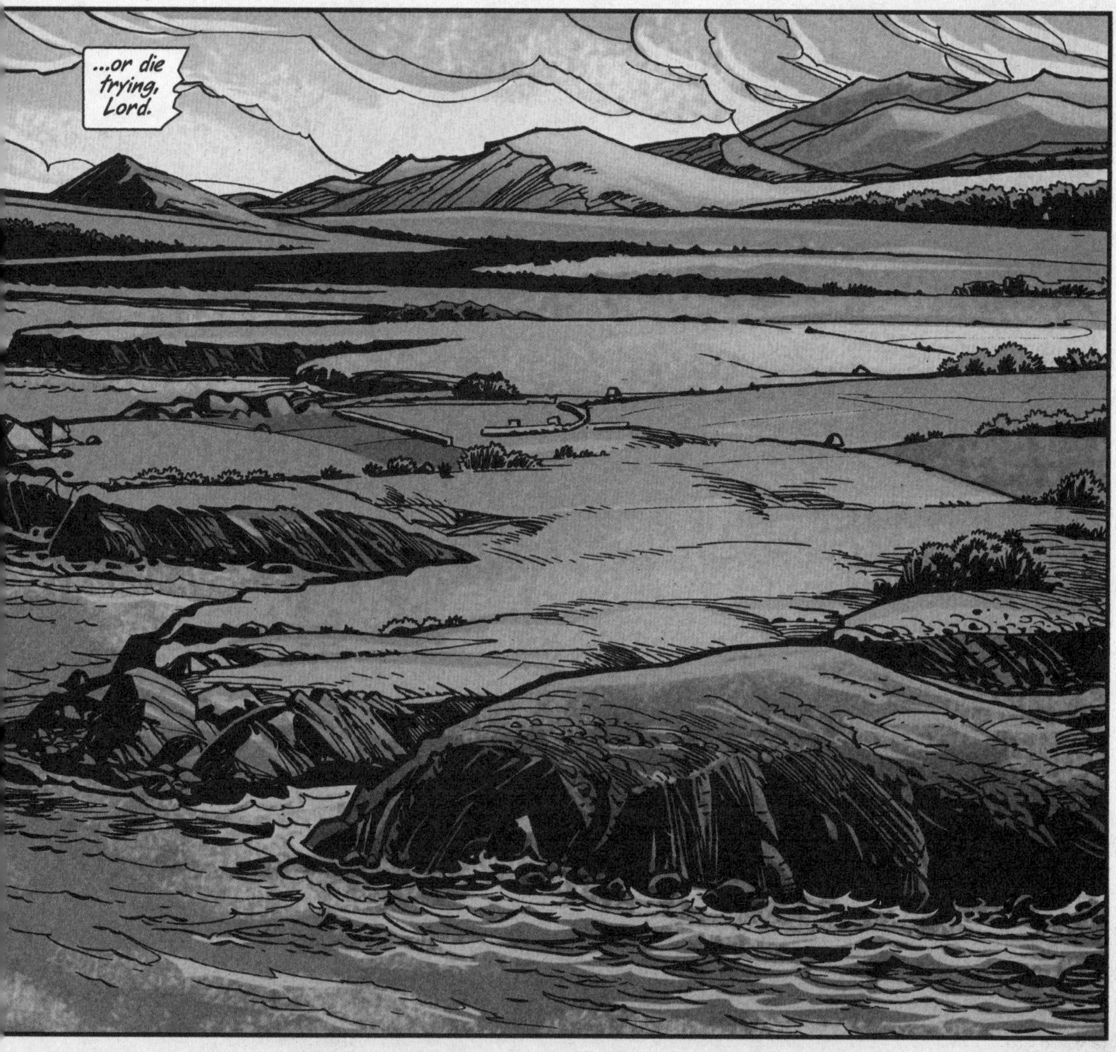
...or die trying, Lord.

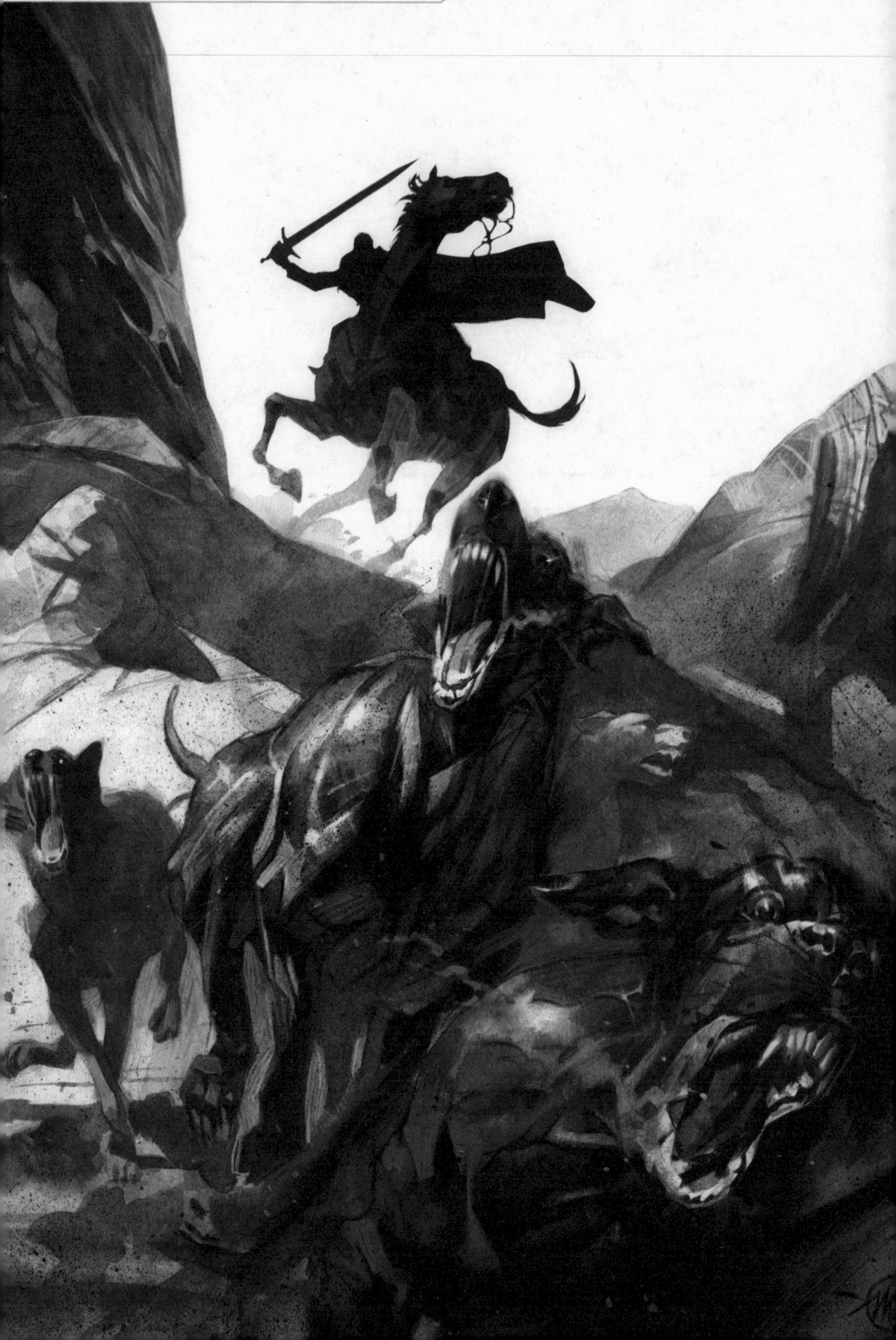

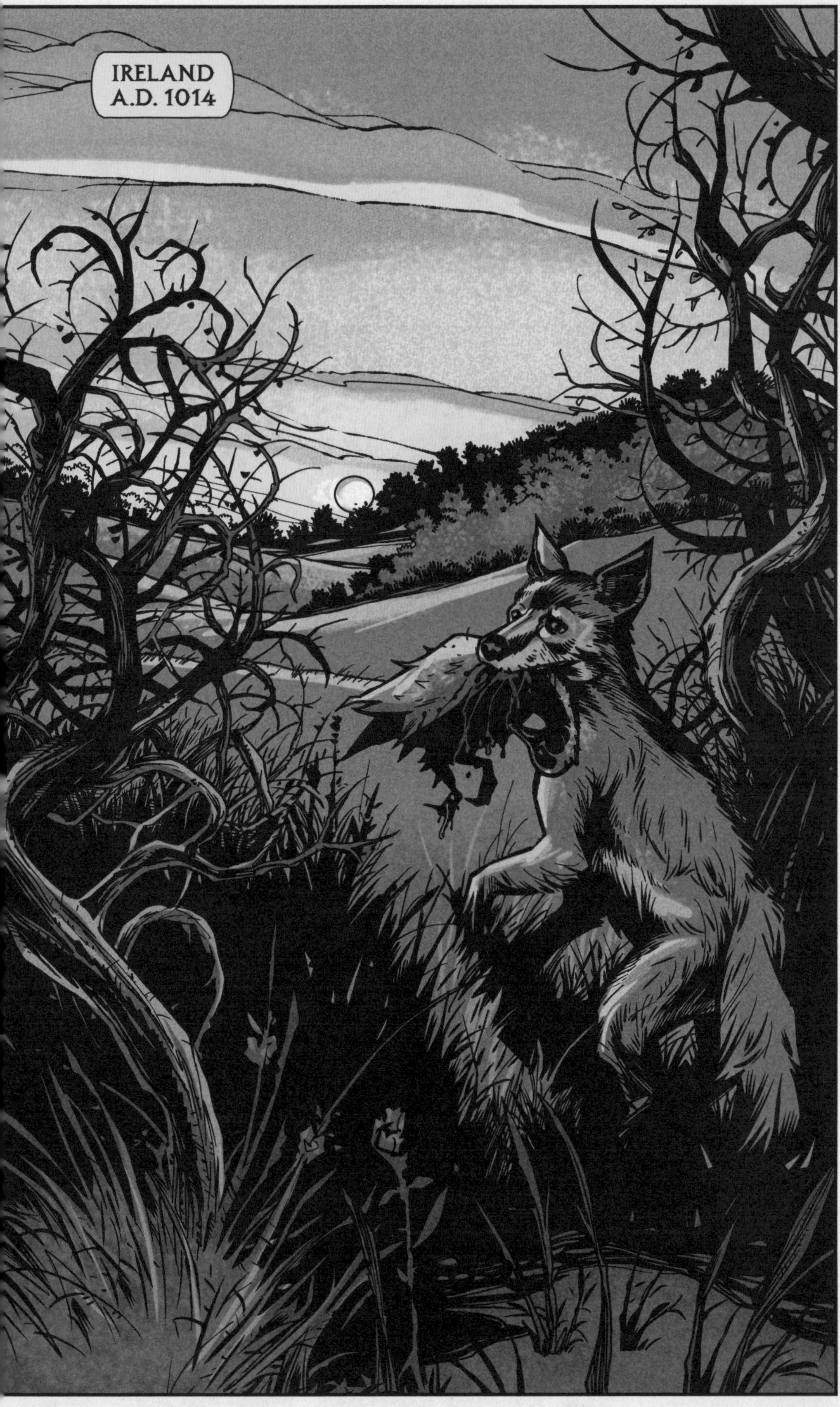
IRELAND
A.D. 1014

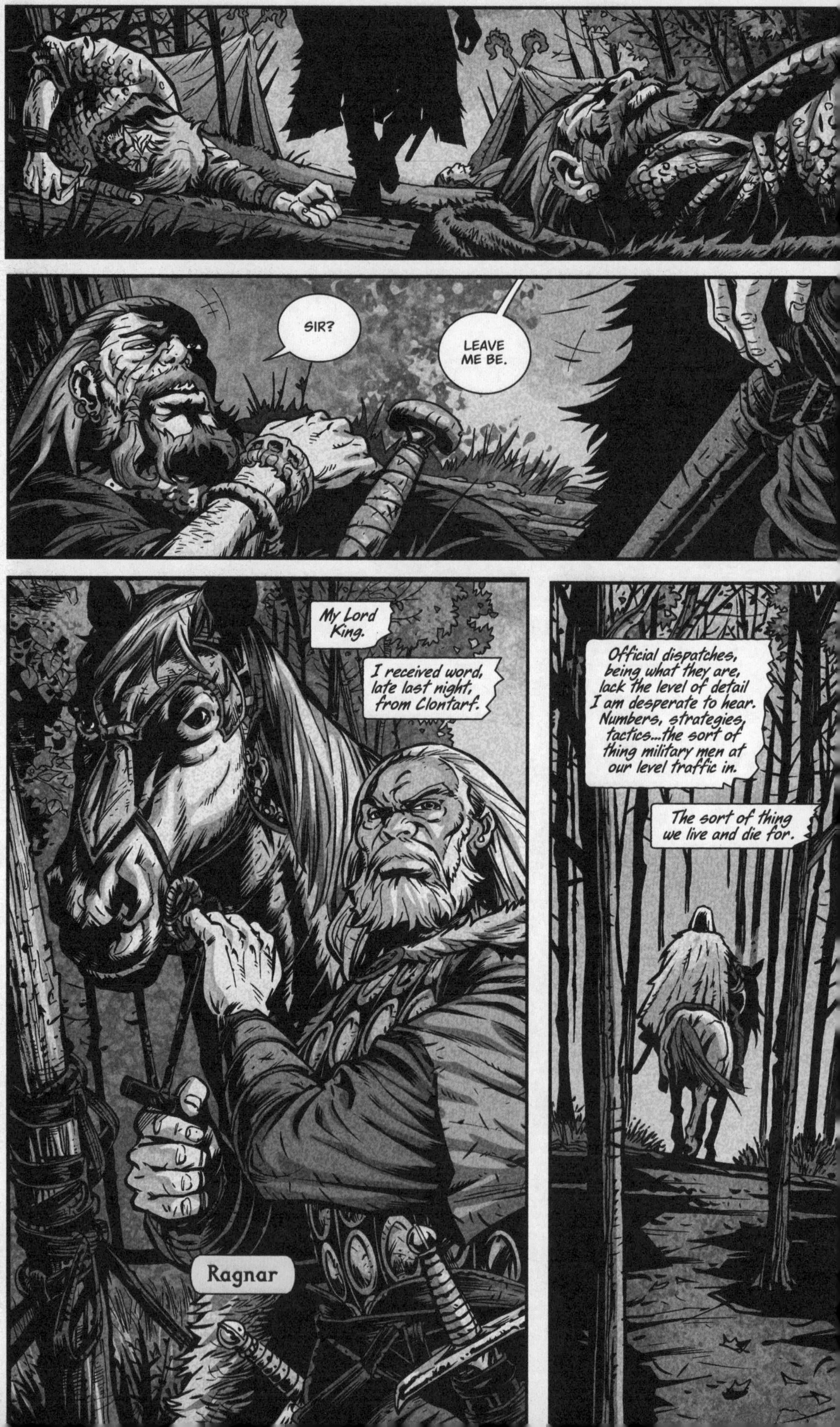
SIR?
LEAVE ME BE.
My Lord King.
I received word, late last night, from Clontarf.
Ragnar
Official dispatches, being what they are, lack the level of detail I am desperate to hear. Numbers, strategies, tactics...the sort of thing military men at our level traffic in.
The sort of thing we live and die for.

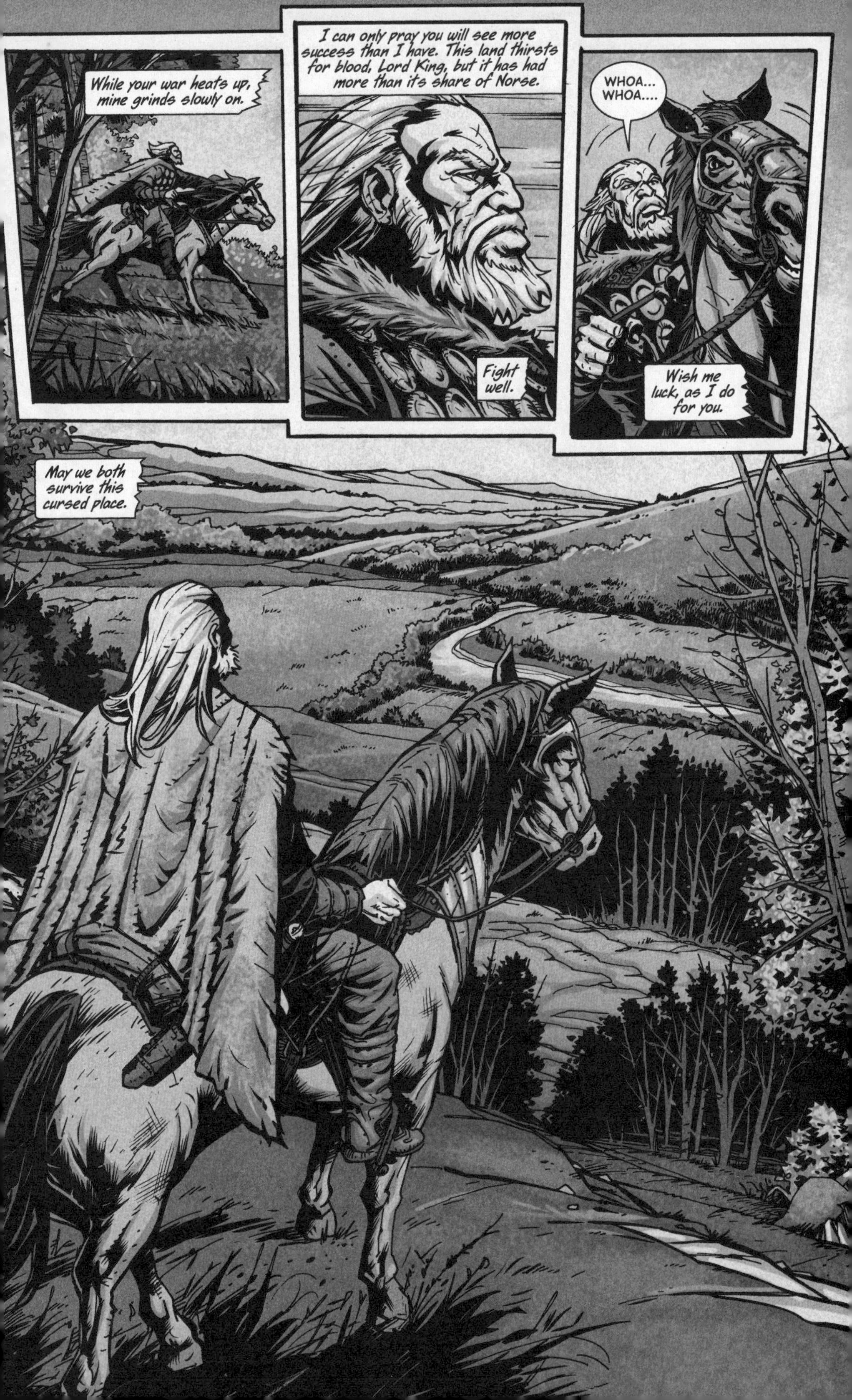
While your war heats up, mine grinds slowly on.
I can only pray you will see more success than I have. This land thirsts for blood, Lord King, but it has had more than its share of Norse.
Fight well.
WHOA... WHOA....
Wish me luck, as I do for you.
May we both survive this cursed place.

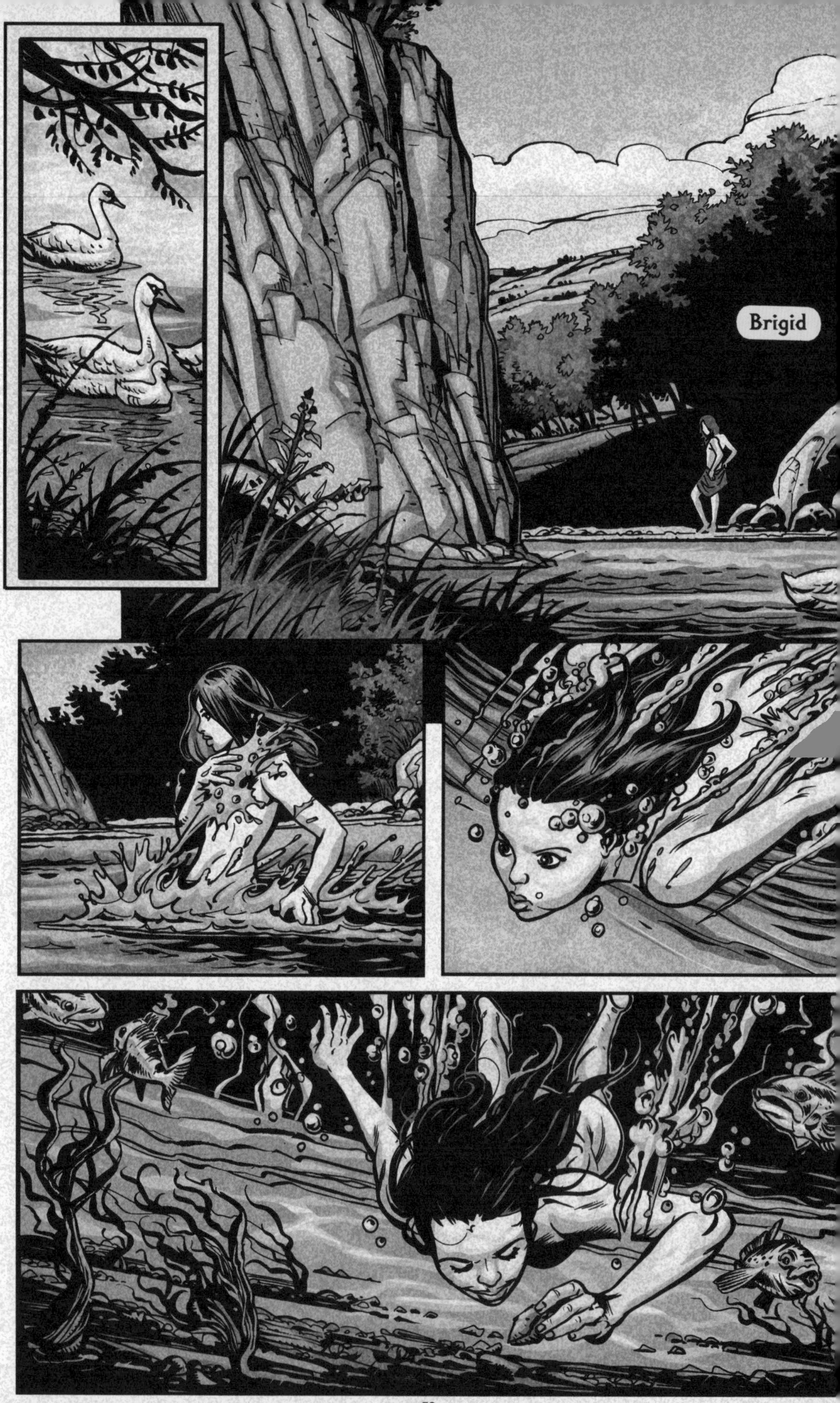
Brigid

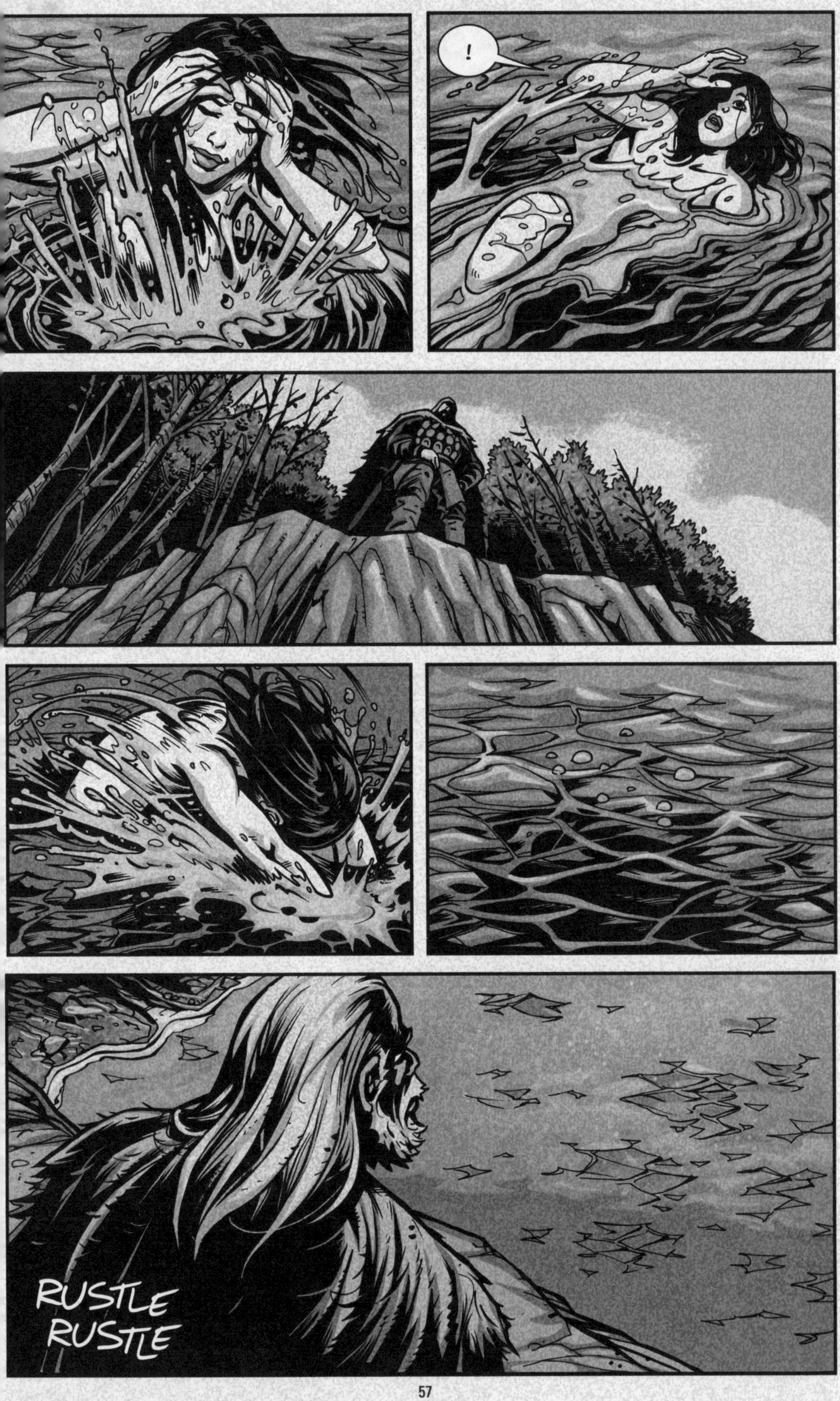
!
RUSTLE
RUSTLE

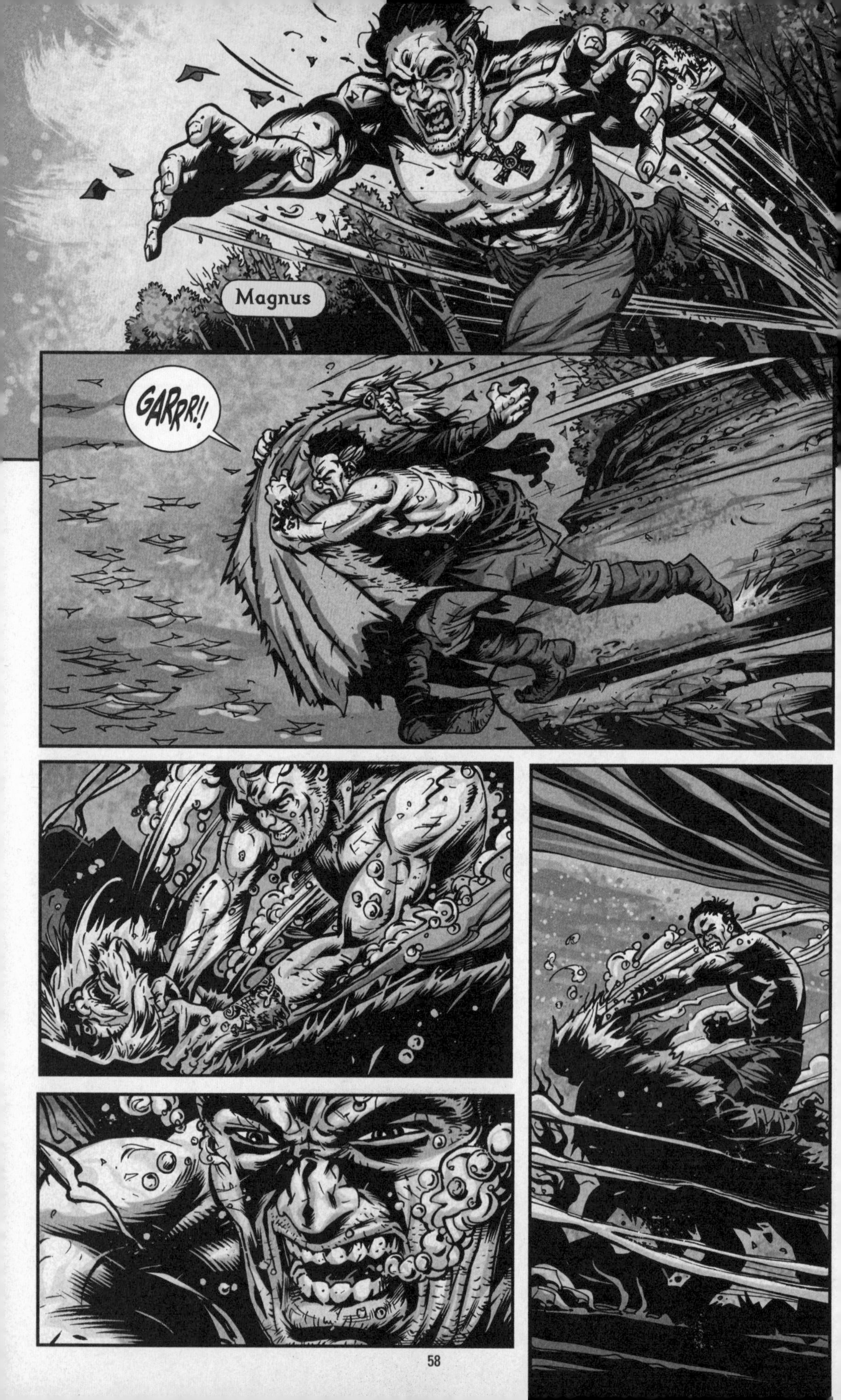
Magnus
GARRR!!

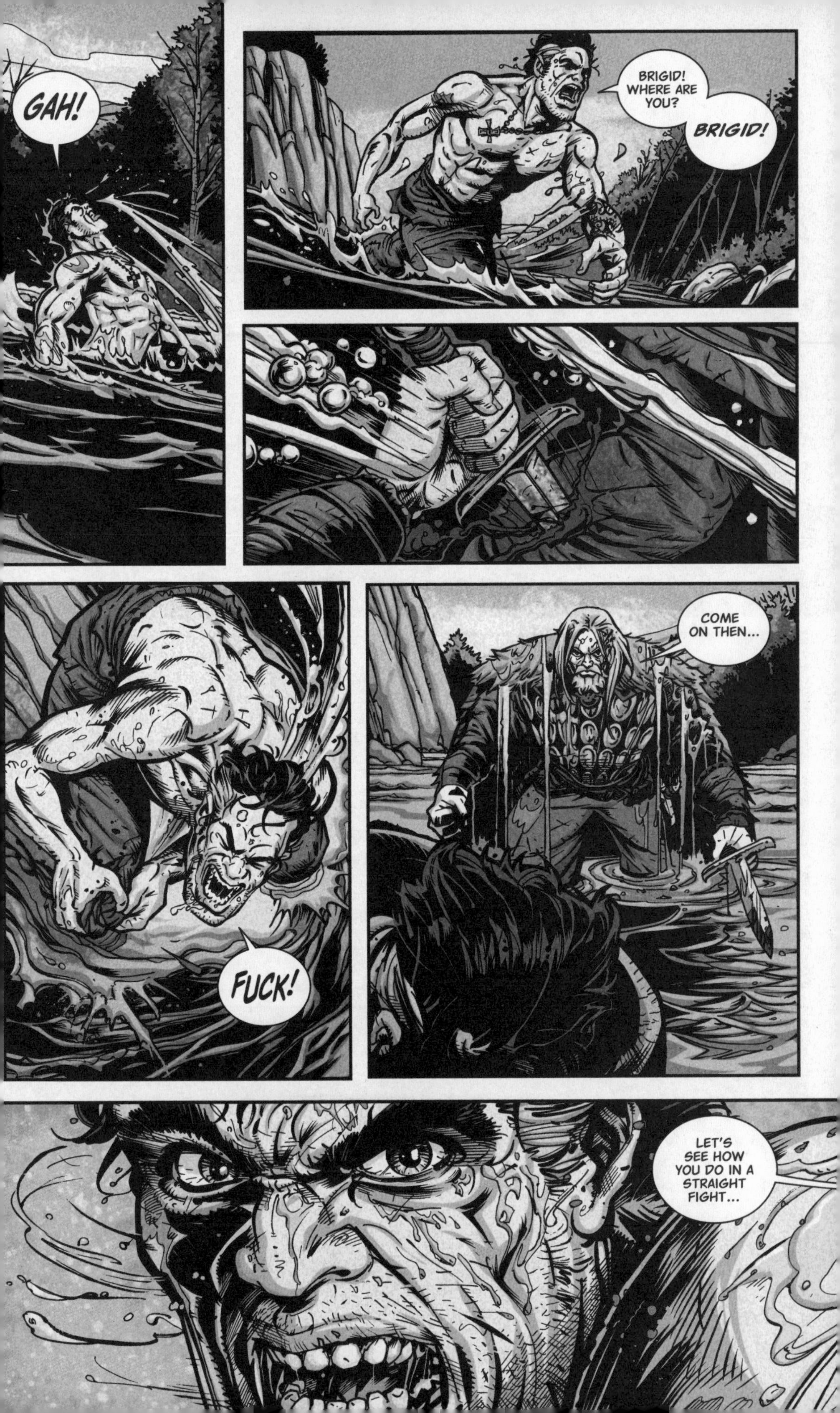
GAH!
BRIGID! WHERE ARE YOU?
BRIGID!
FUCK!
COME ON THEN...
LET'S SEE HOW YOU DO IN A STRAIGHT FIGHT...

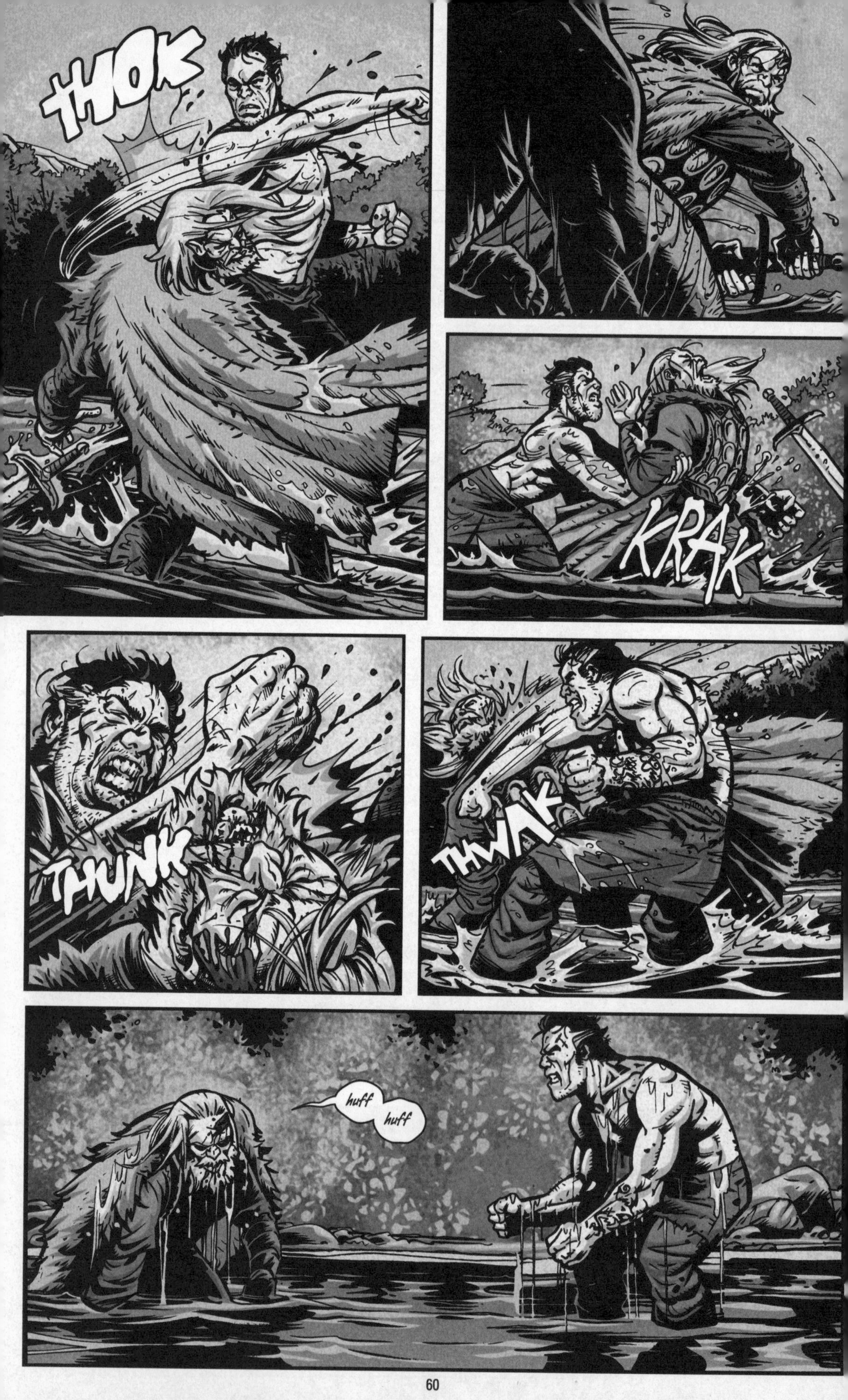

THOK
KRAK
THUNK
THWAK
huff
huff

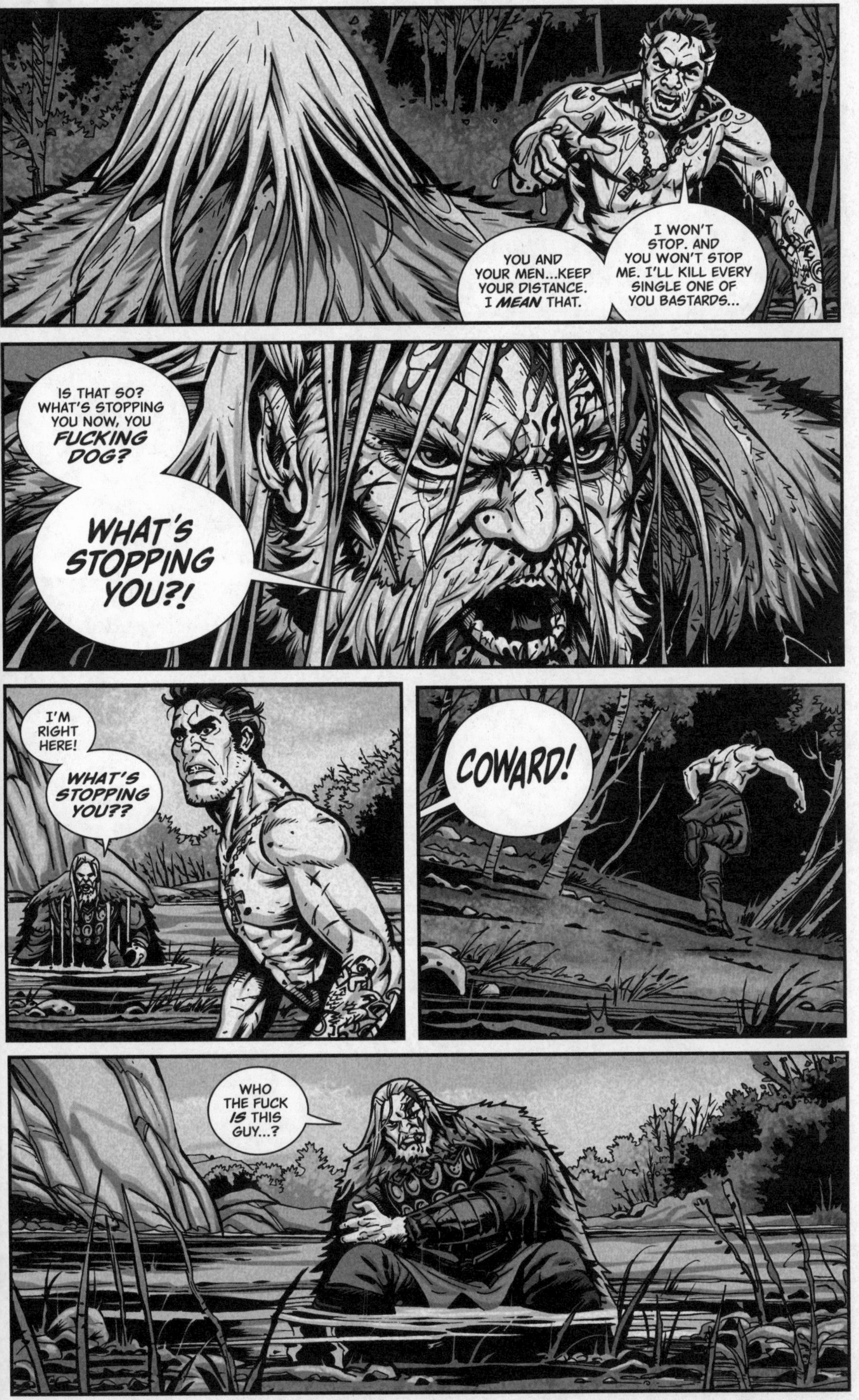
YOU AND YOUR MEN...KEEP YOUR DISTANCE. I *MEAN* THAT.
I WON'T STOP. AND YOU WON'T STOP ME. I'LL KILL EVERY SINGLE ONE OF YOU BASTARDS...
IS THAT SO? WHAT'S STOPPING YOU NOW, YOU *FUCKING DOG?*
WHAT'S STOPPING YOU?!
I'M RIGHT HERE!
WHAT'S STOPPING YOU??
COWARD!
WHO THE FUCK *IS* THIS GUY...?

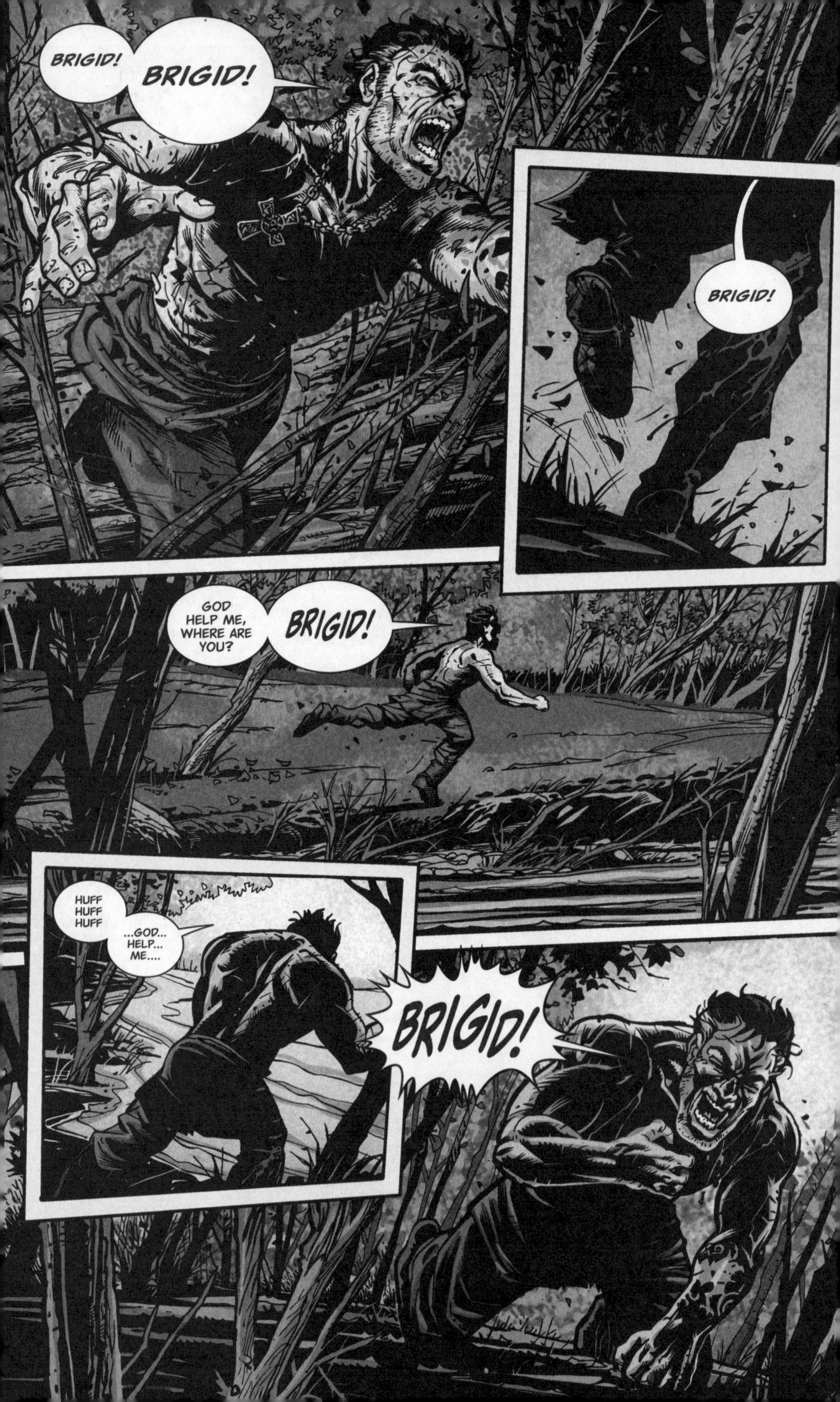
BRIGID!
BRIGID!
BRIGID!
GOD HELP ME, WHERE ARE YOU?
BRIGID!
HUFF HUFF HUFF
...GOD... HELP... ME....
BRIGID!

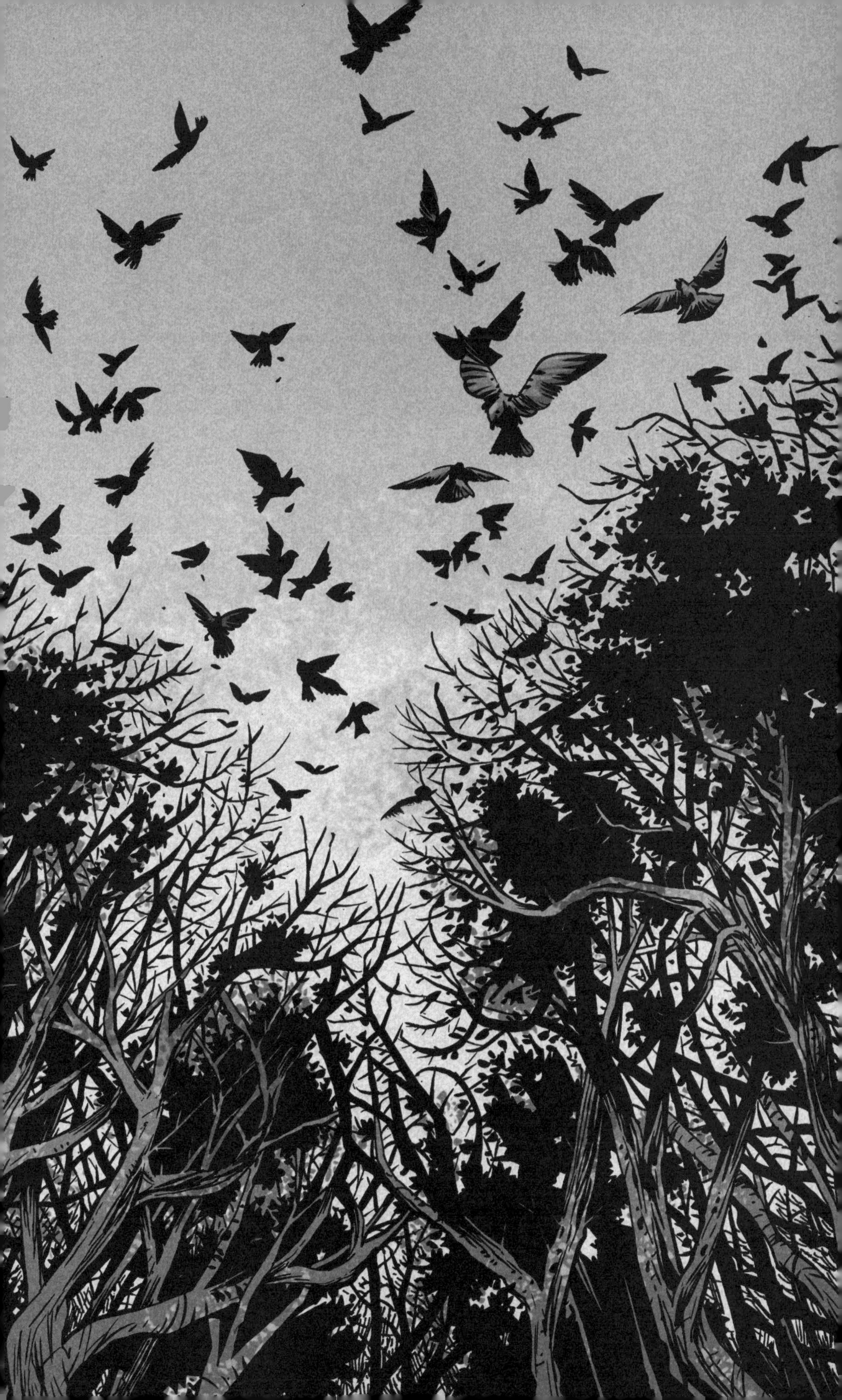

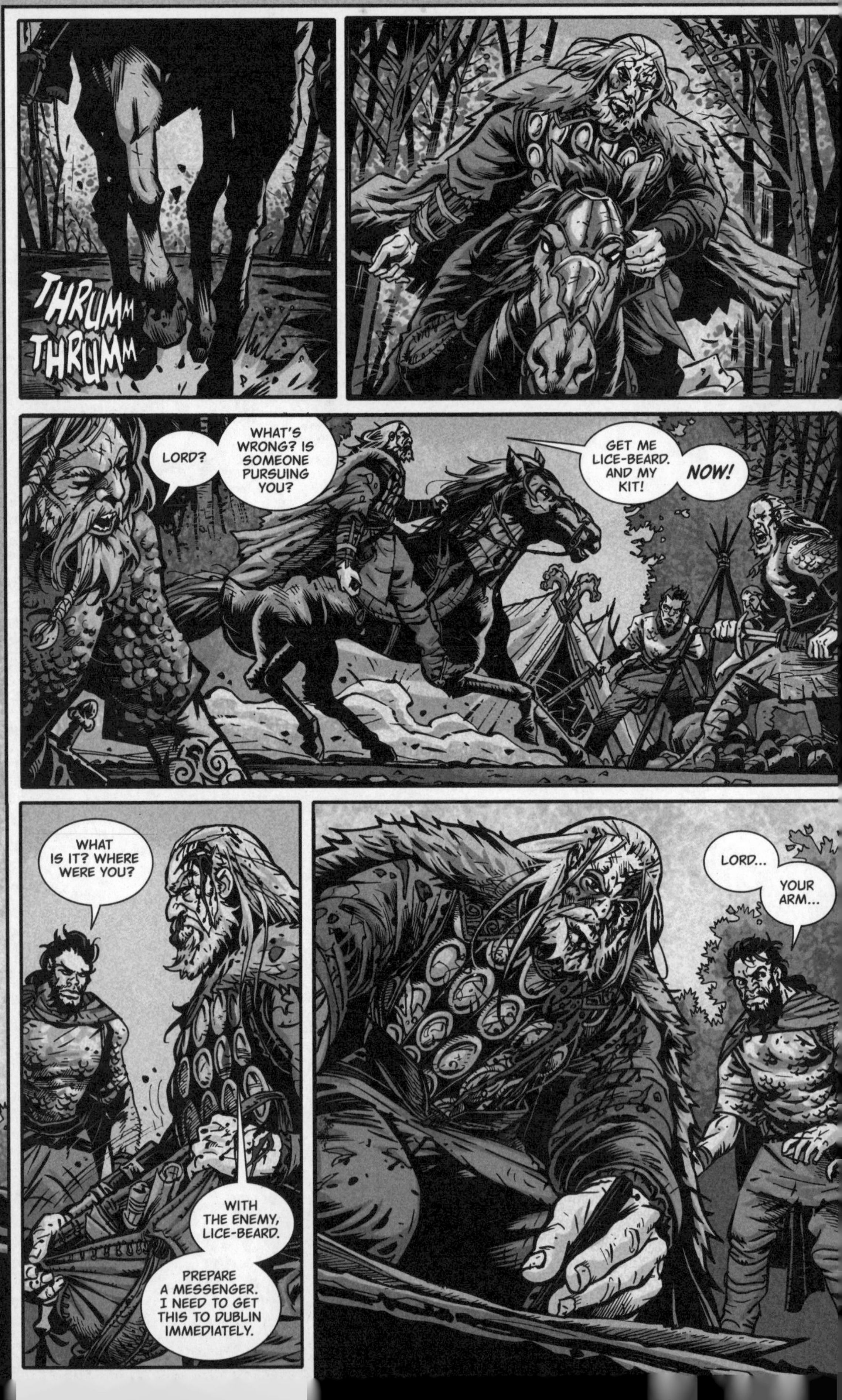
THRUMM
THRUMM
LORD?
WHAT'S WRONG? IS SOMEONE PURSUING YOU?
GET ME LICE-BEARD. AND MY KIT!
NOW!
WHAT IS IT? WHERE WERE YOU?
WITH THE ENEMY, LICE-BEARD.
PREPARE A MESSENGER. I NEED TO GET THIS TO DUBLIN IMMEDIATELY.
LORD...
YOUR ARM...

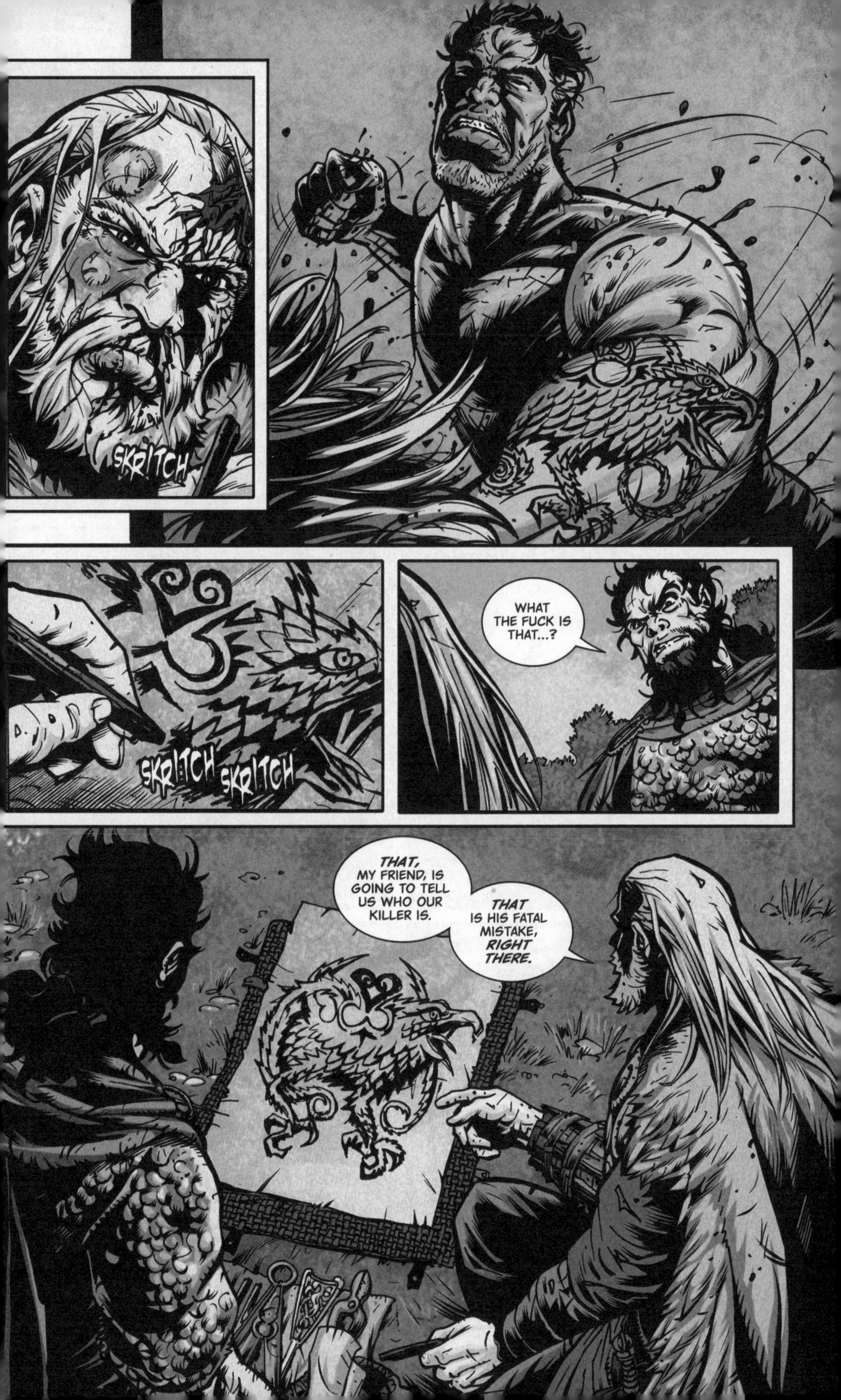
SKRITCH
SKRITCH SKRITCH
WHAT THE FUCK IS THAT...?
THAT, MY FRIEND, IS GOING TO TELL US WHO OUR KILLER IS.
THAT IS HIS FATAL MISTAKE, RIGHT THERE.

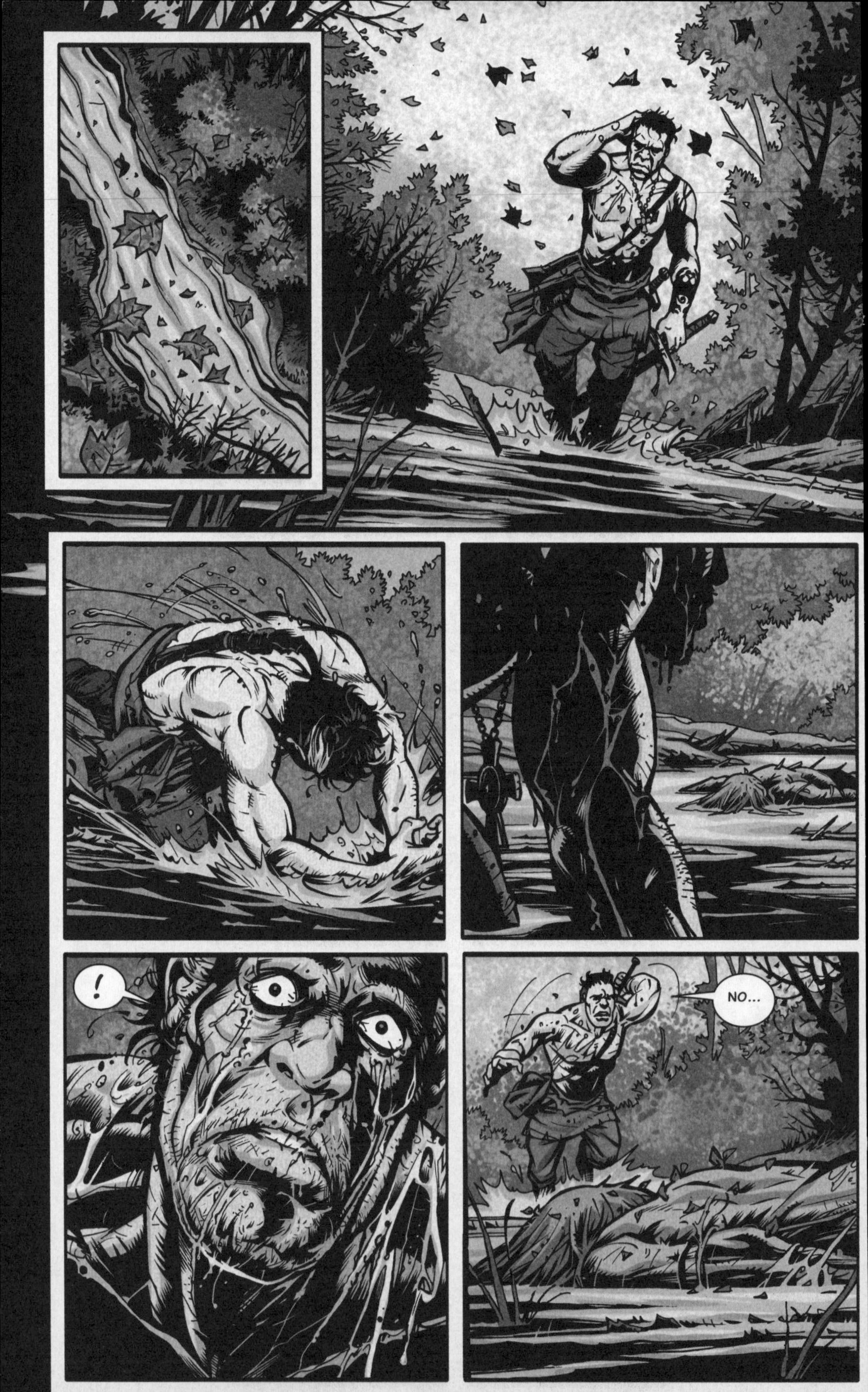
!
NO...

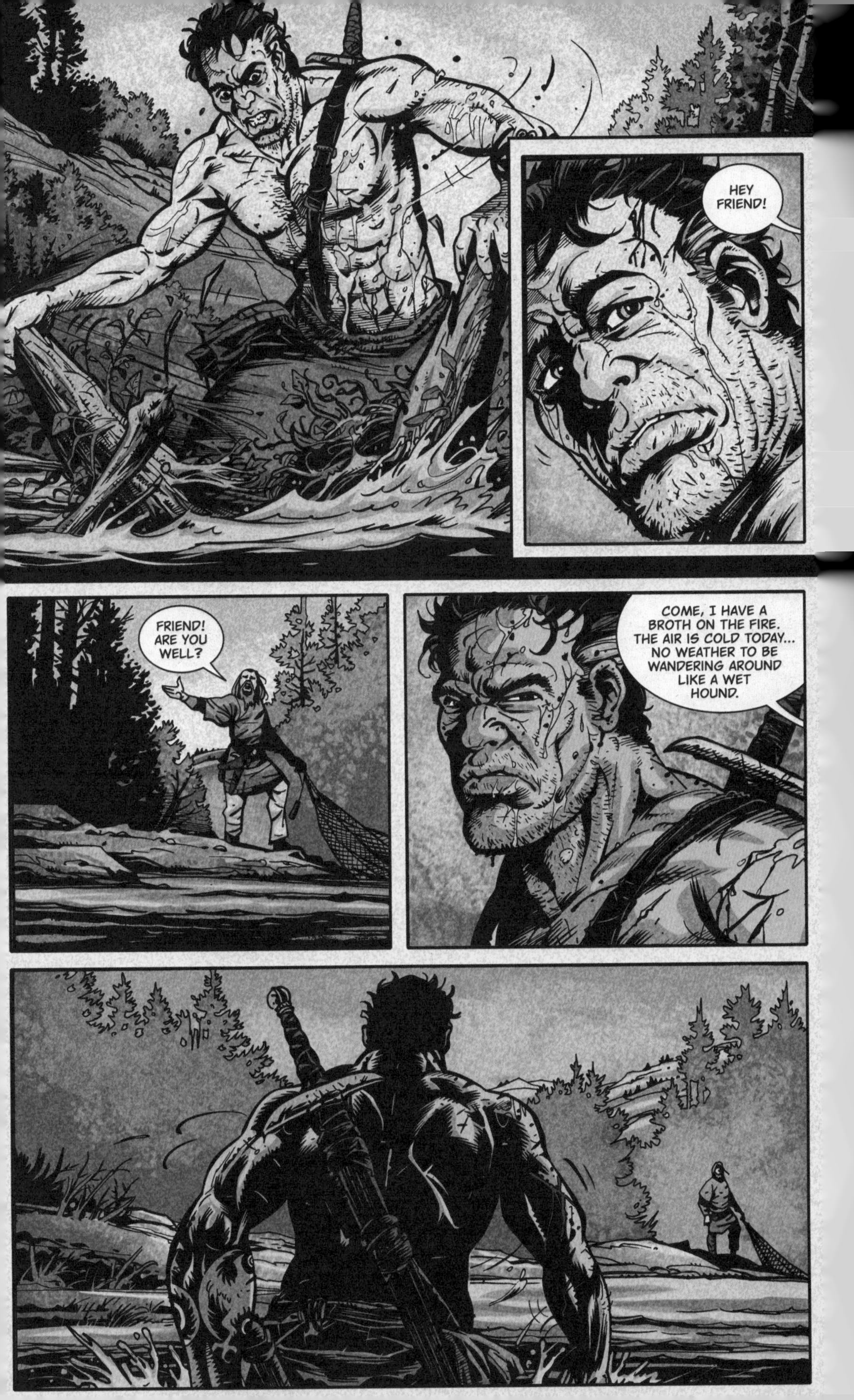
HEY FRIEND!
FRIEND! ARE YOU WELL?
COME, I HAVE A BROTH ON THE FIRE. THE AIR IS COLD TODAY... NO WEATHER TO BE WANDERING AROUND LIKE A WET HOUND.

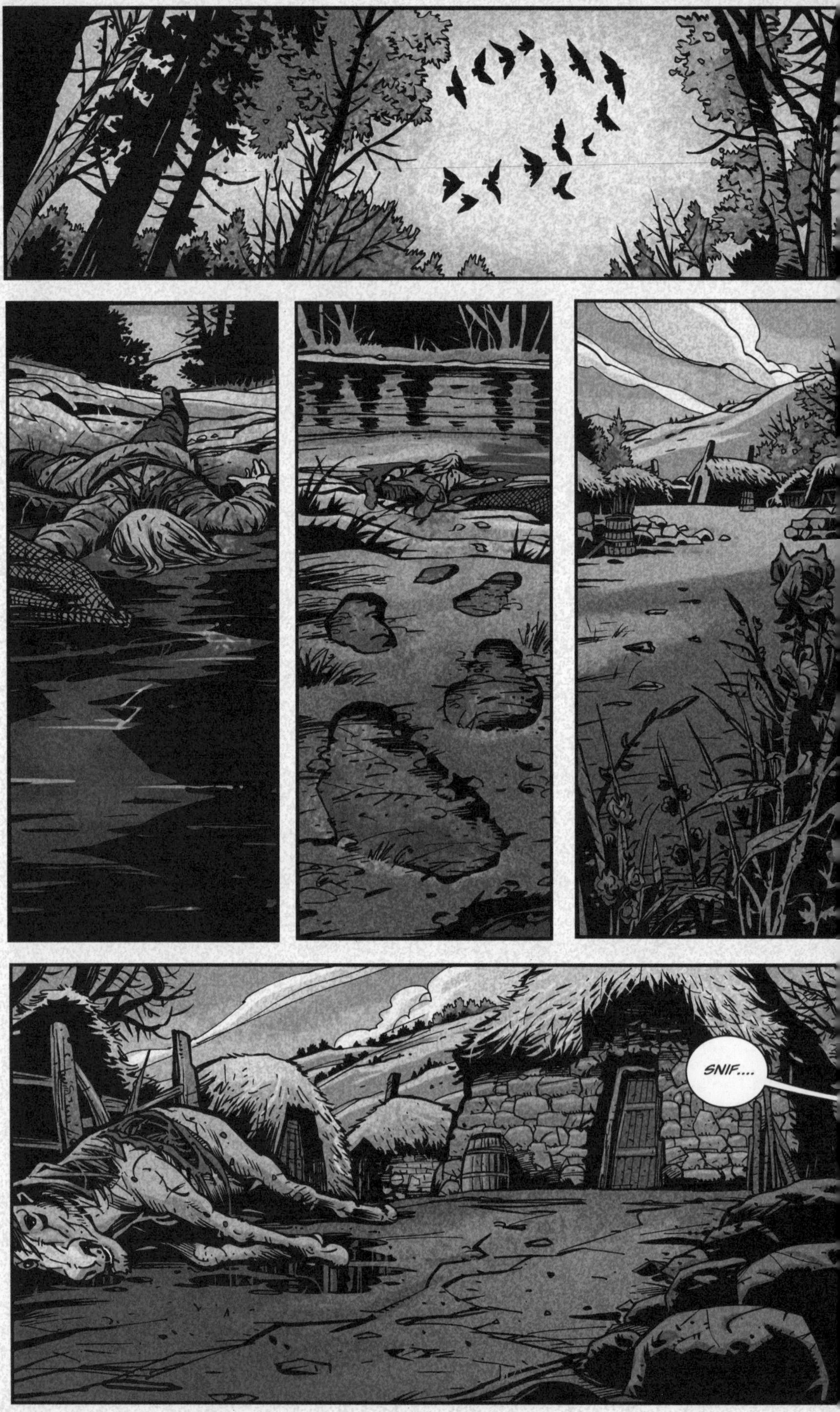
SNIF....

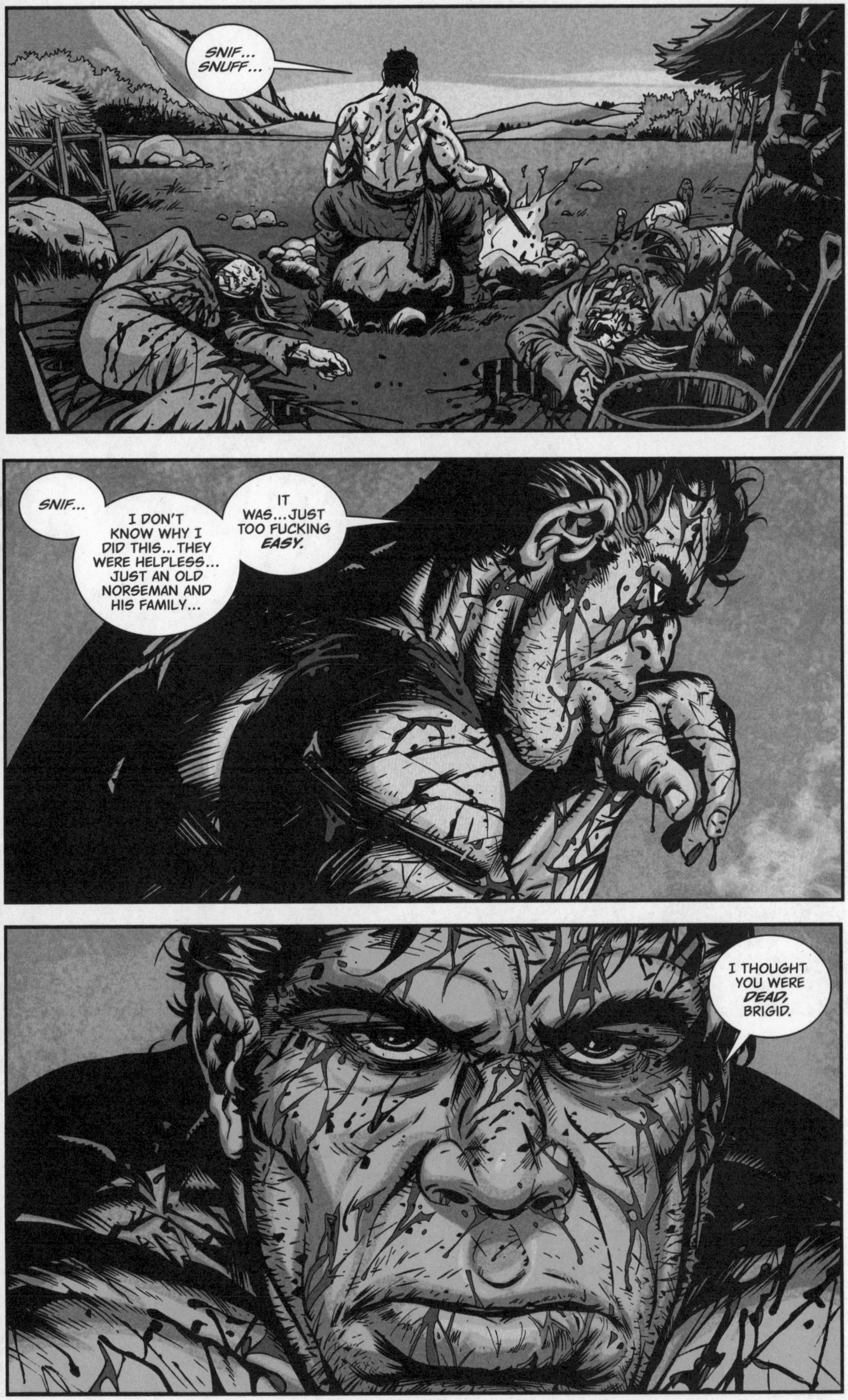
SNIF...
SNUFF...
SNIF...
I DON'T KNOW WHY I DID THIS...THEY WERE HELPLESS... JUST AN OLD NORSEMAN AND HIS FAMILY...
IT WAS...JUST TOO FUCKING *EASY.*
I THOUGHT YOU WERE *DEAD,* BRIGID.

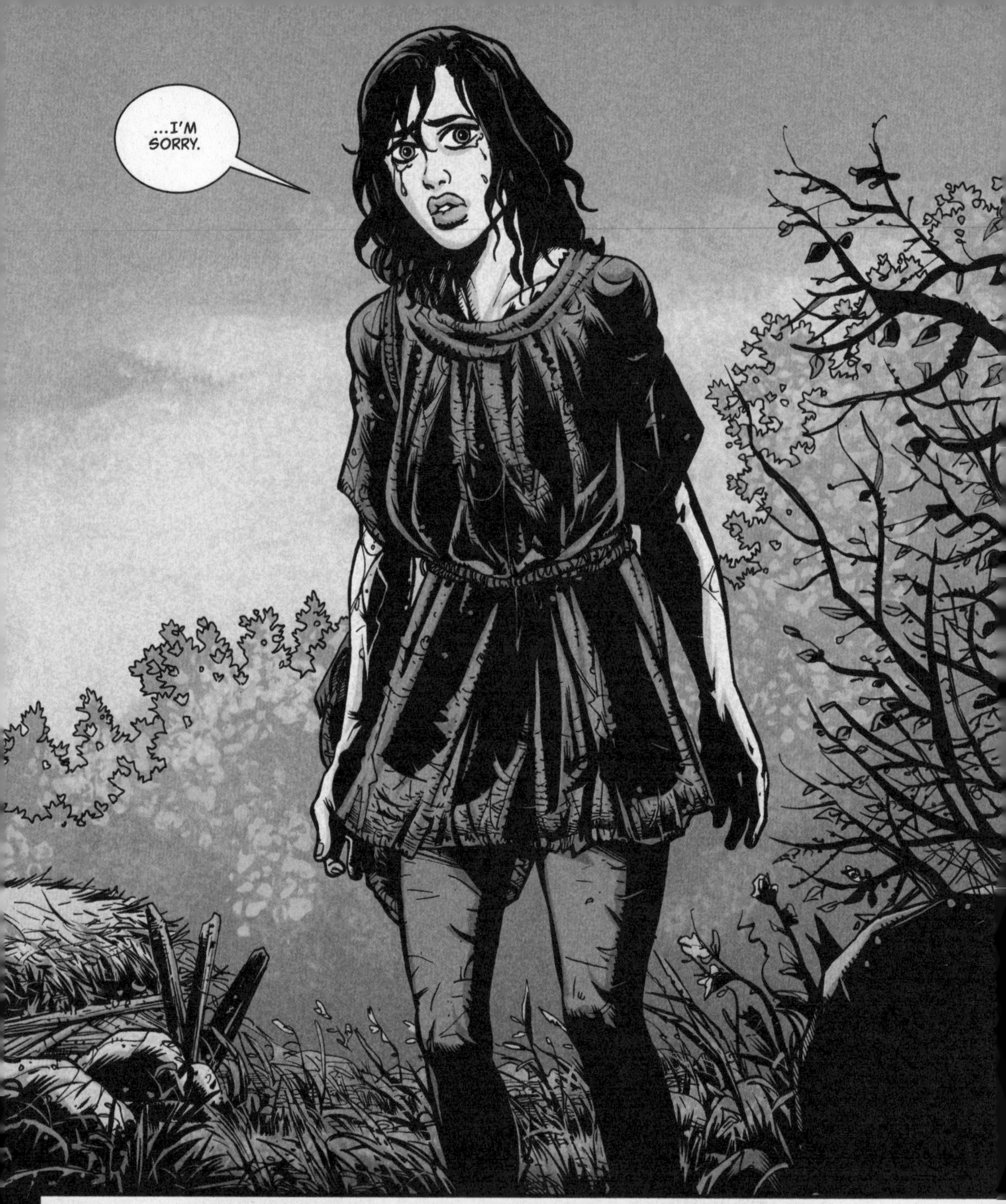
...I'M SORRY.

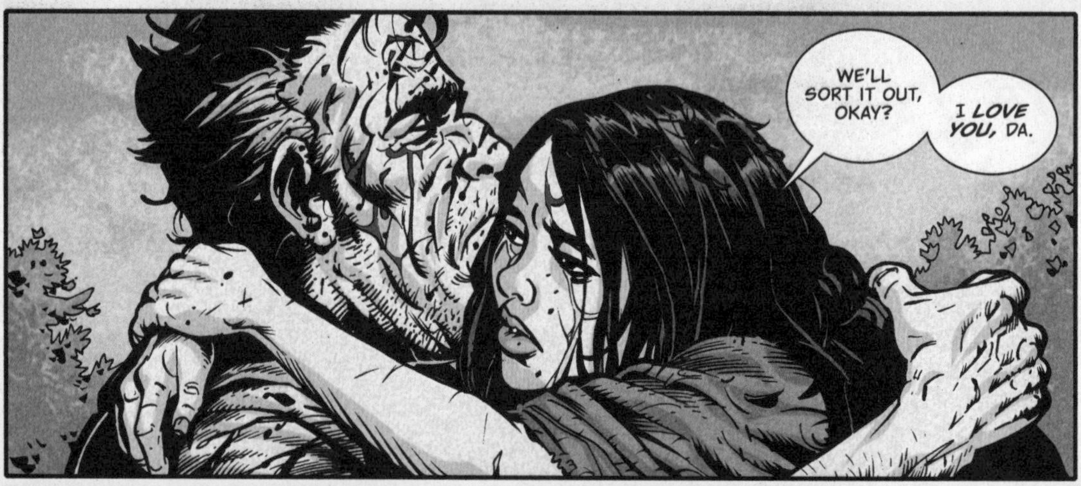
WE'LL SORT IT OUT, OKAY?
I LOVE YOU, DA.

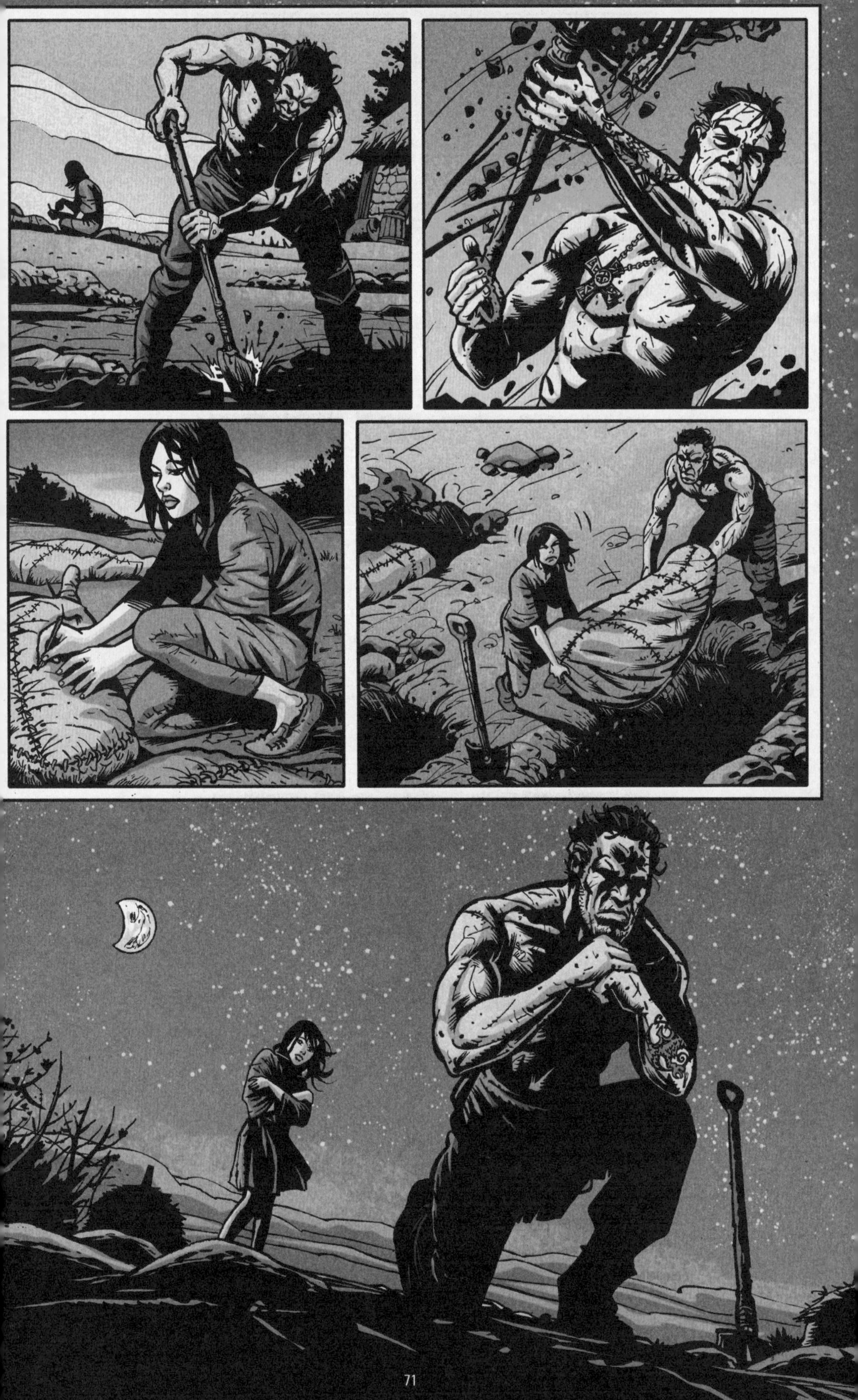

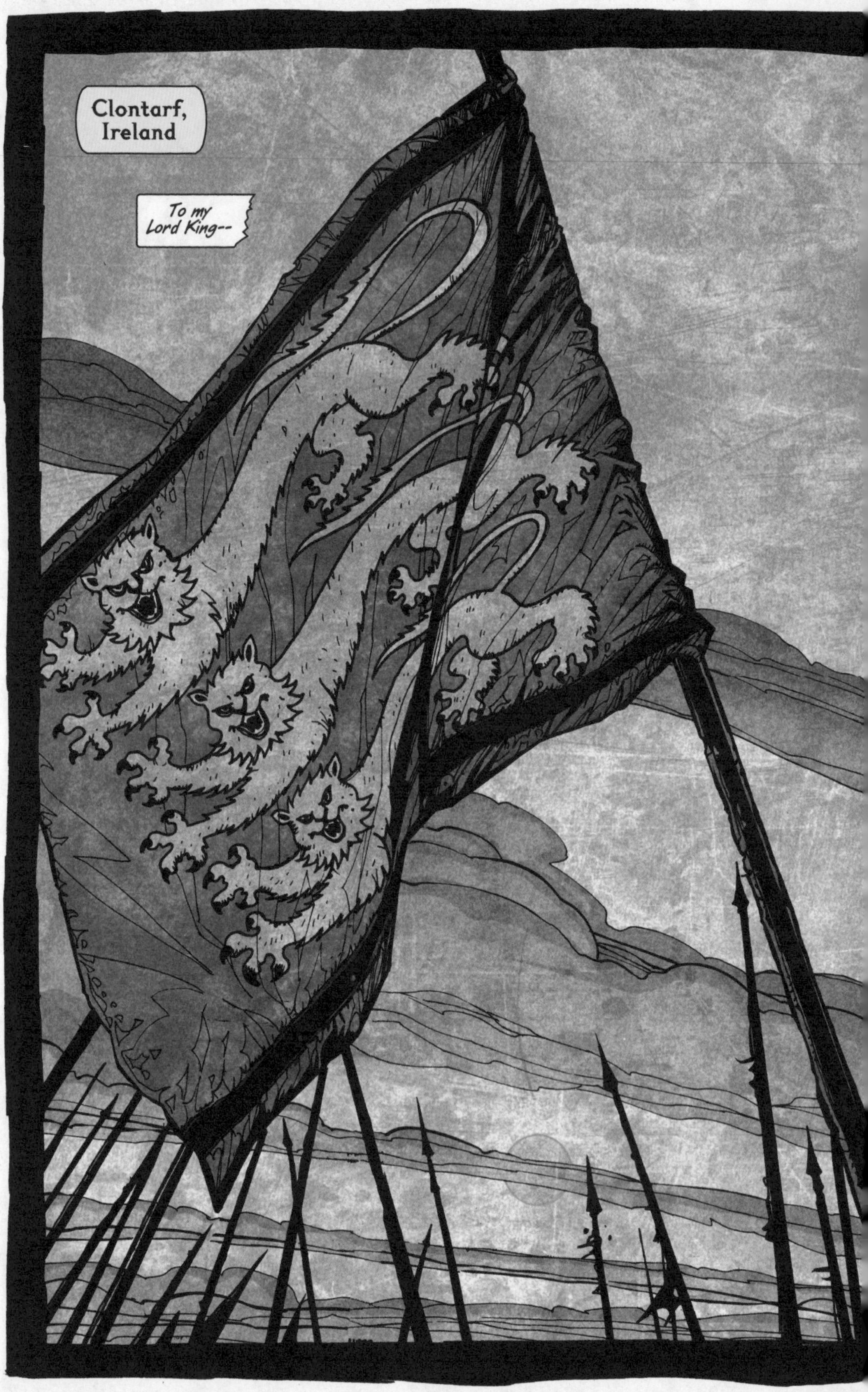
Clontarf, Ireland
To my Lord King--

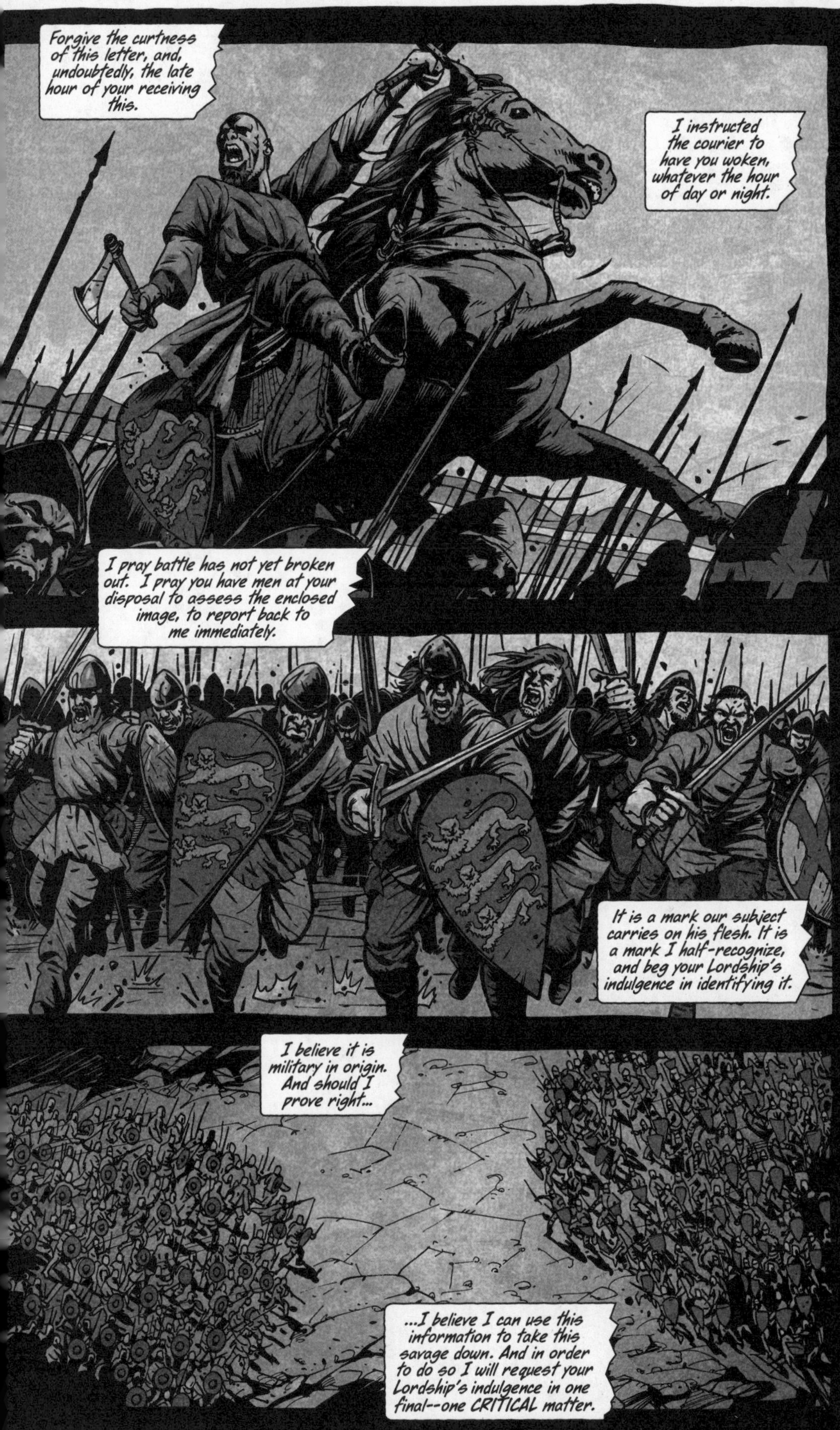
Forgive the curtness of this letter, and, undoubtedly, the late hour of your receiving this.
I instructed the courier to have you woken, whatever the hour of day or night.
I pray battle has not yet broken out. I pray you have men at your disposal to assess the enclosed image, to report back to me immediately.
It is a mark our subject carries on his flesh. It is a mark I half-recognize, and beg your Lordship's indulgence in identifying it.
I believe it is military in origin. And should I prove right...
...I believe I can use this information to take this savage down. And in order to do so I will request your Lordship's indulgence in one final--one CRITICAL matter.

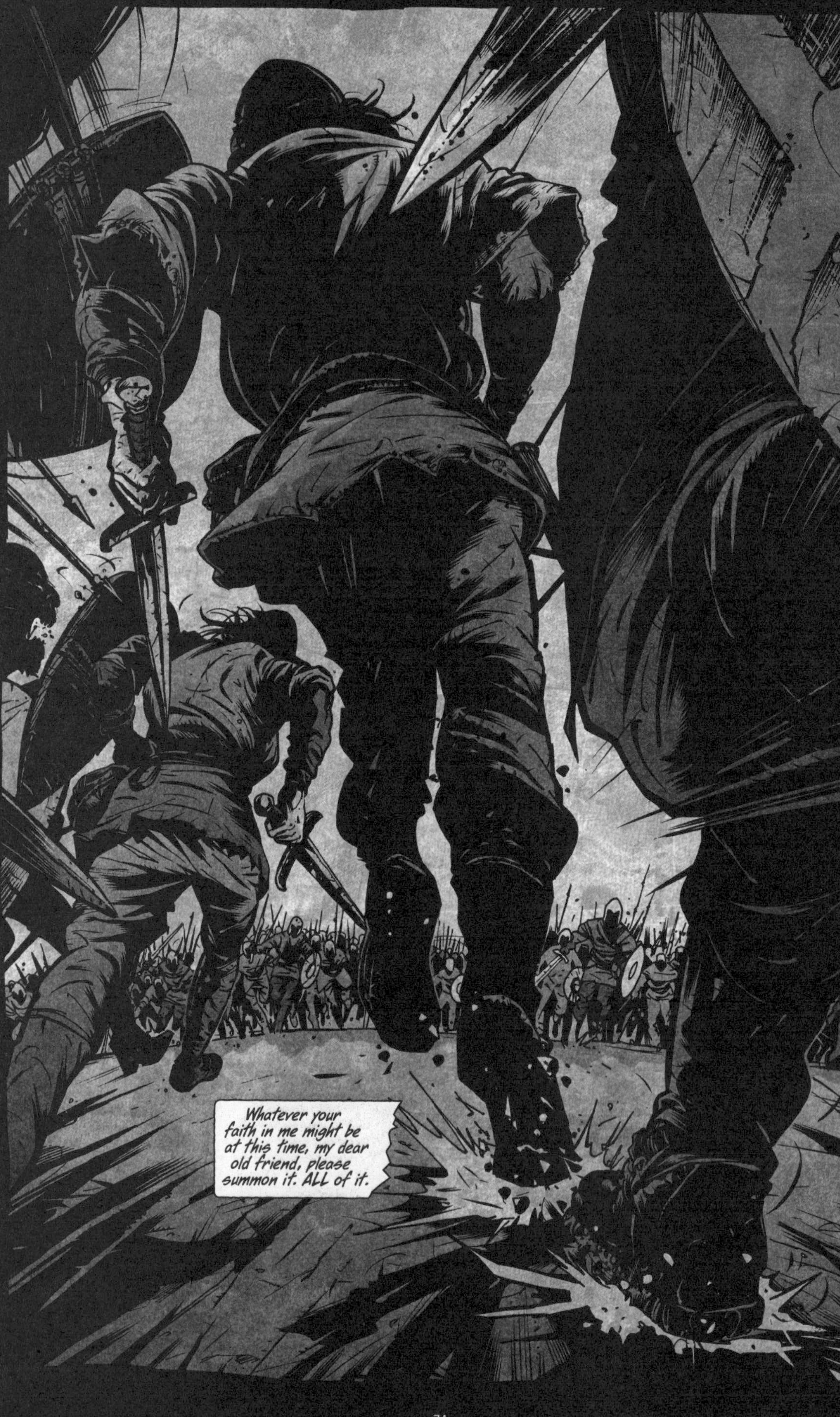
Whatever your faith in me might be at this time, my dear old friend, please summon it. ALL of it.

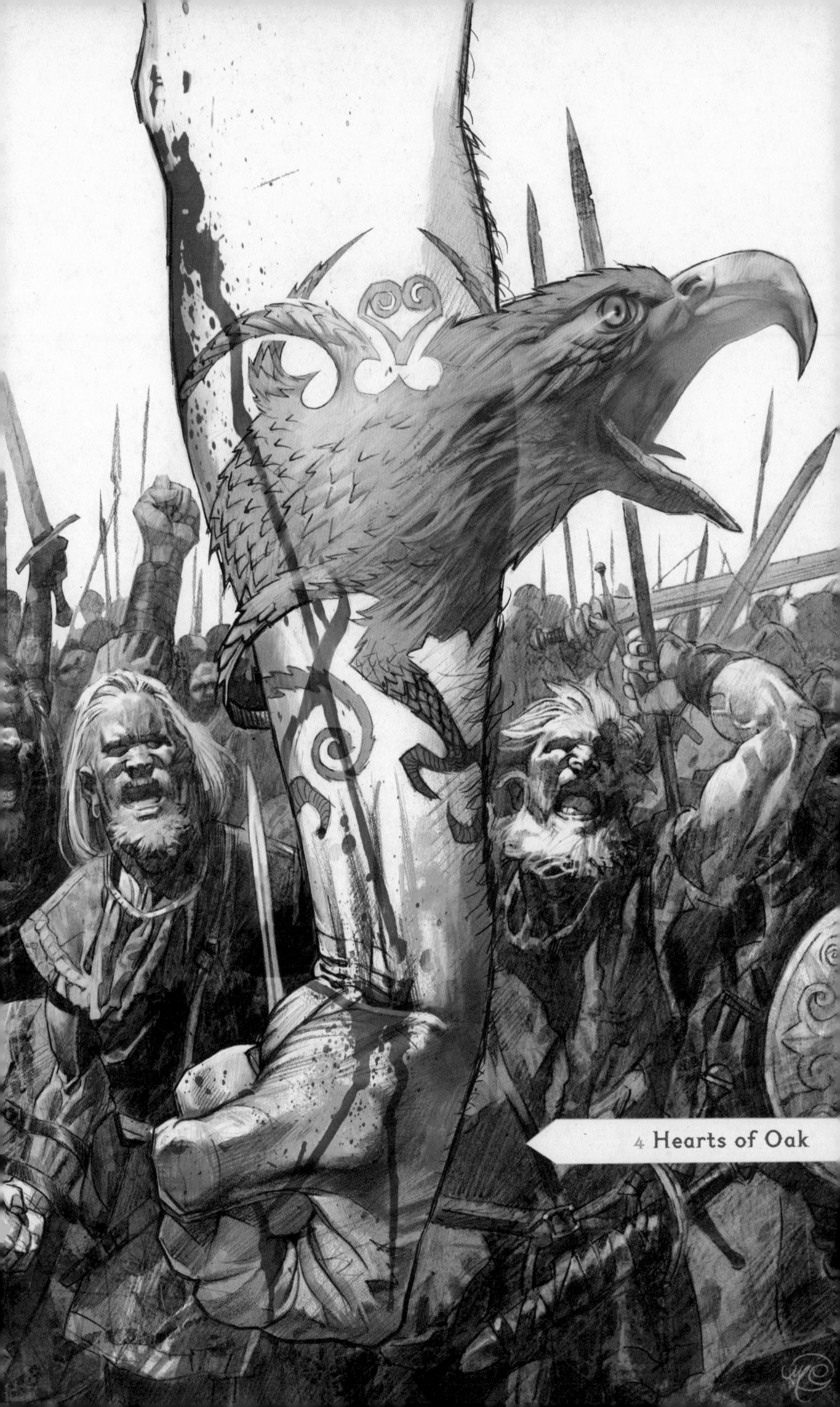

4 Hearts of Oak

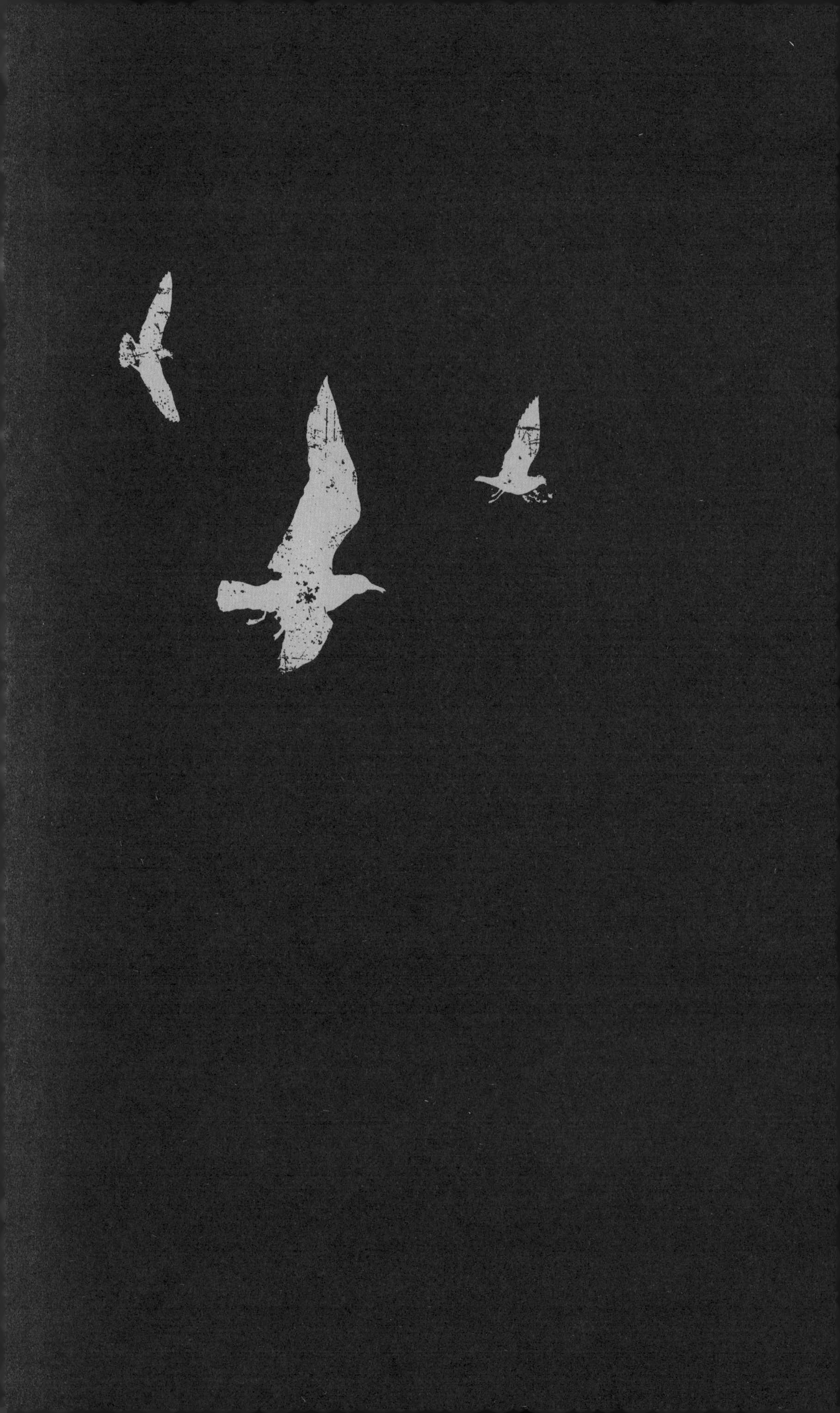

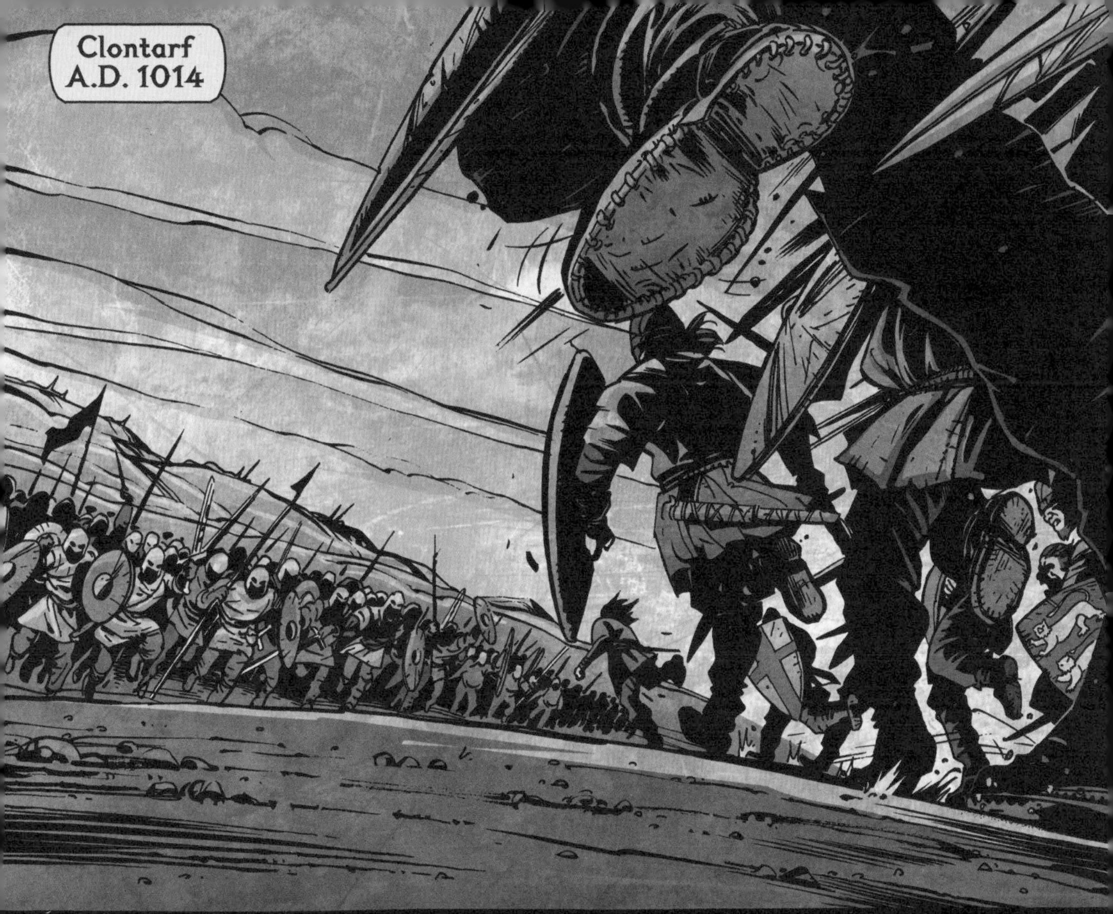
Clontarf
A.D. 1014

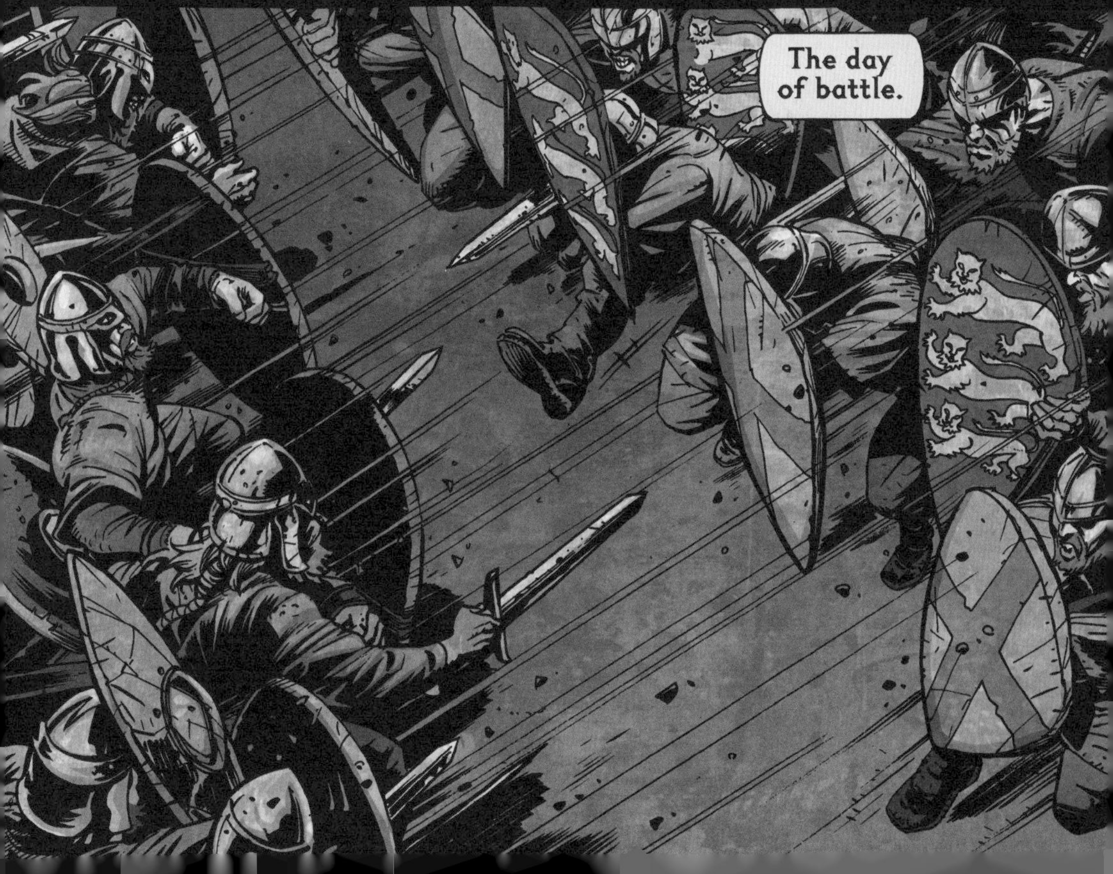
The day
of battle.

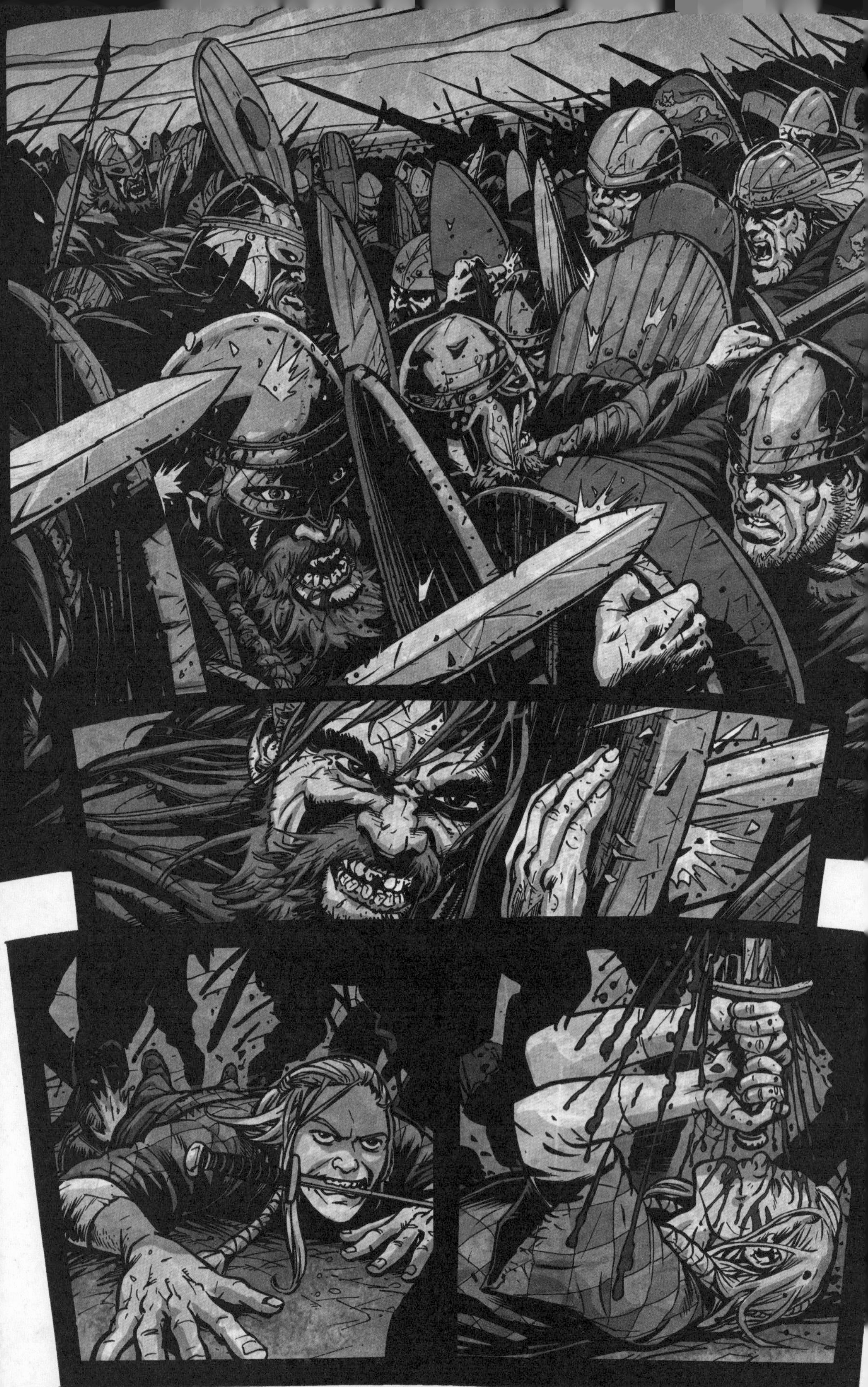

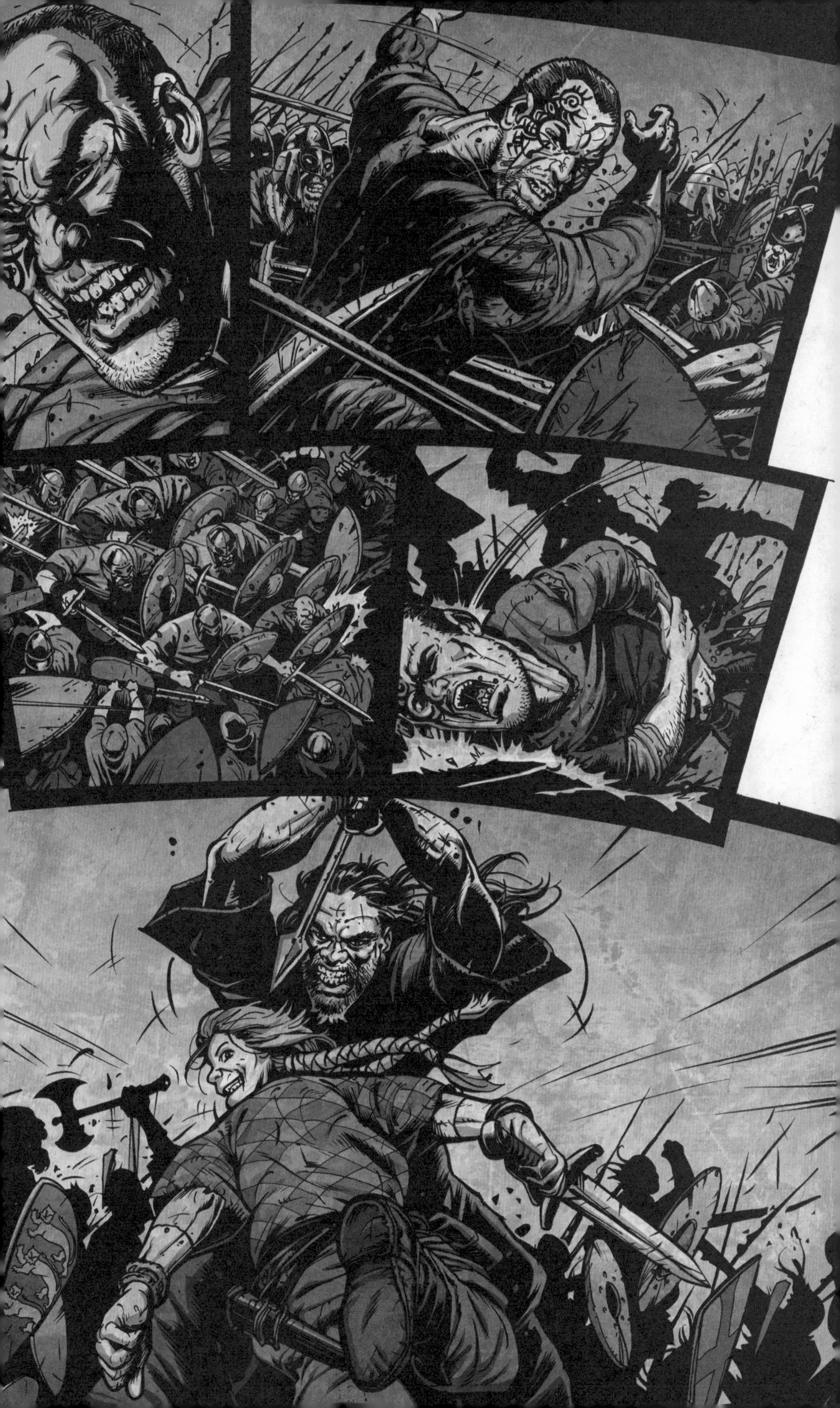

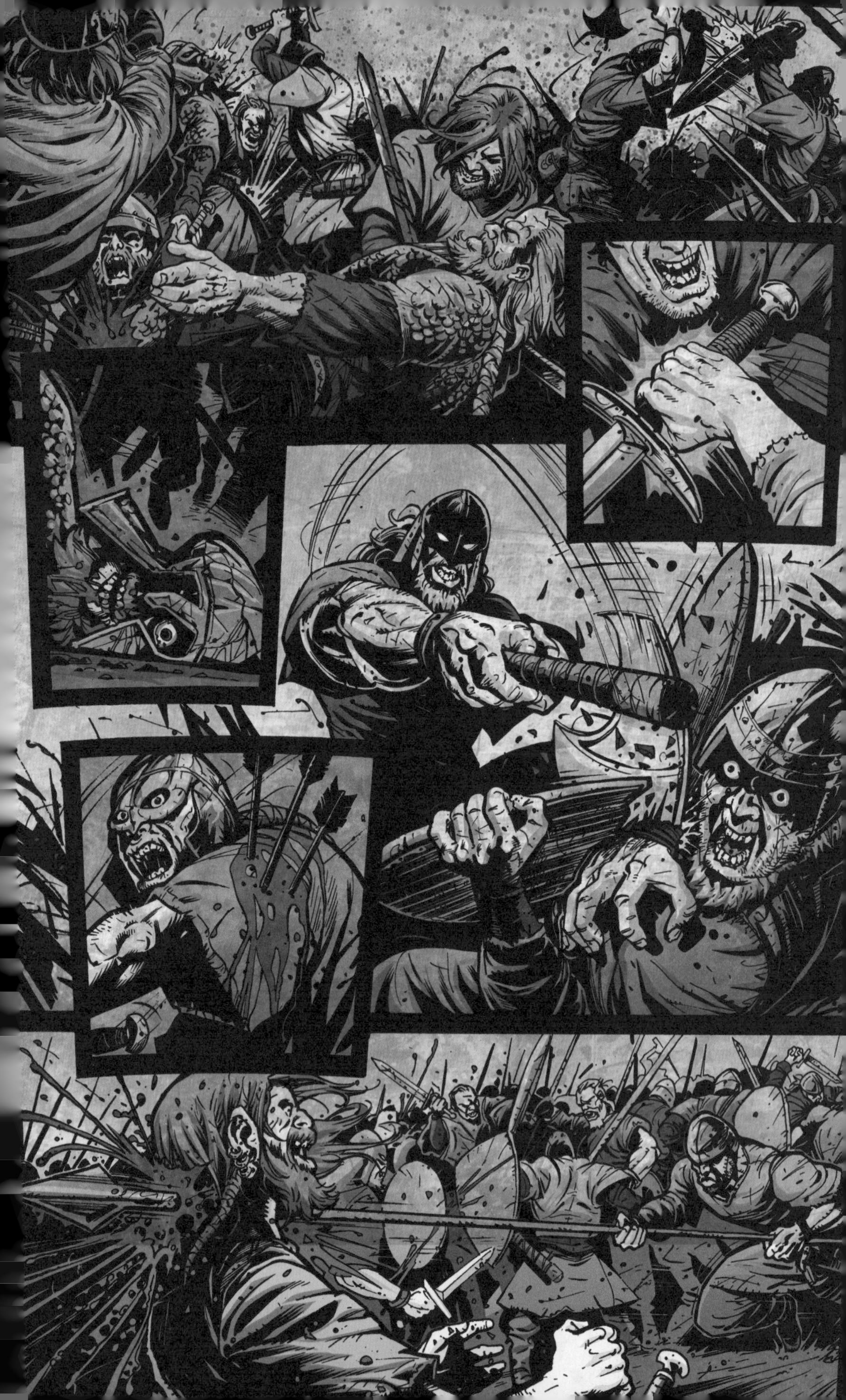

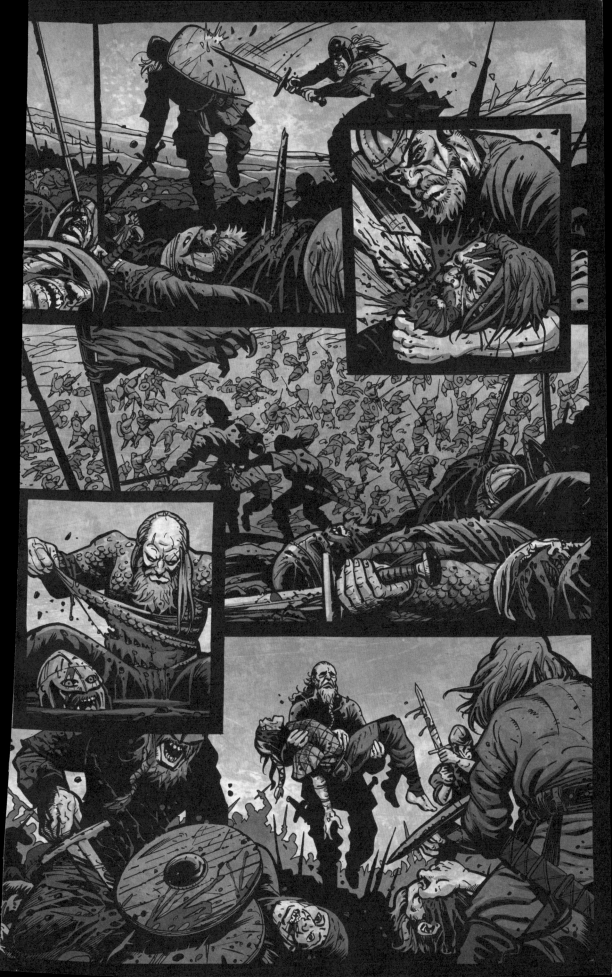

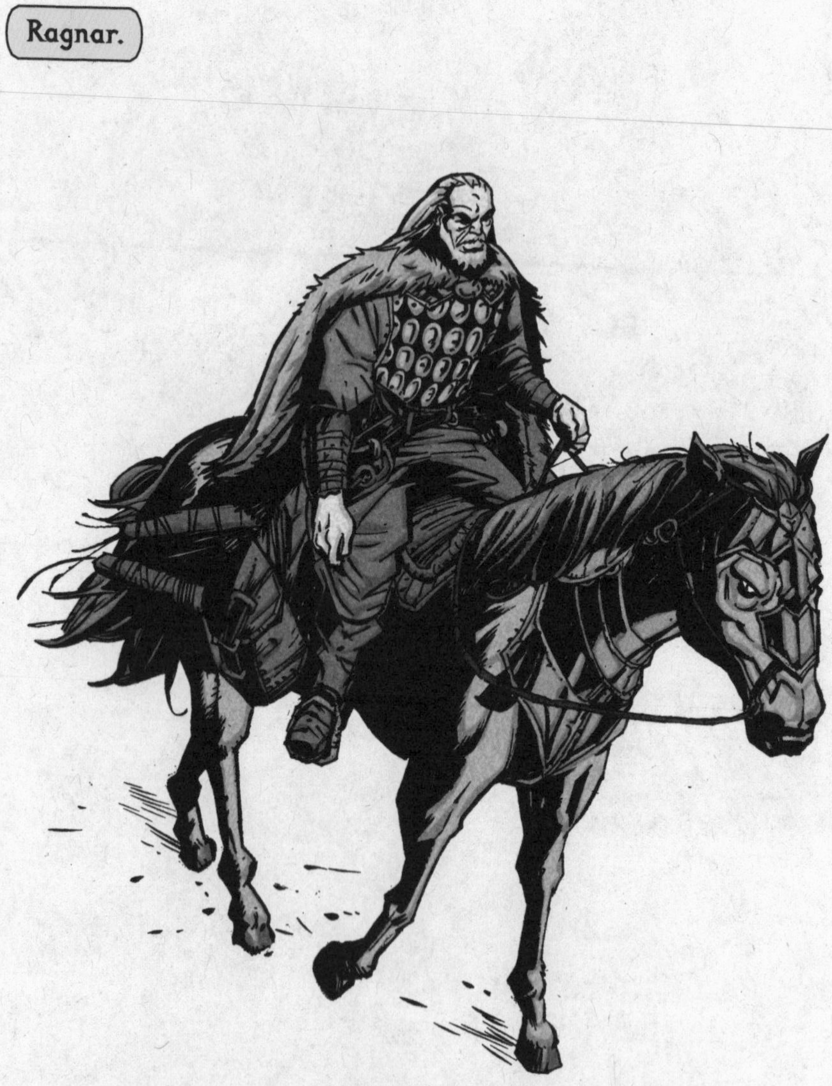
Ragnar.

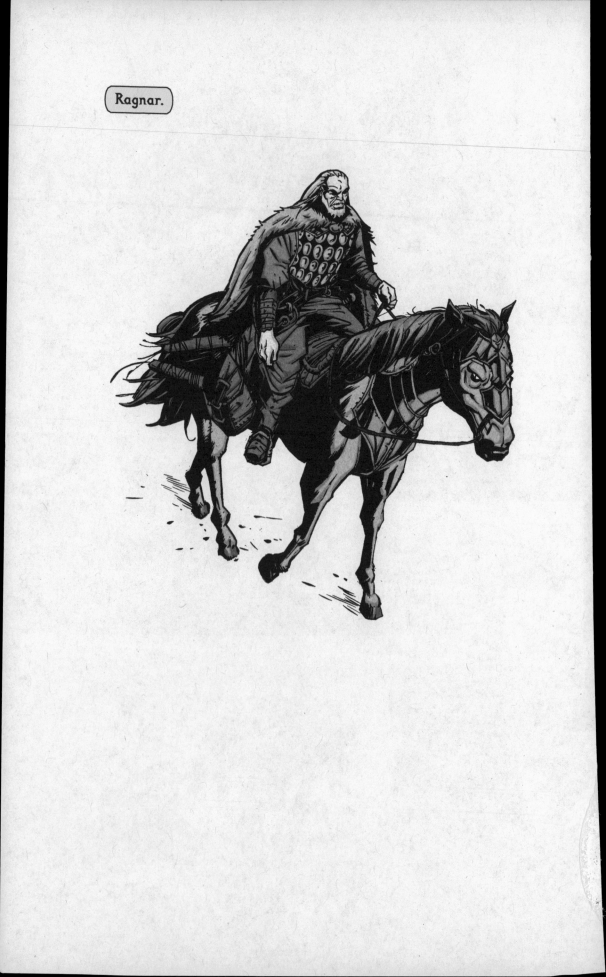

Magnus + Brigid.
Miles away.

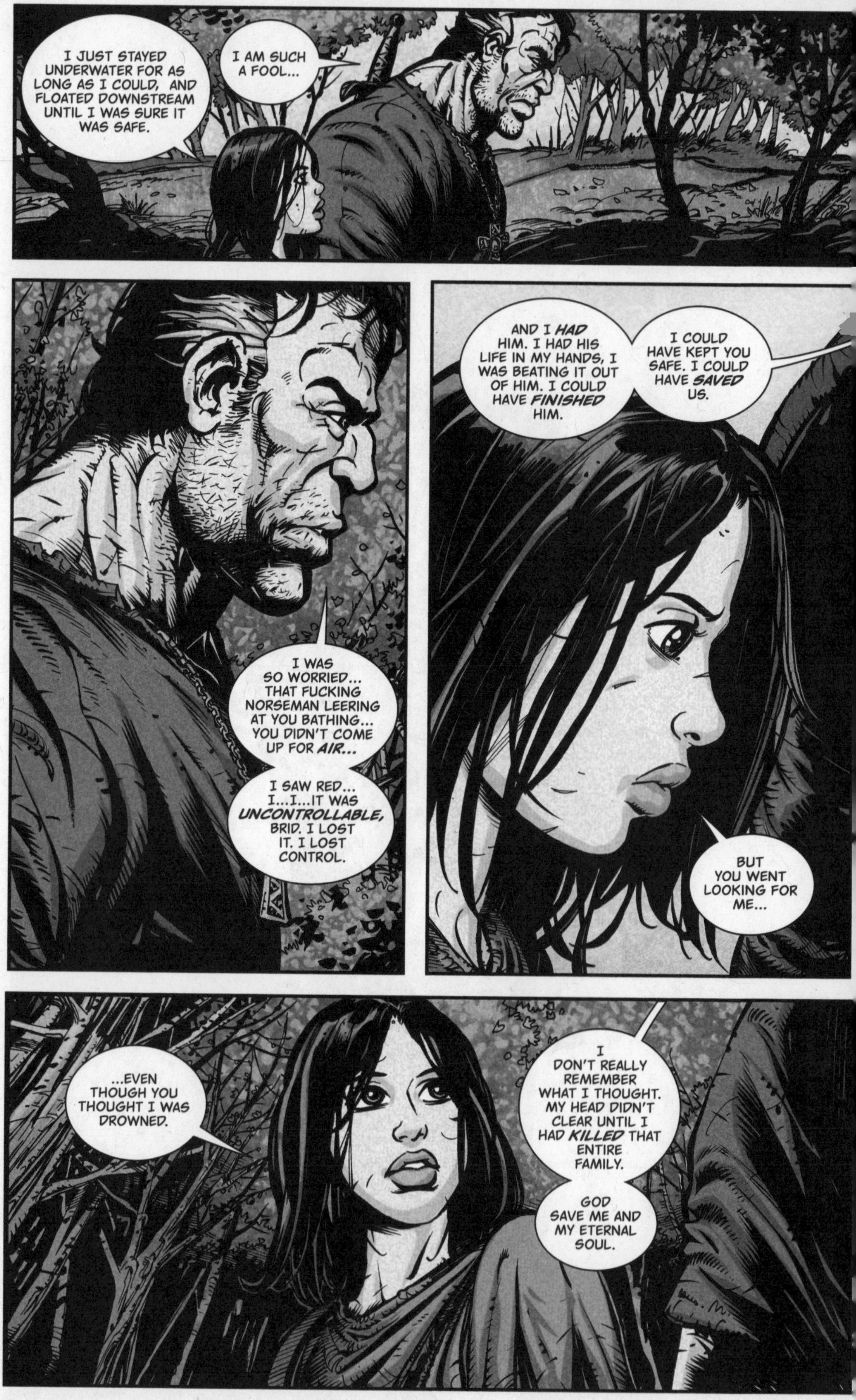
I JUST STAYED UNDERWATER FOR AS LONG AS I COULD, AND FLOATED DOWNSTREAM UNTIL I WAS SURE IT WAS SAFE.
I AM SUCH A FOOL...
I WAS SO WORRIED... THAT FUCKING NORSEMAN LEERING AT YOU BATHING... YOU DIDN'T COME UP FOR AIR...
I SAW RED... I...I...IT WAS UNCONTROLLABLE, BRID. I LOST IT. I LOST CONTROL.
AND I HAD HIM. I HAD HIS LIFE IN MY HANDS, I WAS BEATING IT OUT OF HIM. I COULD HAVE FINISHED HIM.
I COULD HAVE KEPT YOU SAFE. I COULD HAVE SAVED US.
BUT YOU WENT LOOKING FOR ME...
...EVEN THOUGH YOU THOUGHT I WAS DROWNED.
I DON'T REALLY REMEMBER WHAT I THOUGHT. MY HEAD DIDN'T CLEAR UNTIL I HAD KILLED THAT ENTIRE FAMILY.
GOD SAVE ME AND MY ETERNAL SOUL.

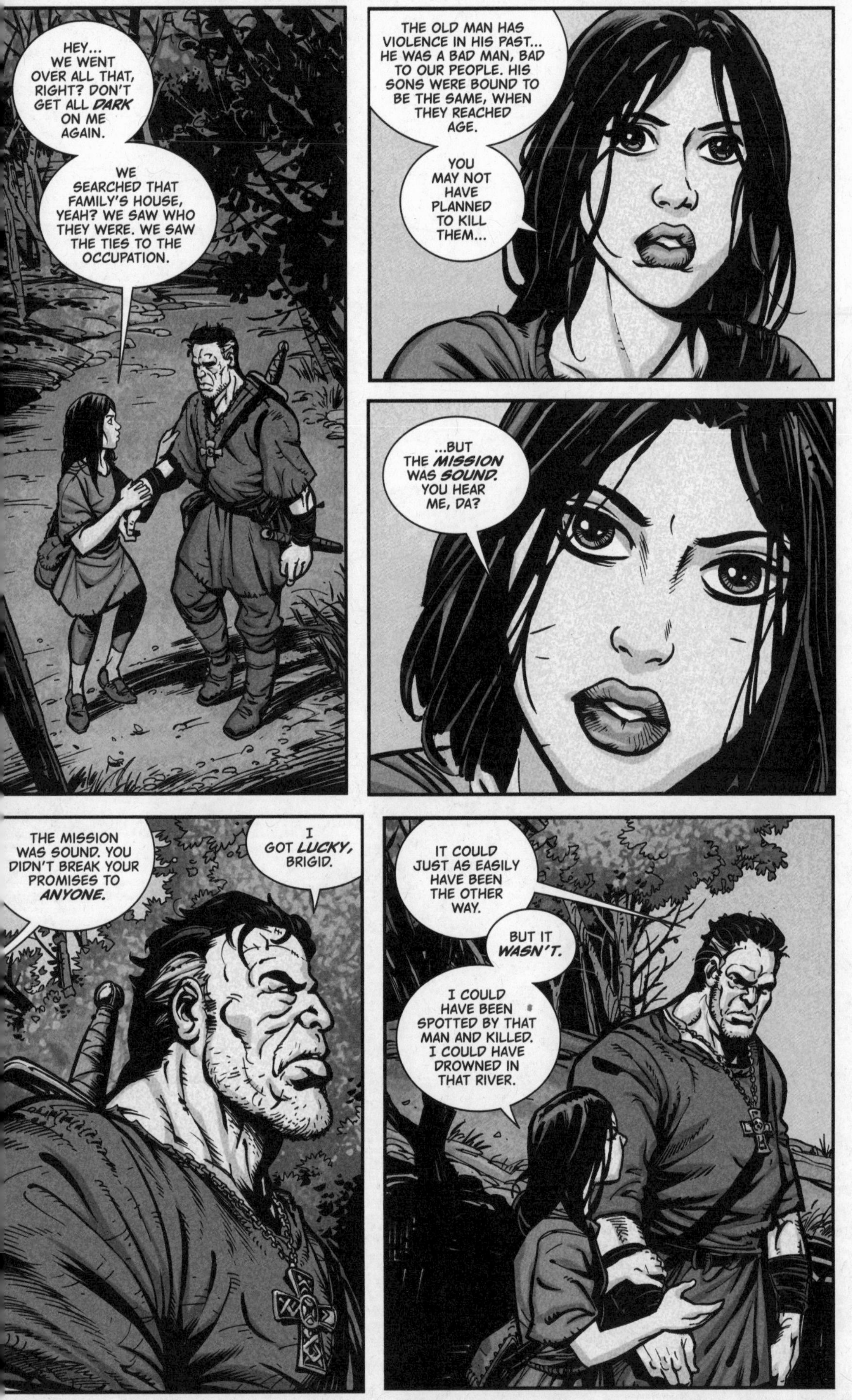

HEY... WE WENT OVER ALL THAT, RIGHT? DON'T GET ALL DARK ON ME AGAIN.
WE SEARCHED THAT FAMILY'S HOUSE, YEAH? WE SAW WHO THEY WERE. WE SAW THE TIES TO THE OCCUPATION.
THE OLD MAN HAS VIOLENCE IN HIS PAST... HE WAS A BAD MAN, BAD TO OUR PEOPLE. HIS SONS WERE BOUND TO BE THE SAME, WHEN THEY REACHED AGE.
YOU MAY NOT HAVE PLANNED TO KILL THEM...
...BUT THE MISSION WAS SOUND. YOU HEAR ME, DA?
THE MISSION WAS SOUND. YOU DIDN'T BREAK YOUR PROMISES TO ANYONE.
I GOT LUCKY, BRIGID.
IT COULD JUST AS EASILY HAVE BEEN THE OTHER WAY.
BUT IT WASN'T.
I COULD HAVE BEEN SPOTTED BY THAT MAN AND KILLED. I COULD HAVE DROWNED IN THAT RIVER.

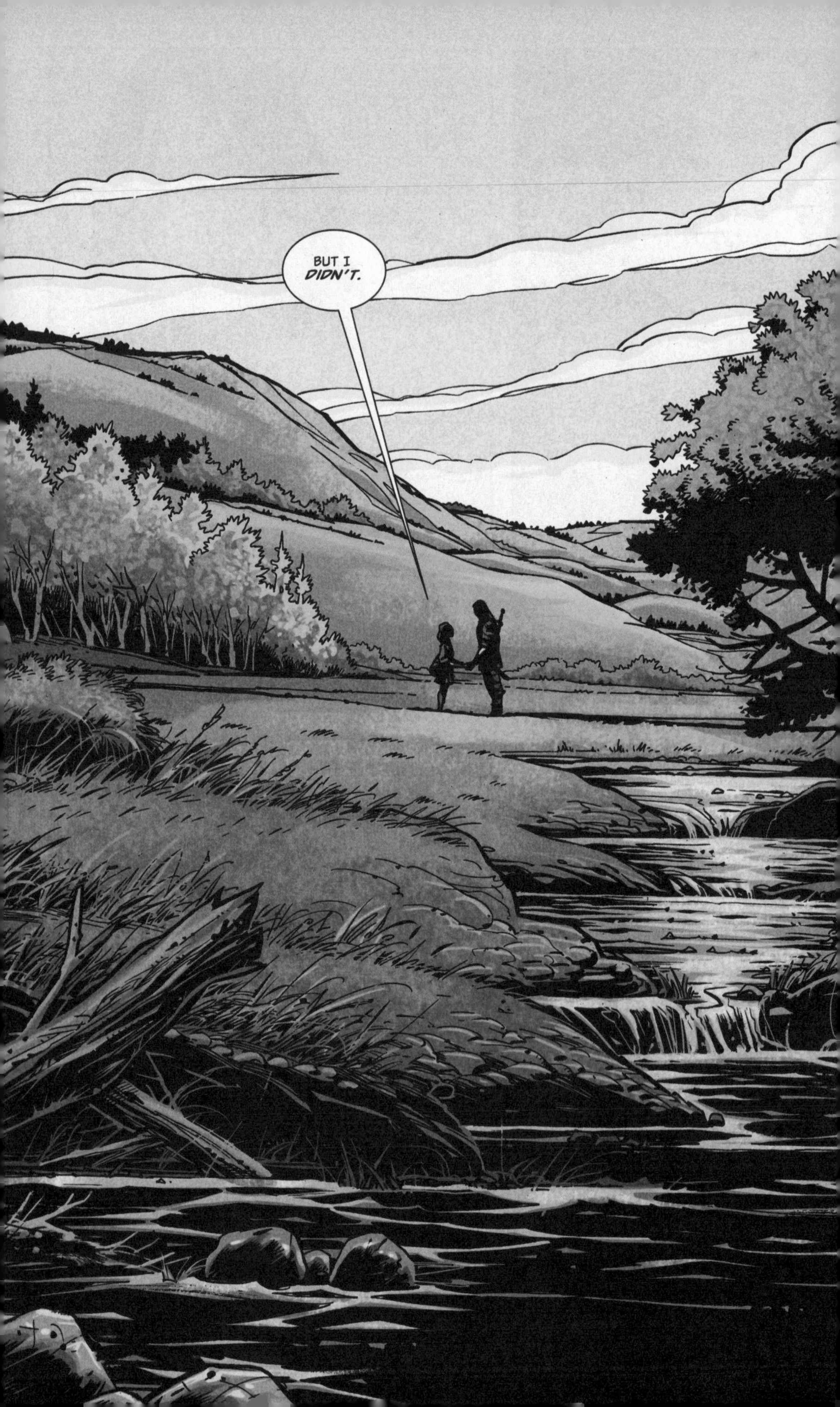
BUT I *DIDN'T.*

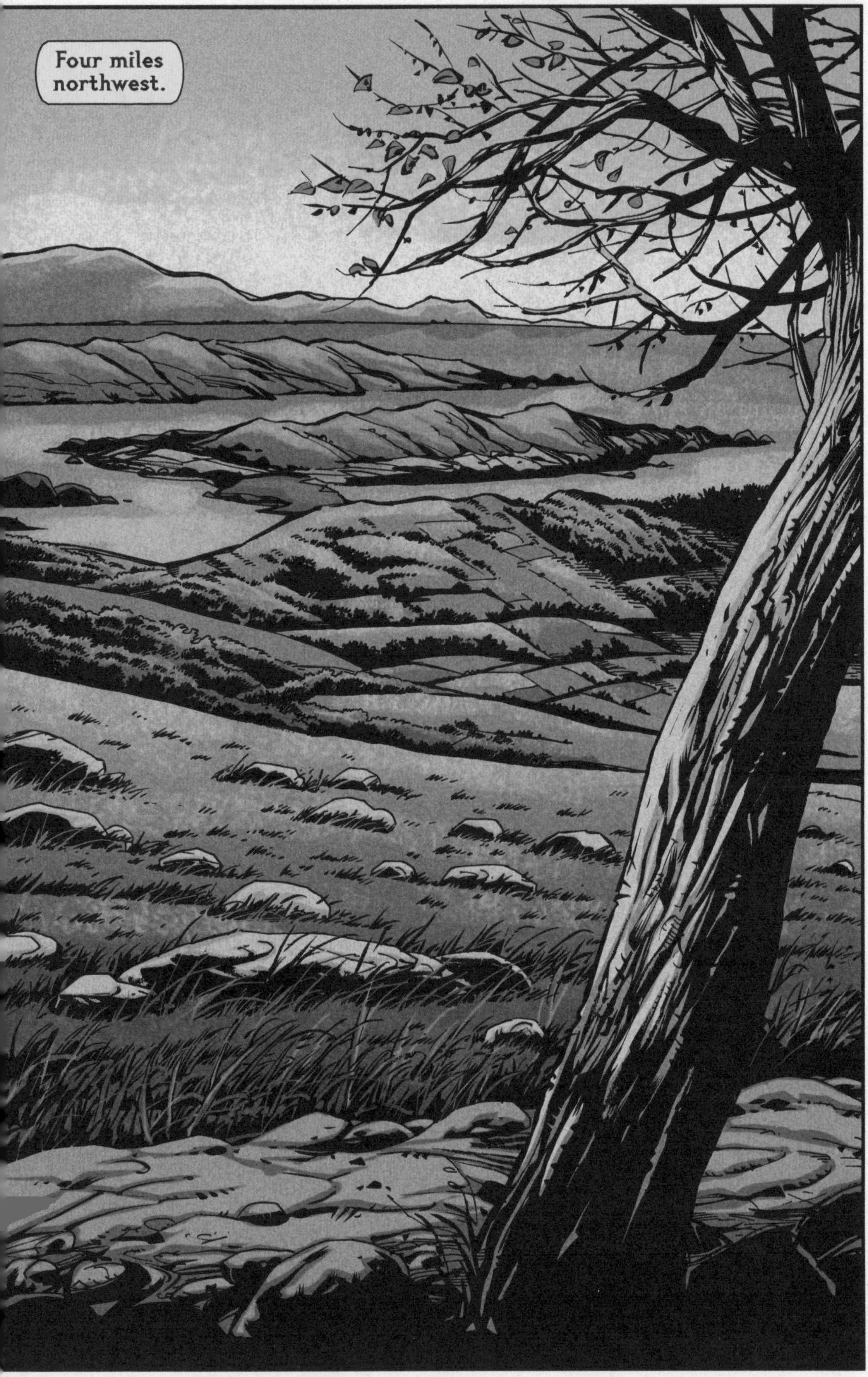
Four miles northwest.

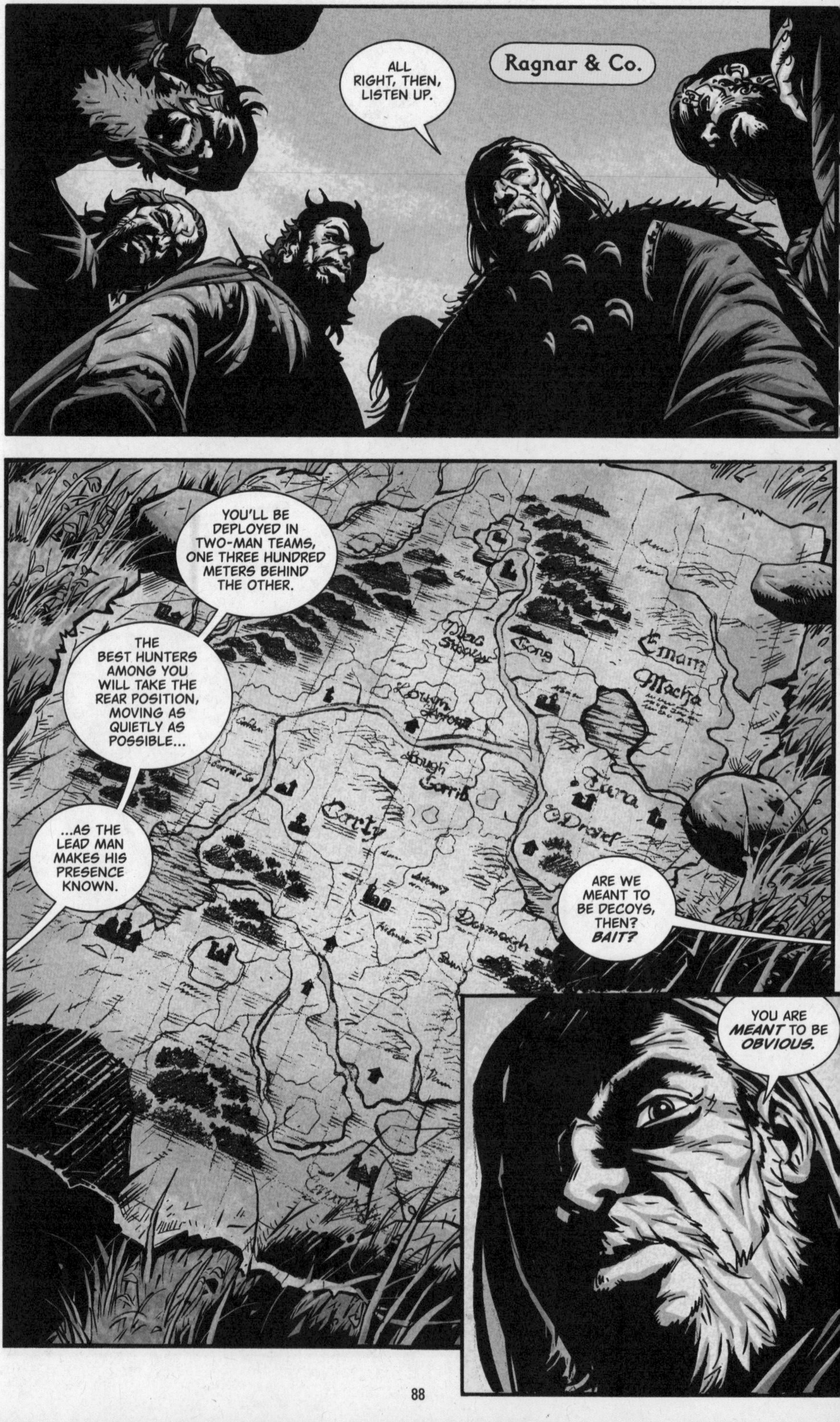
Ragnar & Co.
ALL RIGHT, THEN, LISTEN UP.
YOU'LL BE DEPLOYED IN TWO-MAN TEAMS, ONE THREE HUNDRED METERS BEHIND THE OTHER.
THE BEST HUNTERS AMONG YOU WILL TAKE THE REAR POSITION, MOVING AS QUIETLY AS POSSIBLE...
...AS THE LEAD MAN MAKES HIS PRESENCE KNOWN.
ARE WE MEANT TO BE DECOYS, THEN? *BAIT?*
YOU ARE *MEANT* TO BE *OBVIOUS.*

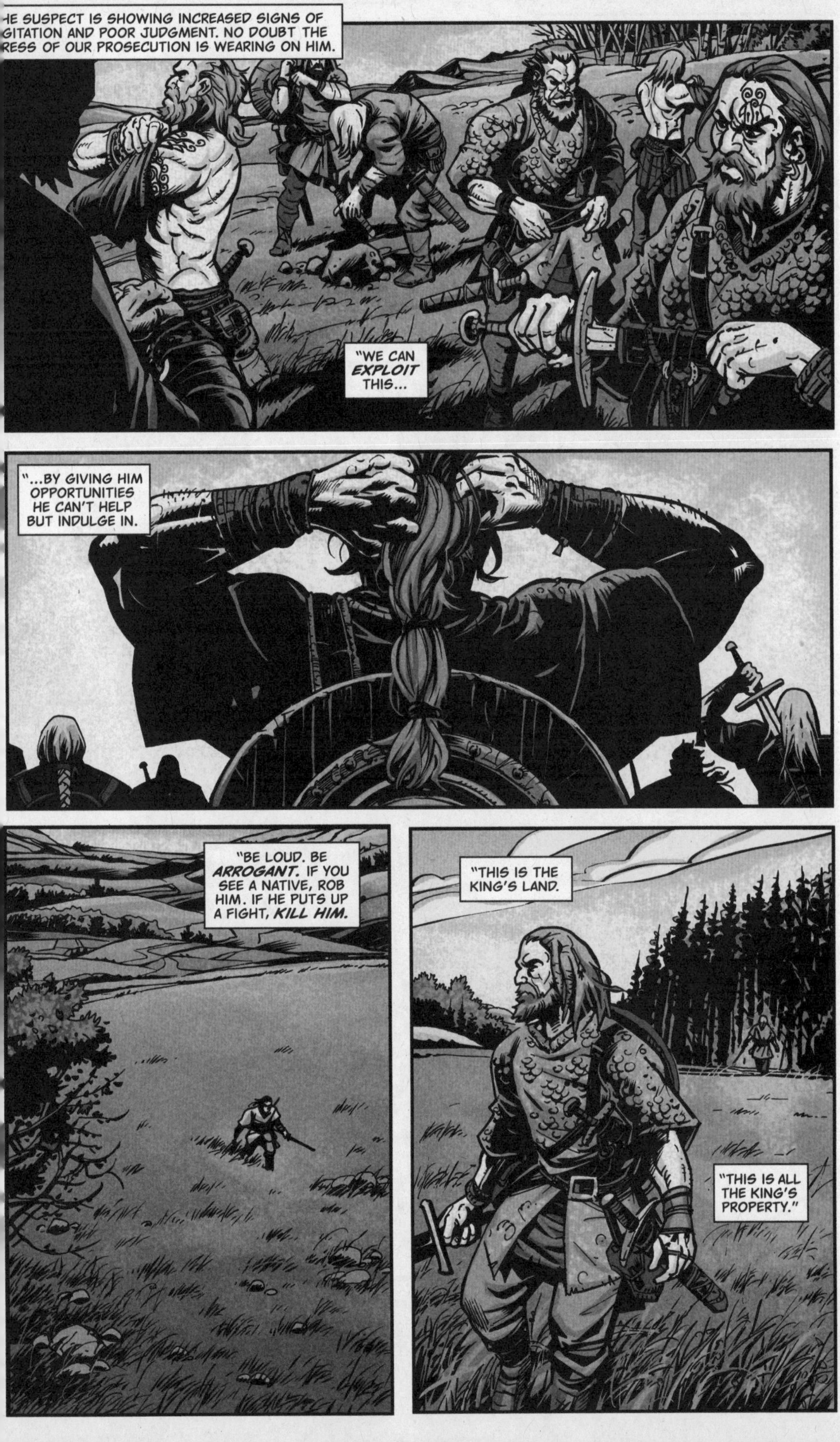
HE SUSPECT IS SHOWING INCREASED SIGNS OF
GITATION AND POOR JUDGMENT. NO DOUBT THE
RESS OF OUR PROSECUTION IS WEARING ON HIM.
"WE CAN EXPLOIT THIS...
"...BY GIVING HIM OPPORTUNITIES HE CAN'T HELP BUT INDULGE IN.
"BE LOUD. BE ARROGANT. IF YOU SEE A NATIVE, ROB HIM. IF HE PUTS UP A FIGHT, KILL HIM.
"THIS IS THE KING'S LAND.
"THIS IS ALL THE KING'S PROPERTY."

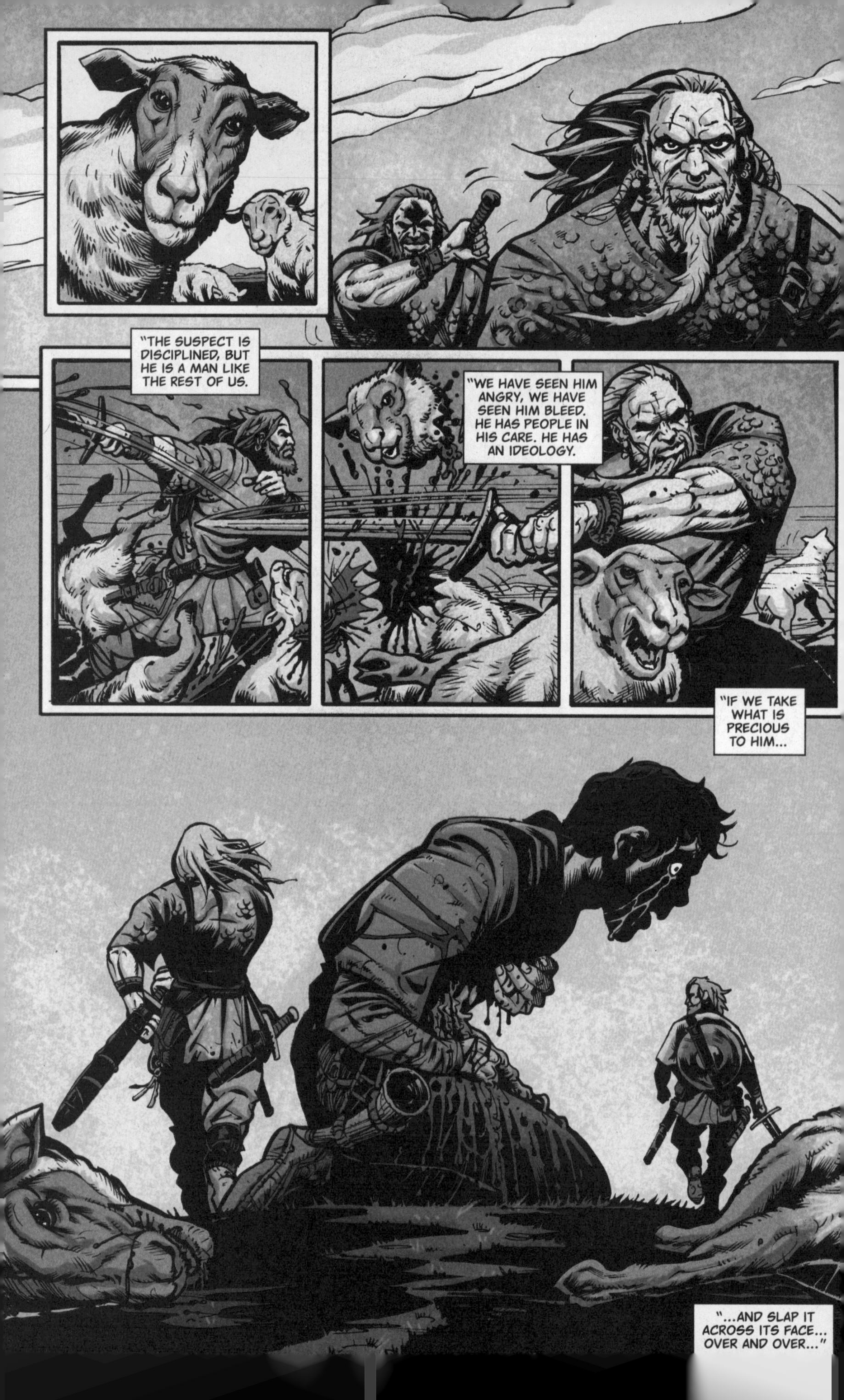
"THE SUSPECT IS DISCIPLINED, BUT HE IS A MAN LIKE THE REST OF US.
"WE HAVE SEEN HIM ANGRY, WE HAVE SEEN HIM BLEED. HE HAS PEOPLE IN HIS CARE. HE HAS AN IDEOLOGY.
"IF WE TAKE WHAT IS PRECIOUS TO HIM...
"...AND SLAP IT ACROSS ITS FACE... OVER AND OVER..."

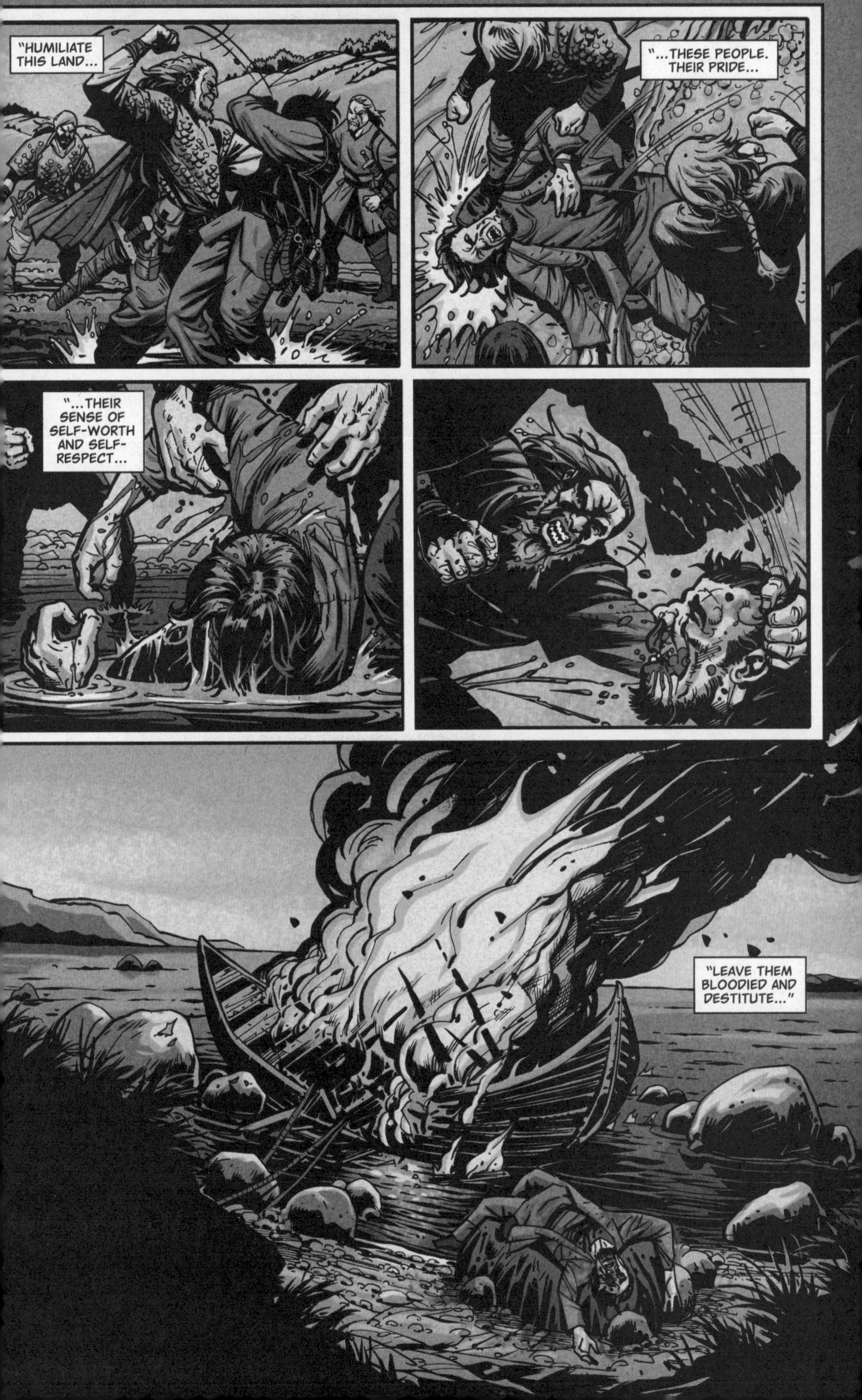

"HUMILIATE THIS LAND...
"...THESE PEOPLE. THEIR PRIDE...
"...THEIR SENSE OF SELF-WORTH AND SELF-RESPECT...
"LEAVE THEM BLOODIED AND DESTITUTE..."

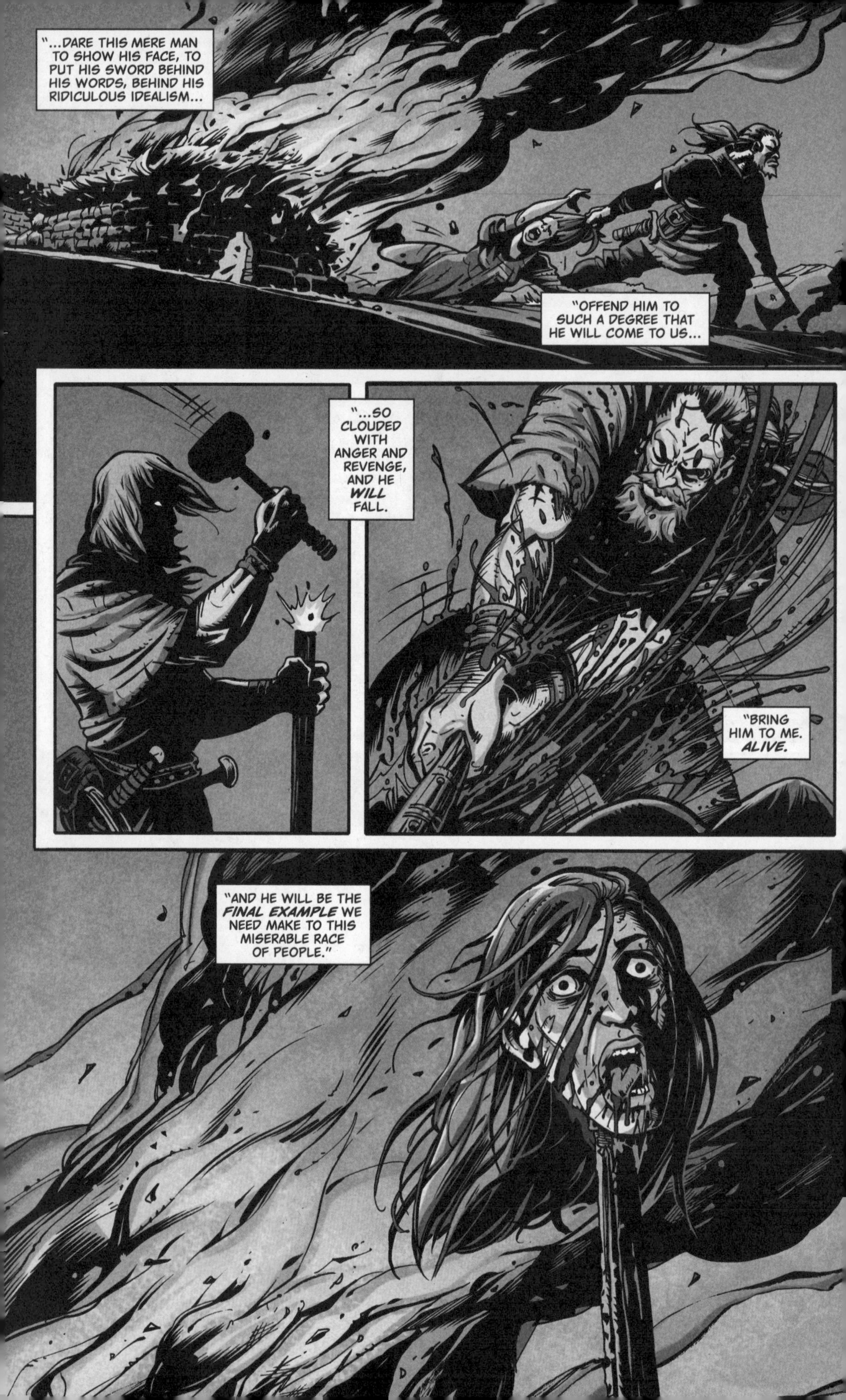
"...DARE THIS MERE MAN TO SHOW HIS FACE, TO PUT HIS SWORD BEHIND HIS WORDS, BEHIND HIS RIDICULOUS IDEALISM...
"OFFEND HIM TO SUCH A DEGREE THAT HE WILL COME TO US...
"...SO CLOUDED WITH ANGER AND REVENGE, AND HE WILL FALL.
"BRING HIM TO ME. ALIVE.
"AND HE WILL BE THE FINAL EXAMPLE WE NEED MAKE TO THIS MISERABLE RACE OF PEOPLE."

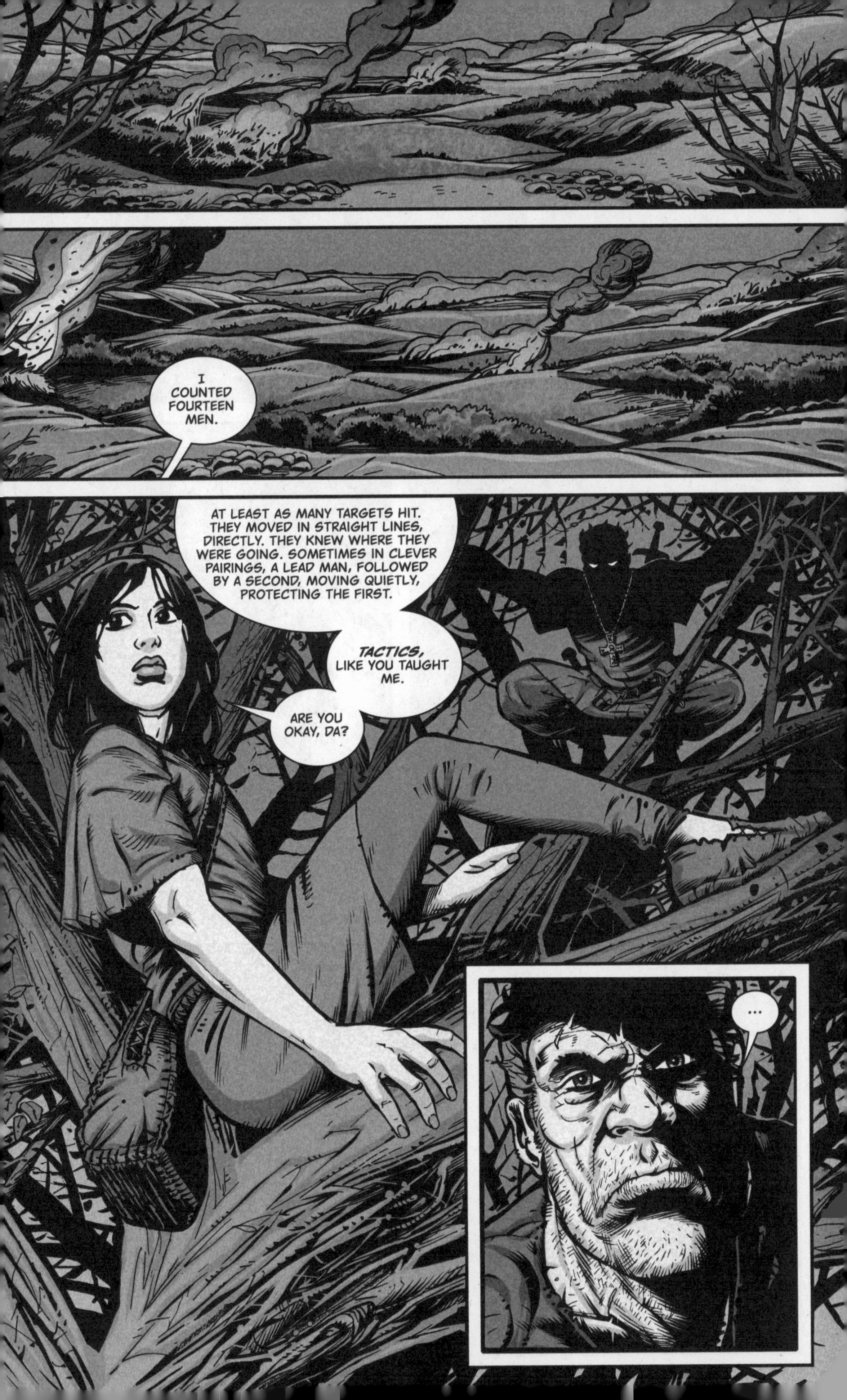

I COUNTED FOURTEEN MEN.
AT LEAST AS MANY TARGETS HIT. THEY MOVED IN STRAIGHT LINES, DIRECTLY. THEY KNEW WHERE THEY WERE GOING. SOMETIMES IN CLEVER PAIRINGS, A LEAD MAN, FOLLOWED BY A SECOND, MOVING QUIETLY, PROTECTING THE FIRST.
TACTICS, LIKE YOU TAUGHT ME.
ARE YOU OKAY, DA?
...

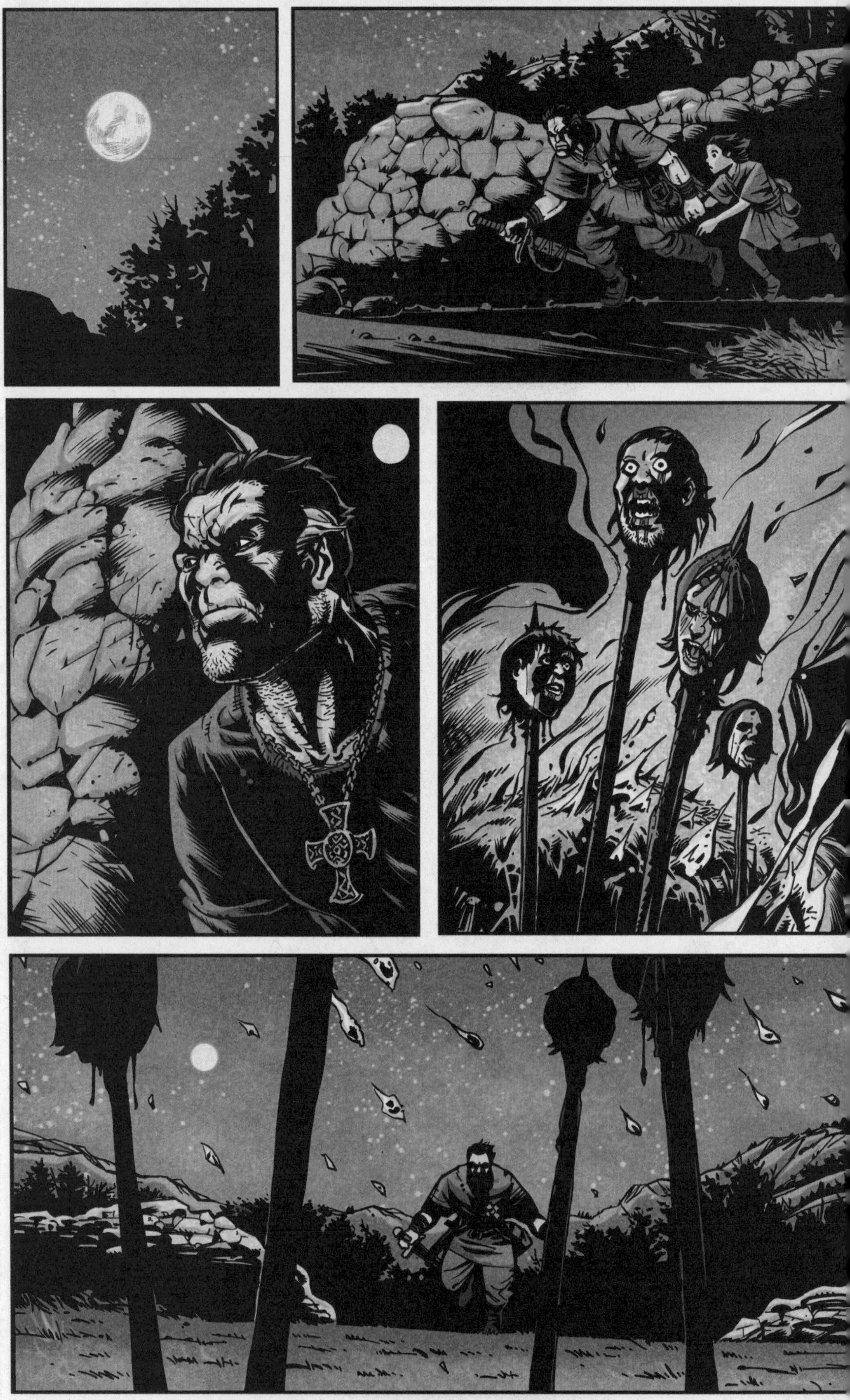

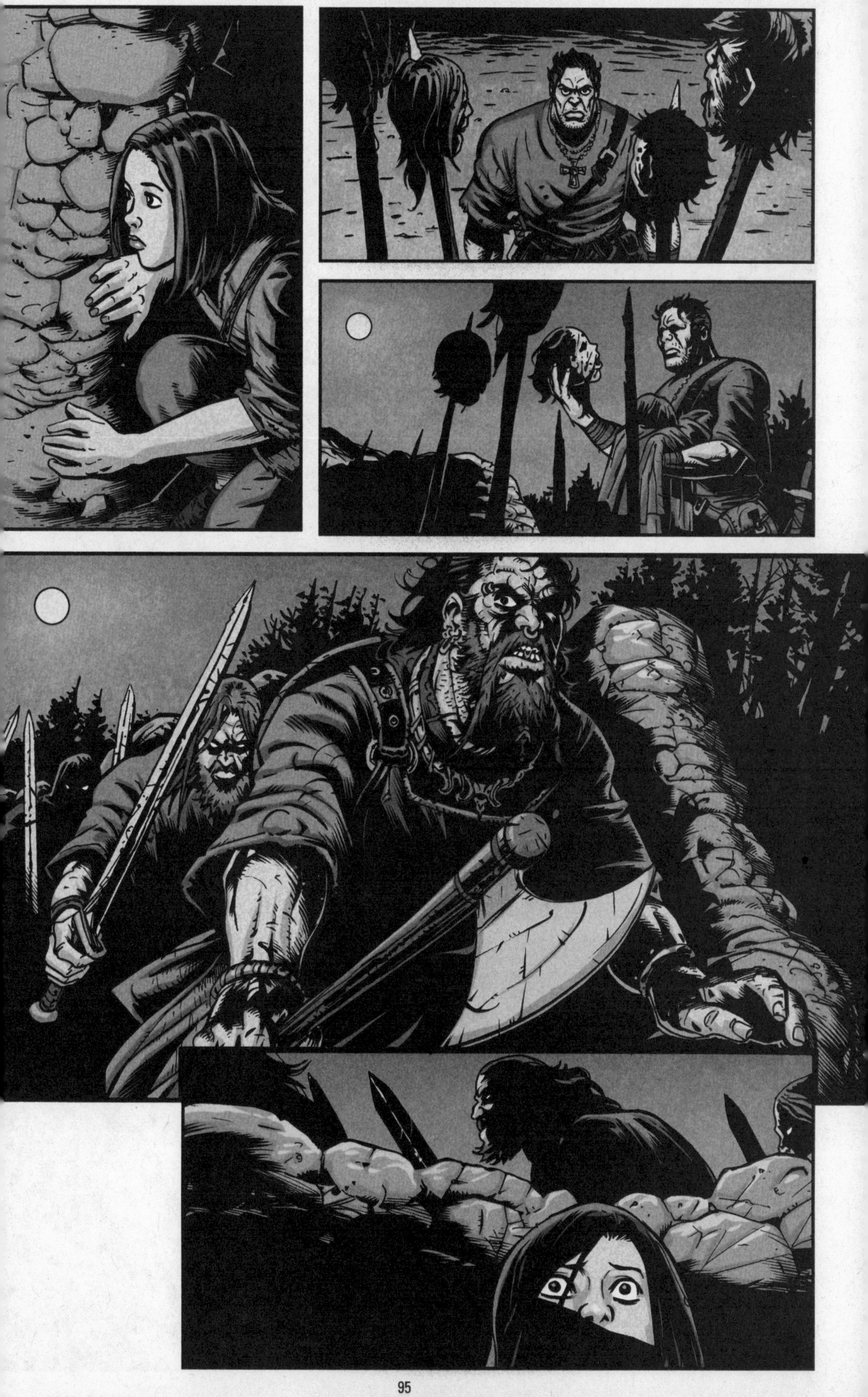

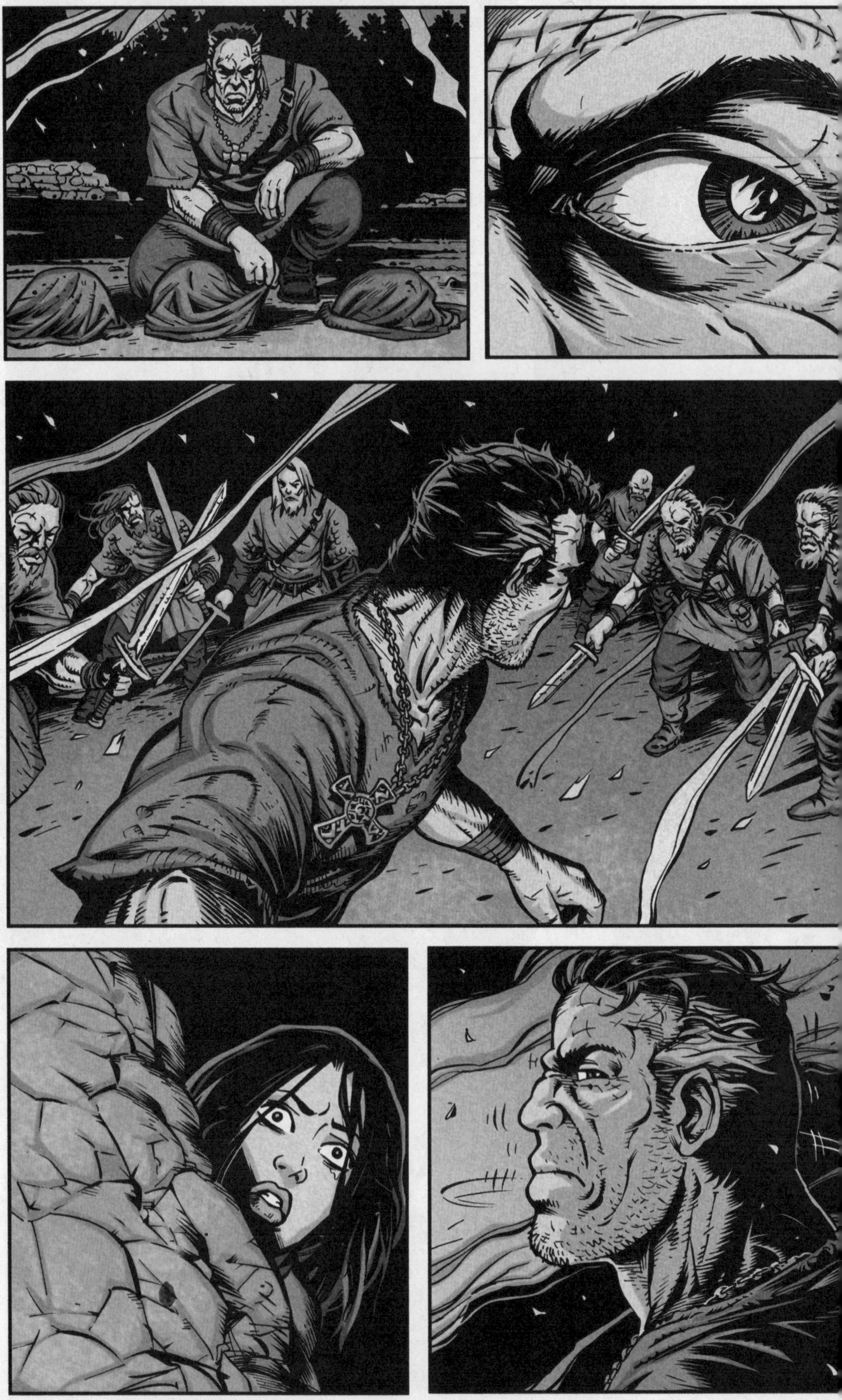

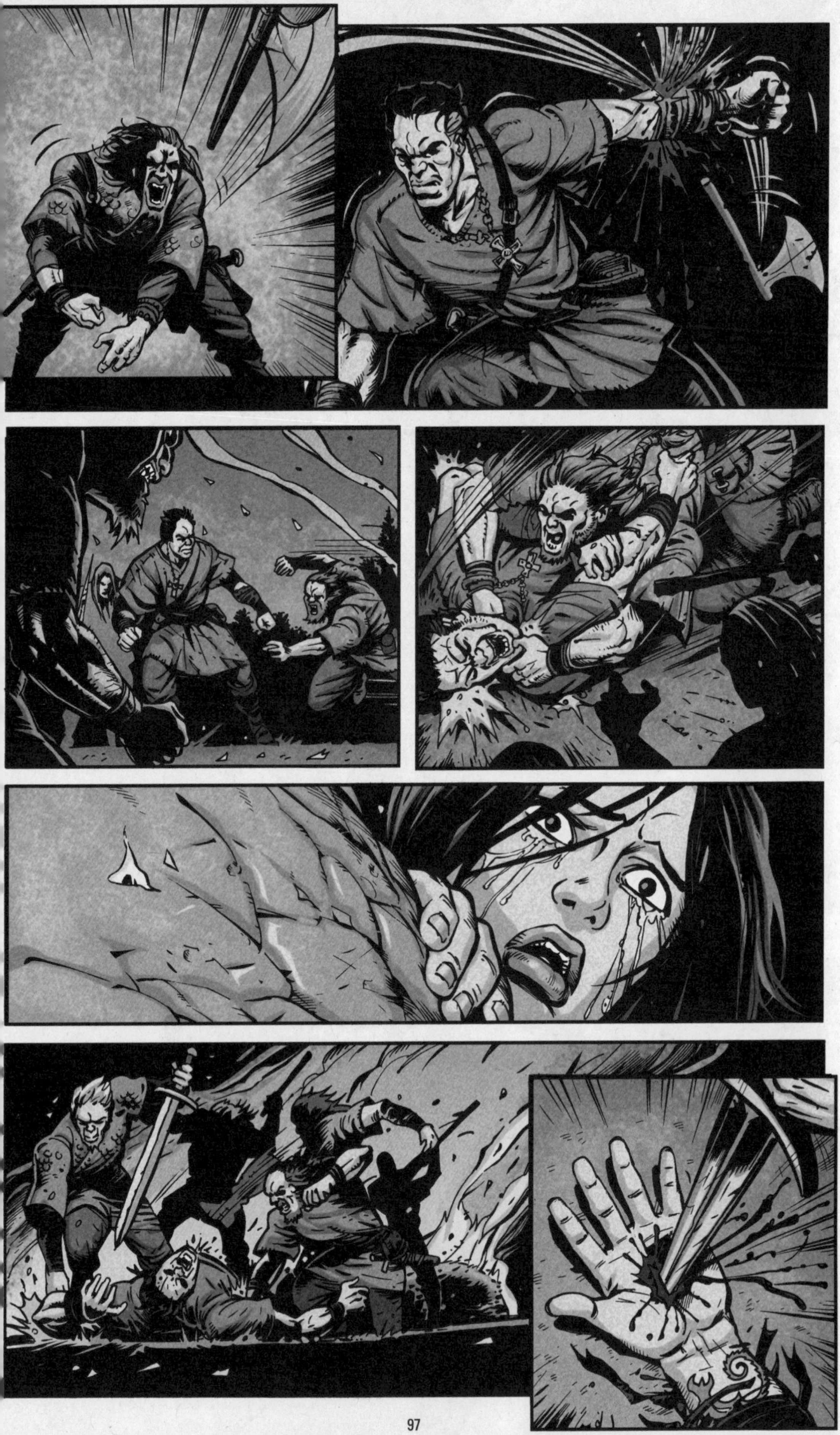

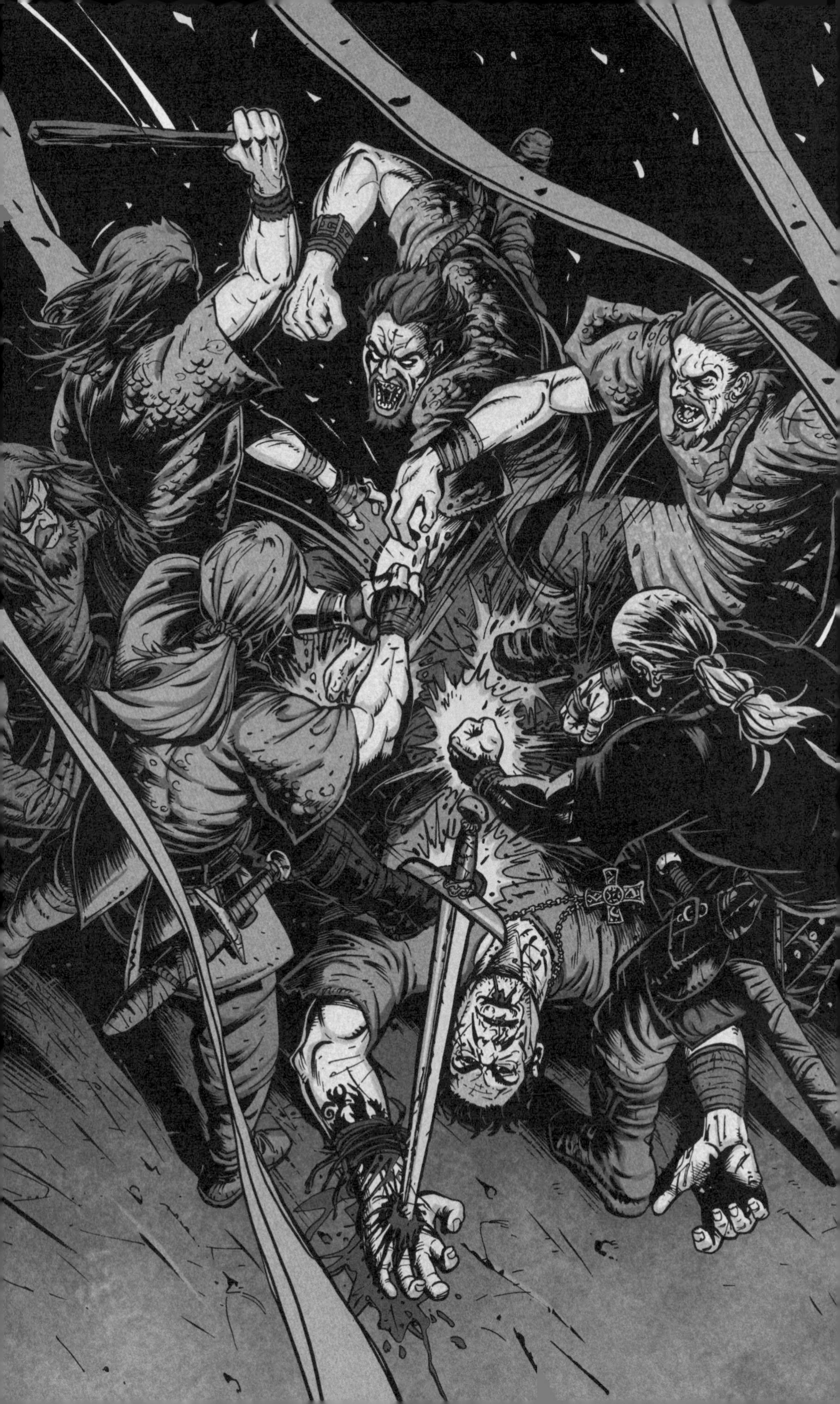

5 The Red Road

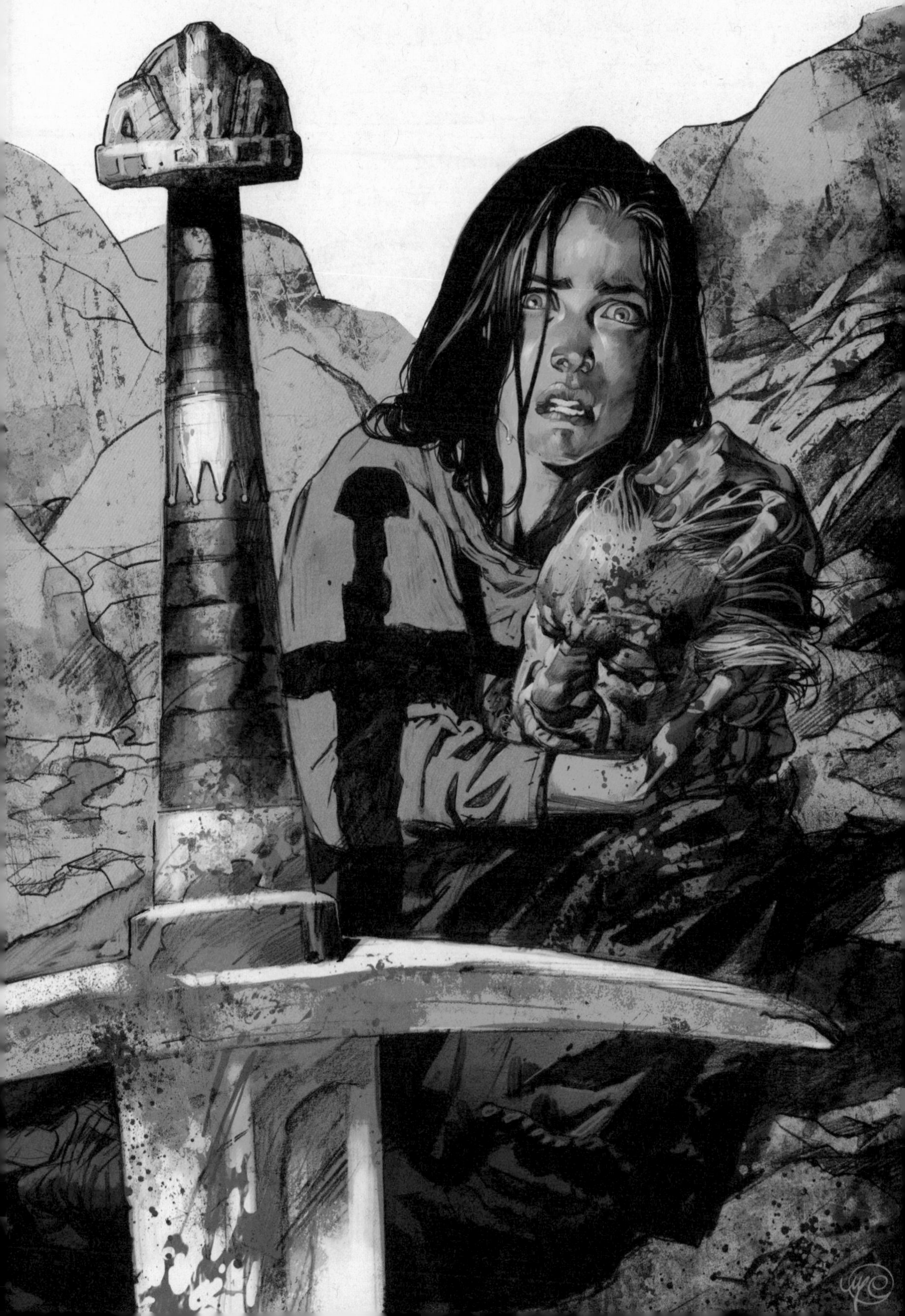

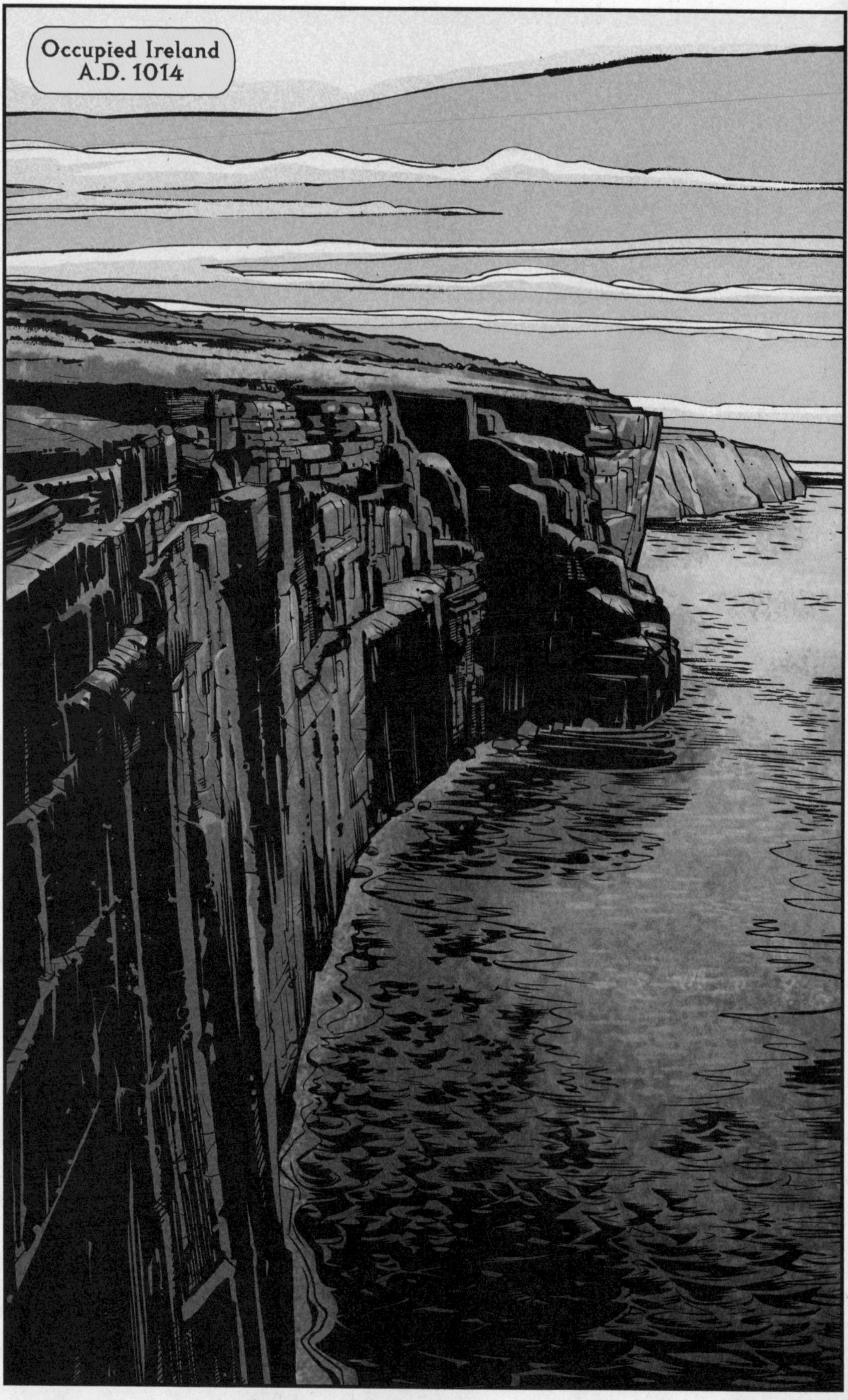
Occupied Ireland
A.D. 1014

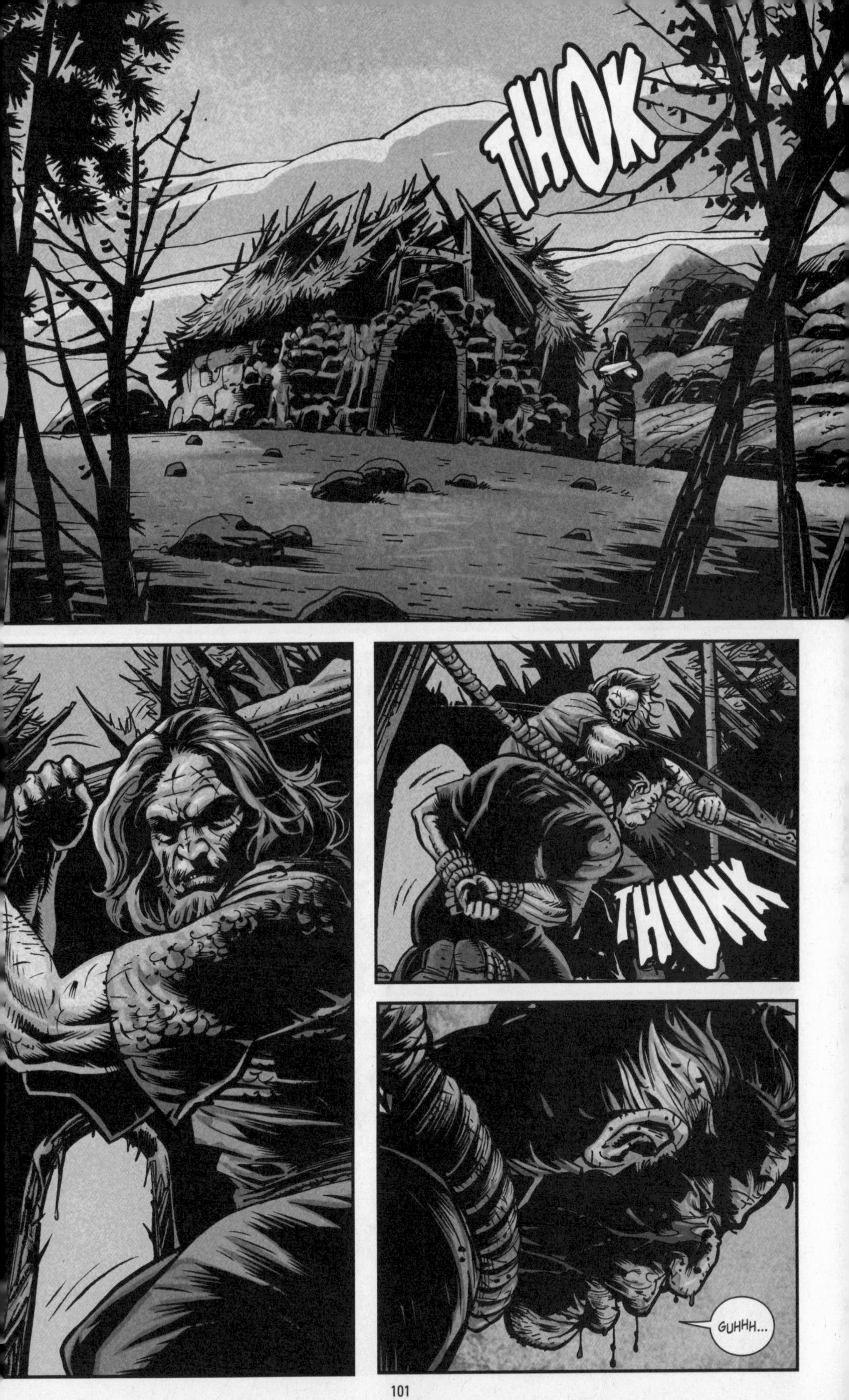
THOK
THUNK
GUHHH...

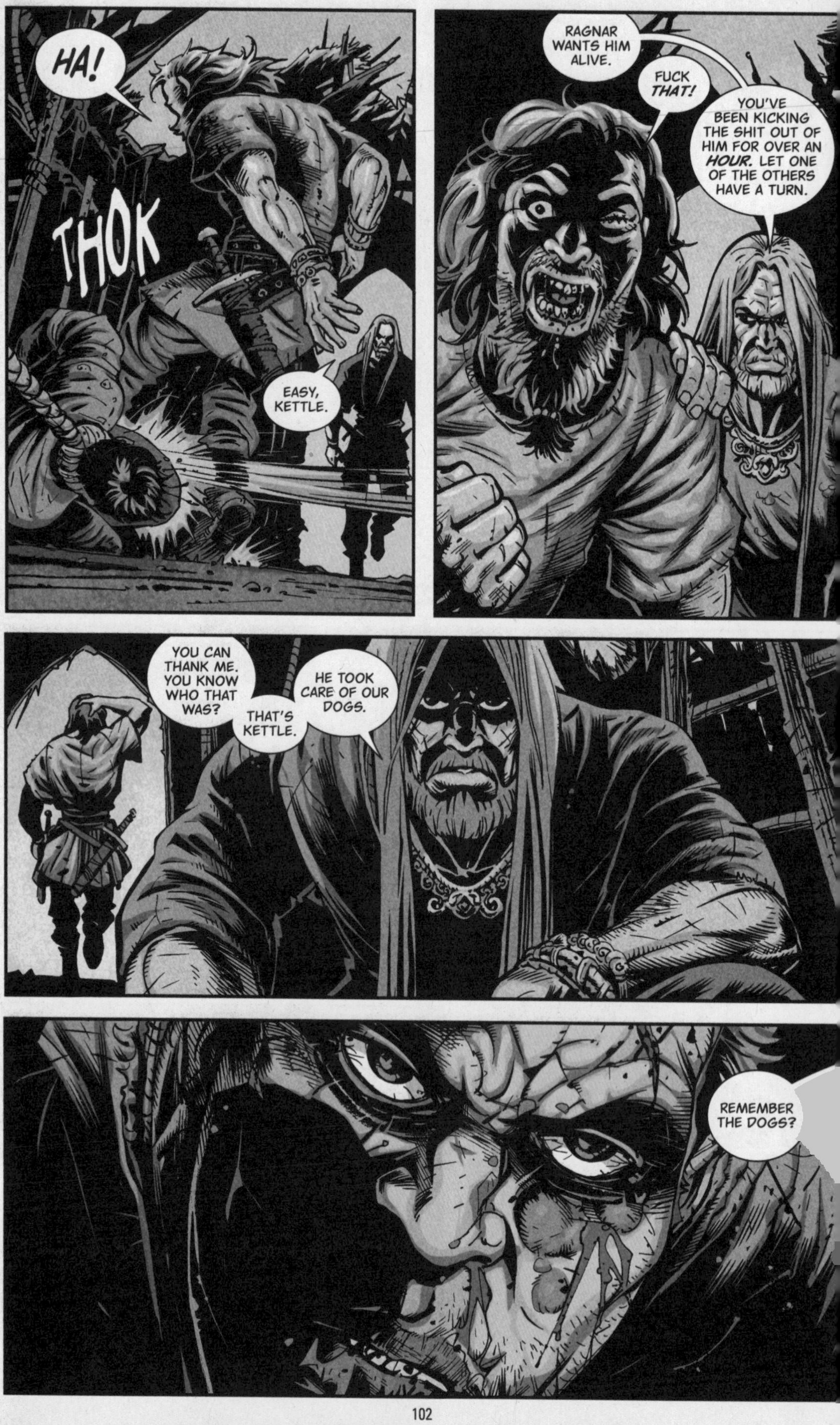
HA!
THOK
EASY, KETTLE.
RAGNAR WANTS HIM ALIVE.
FUCK THAT!
YOU'VE BEEN KICKING THE SHIT OUT OF HIM FOR OVER AN HOUR. LET ONE OF THE OTHERS HAVE A TURN.
YOU CAN THANK ME. YOU KNOW WHO THAT WAS?
THAT'S KETTLE.
HE TOOK CARE OF OUR DOGS.
REMEMBER THE DOGS?

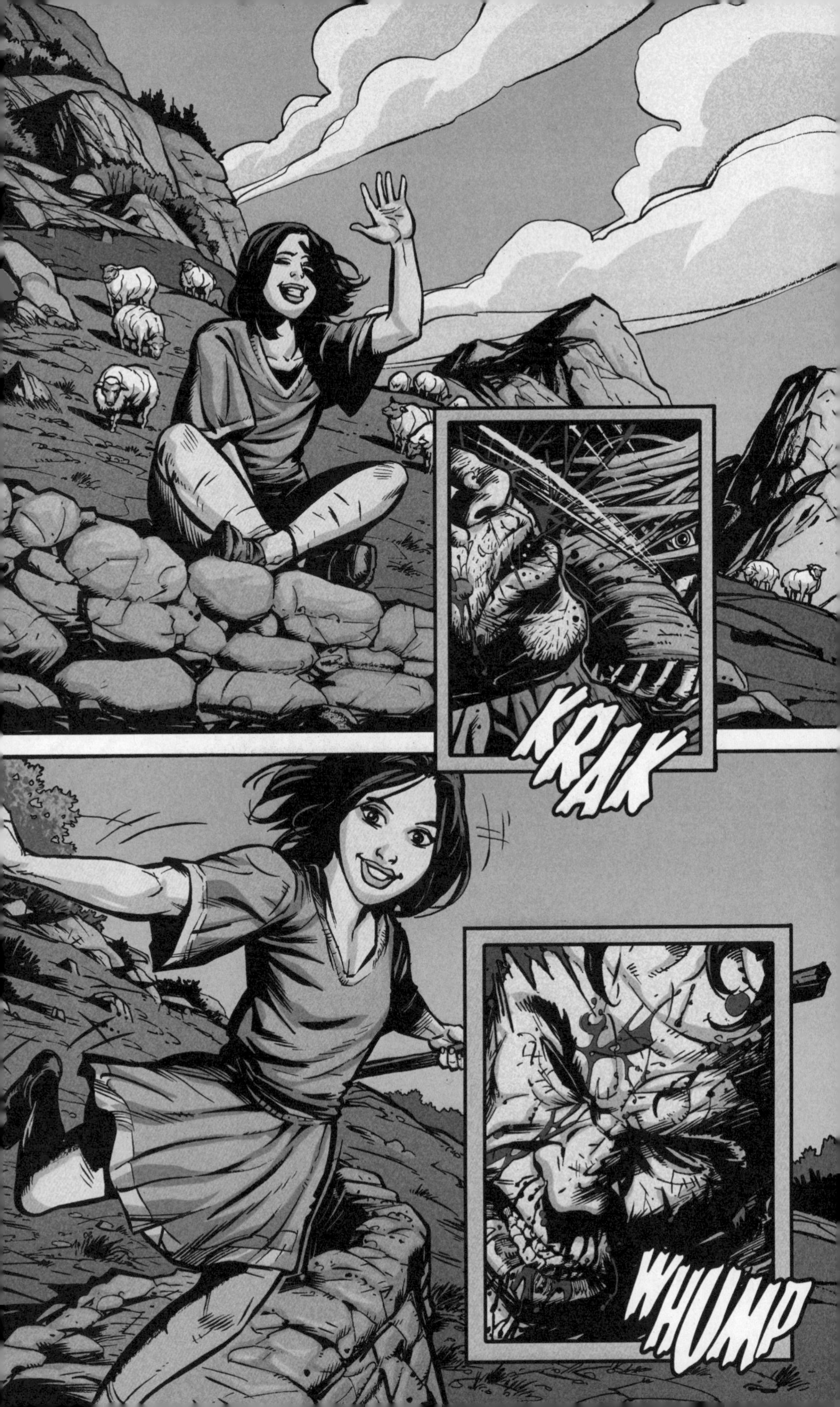

KRAK
WHUMP

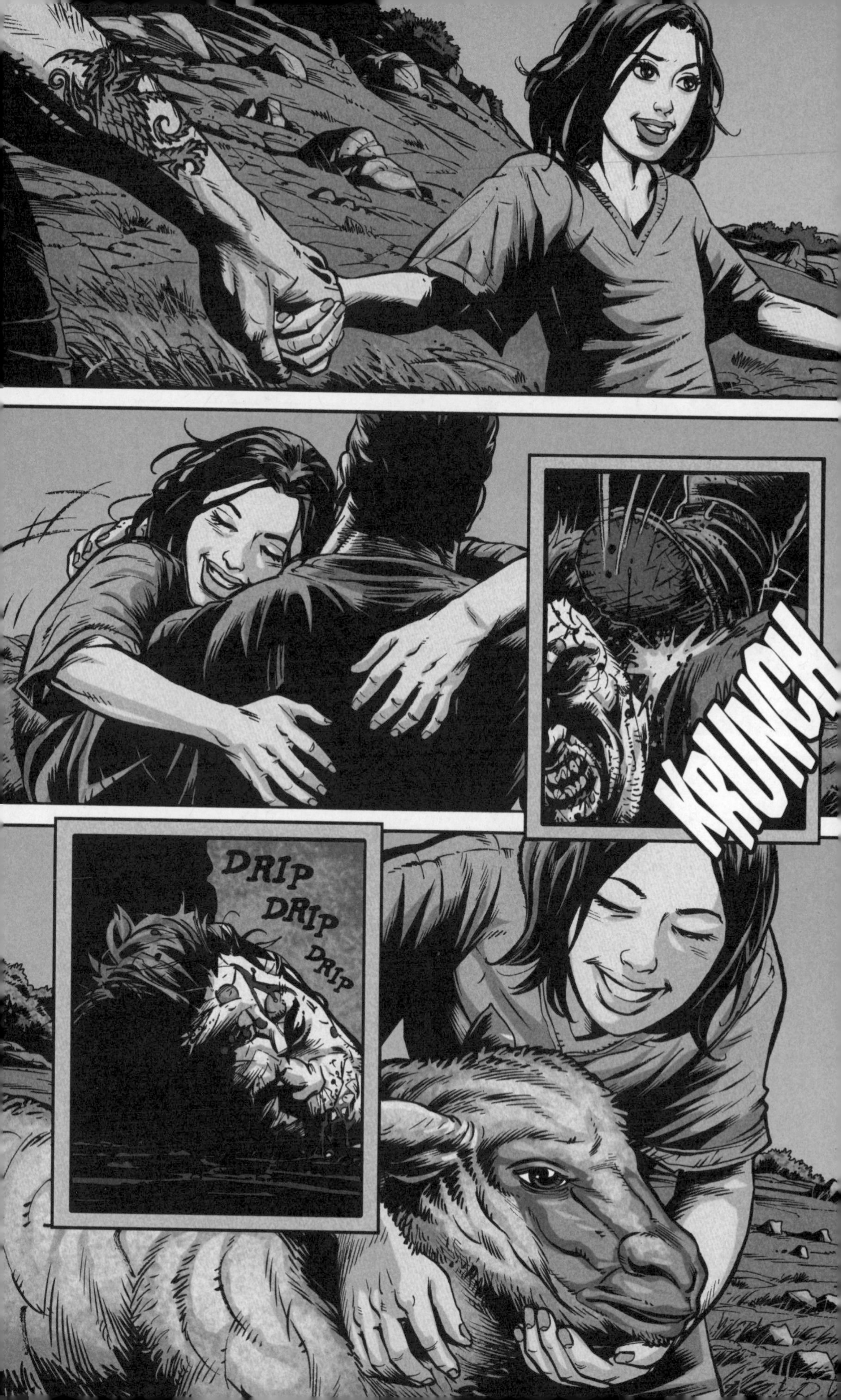
KRUNCH
DRIP
DRIP
DRIP

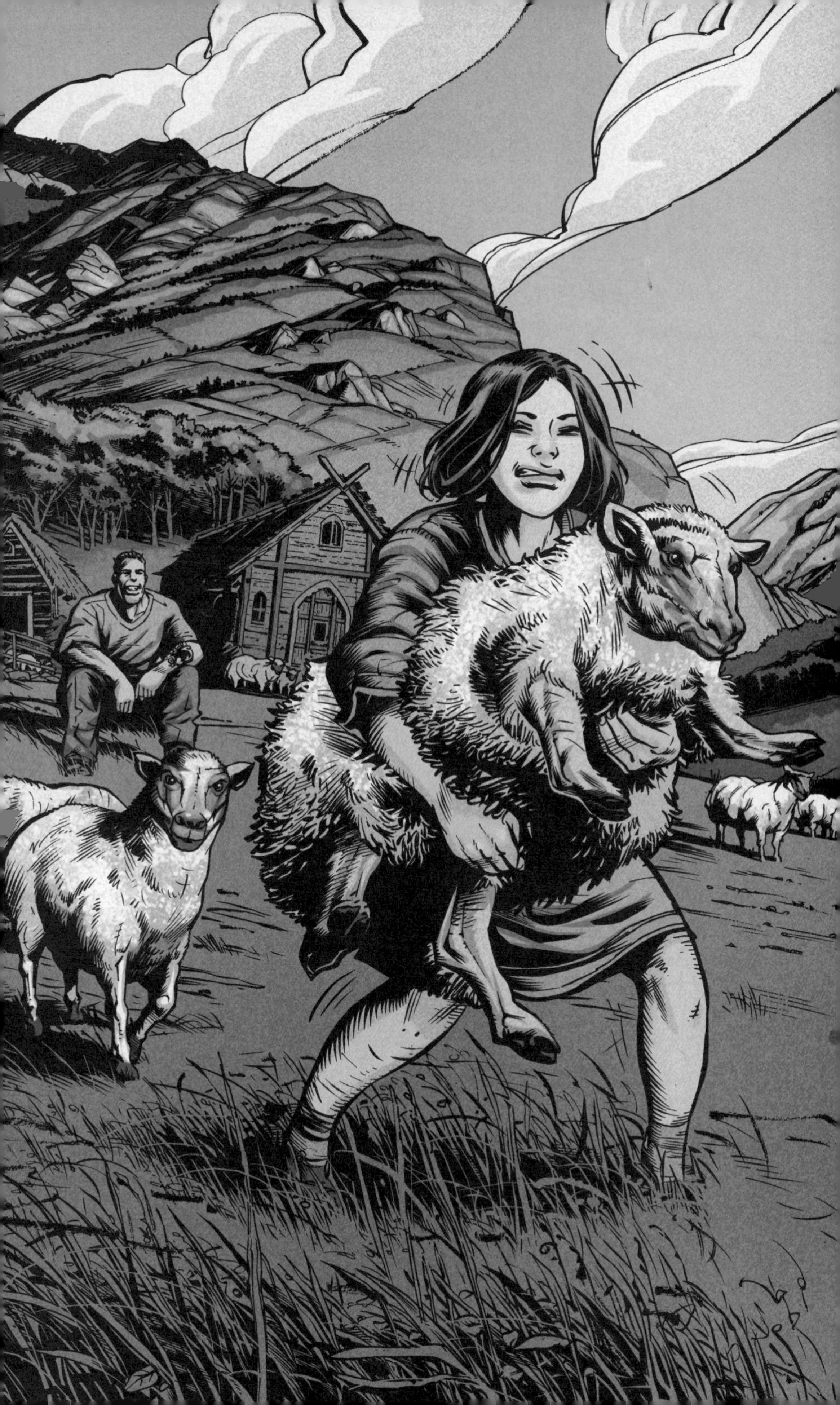

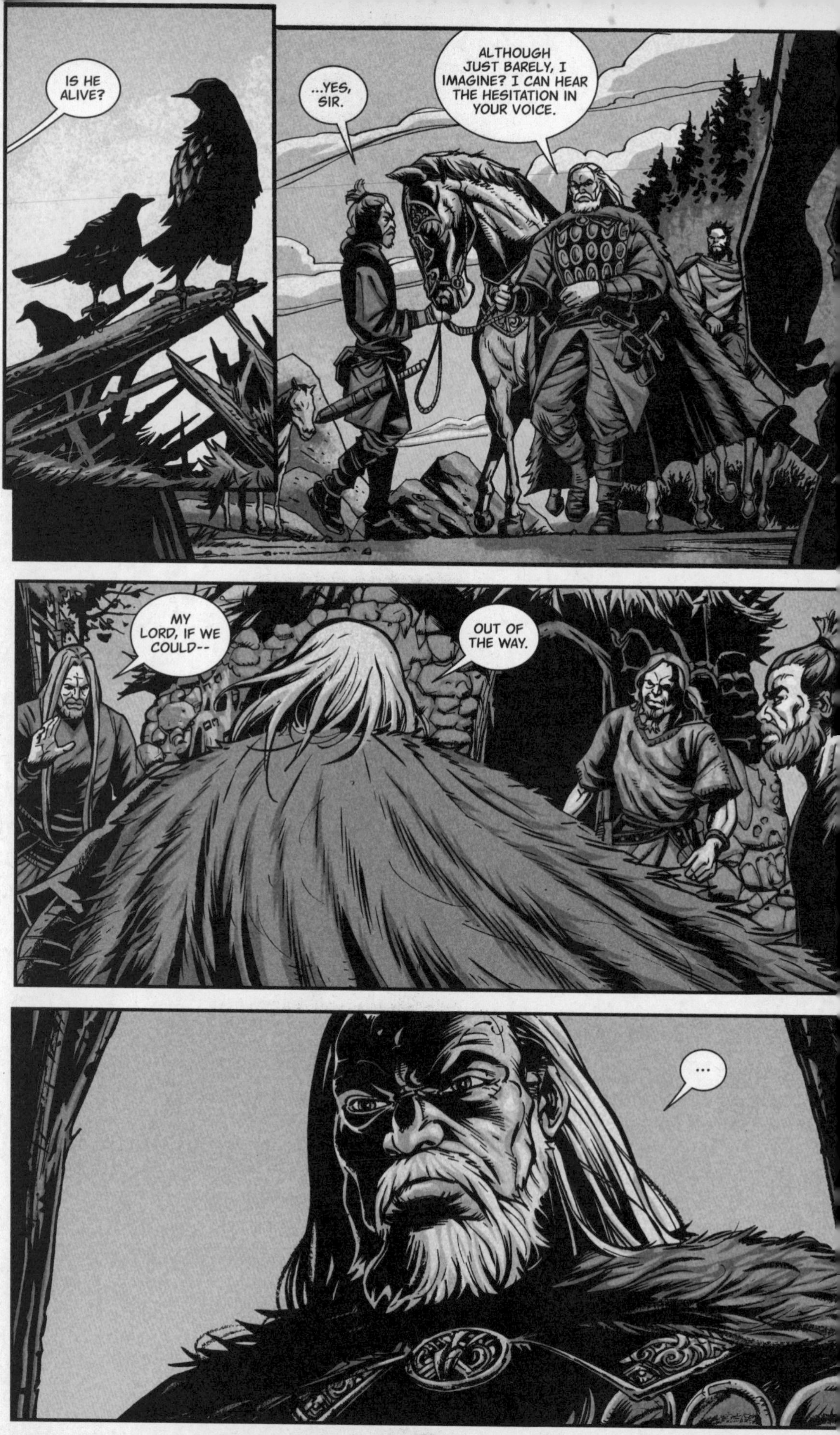
IS HE ALIVE?
...YES, SIR.
ALTHOUGH JUST BARELY, I IMAGINE? I CAN HEAR THE HESITATION IN YOUR VOICE.
MY LORD, IF WE COULD--
OUT OF THE WAY.
...

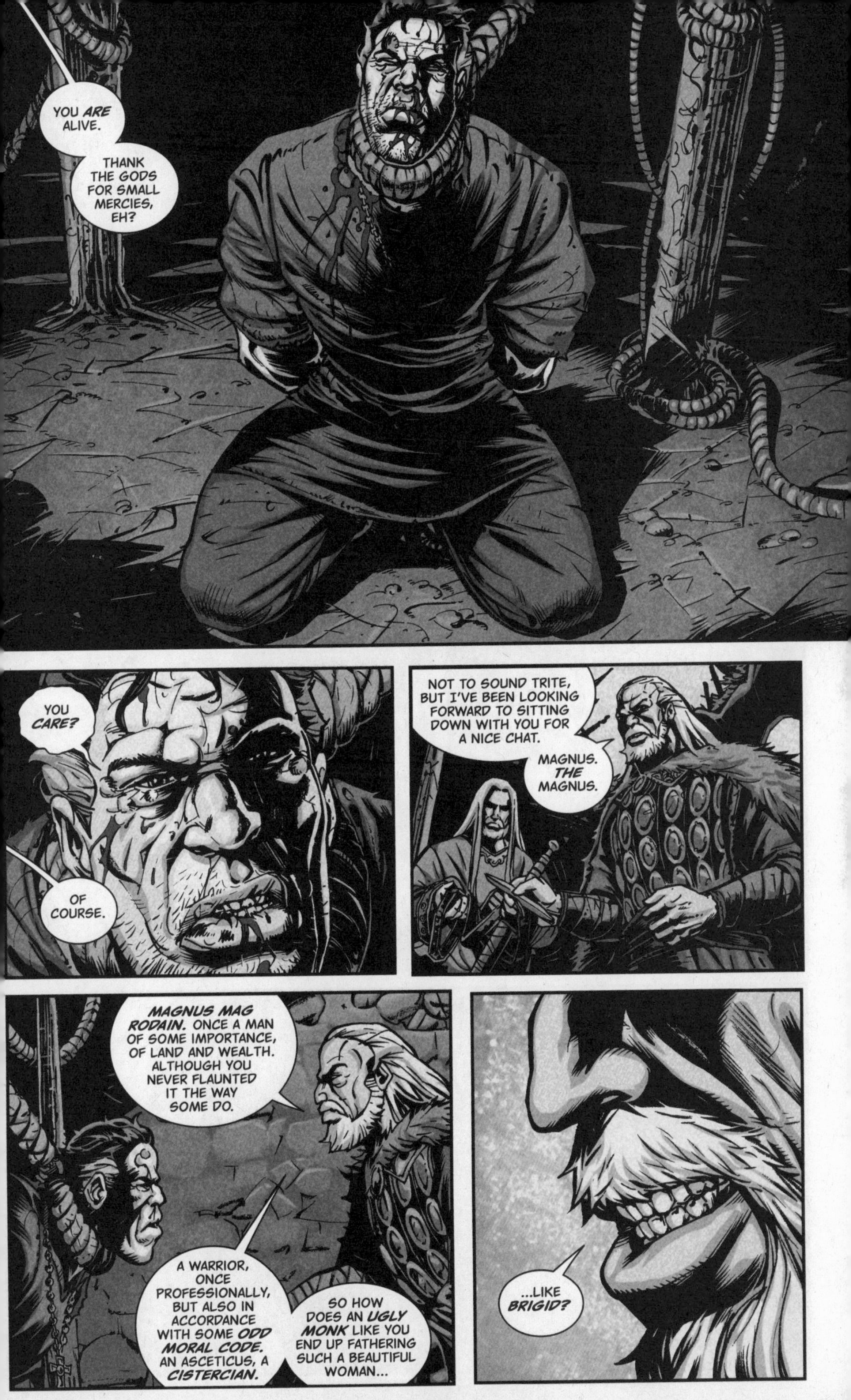
YOU ARE ALIVE.
THANK THE GODS FOR SMALL MERCIES, EH?
YOU CARE?
OF COURSE.
NOT TO SOUND TRITE, BUT I'VE BEEN LOOKING FORWARD TO SITTING DOWN WITH YOU FOR A NICE CHAT.
MAGNUS. THE MAGNUS.
MAGNUS MAG RODAIN. ONCE A MAN OF SOME IMPORTANCE, OF LAND AND WEALTH. ALTHOUGH YOU NEVER FLAUNTED IT THE WAY SOME DO.
A WARRIOR, ONCE PROFESSIONALLY, BUT ALSO IN ACCORDANCE WITH SOME ODD MORAL CODE. AN ASCETICUS, A CISTERCIAN.
SO HOW DOES AN UGLY MONK LIKE YOU END UP FATHERING SUCH A BEAUTIFUL WOMAN...
...LIKE BRIGID?

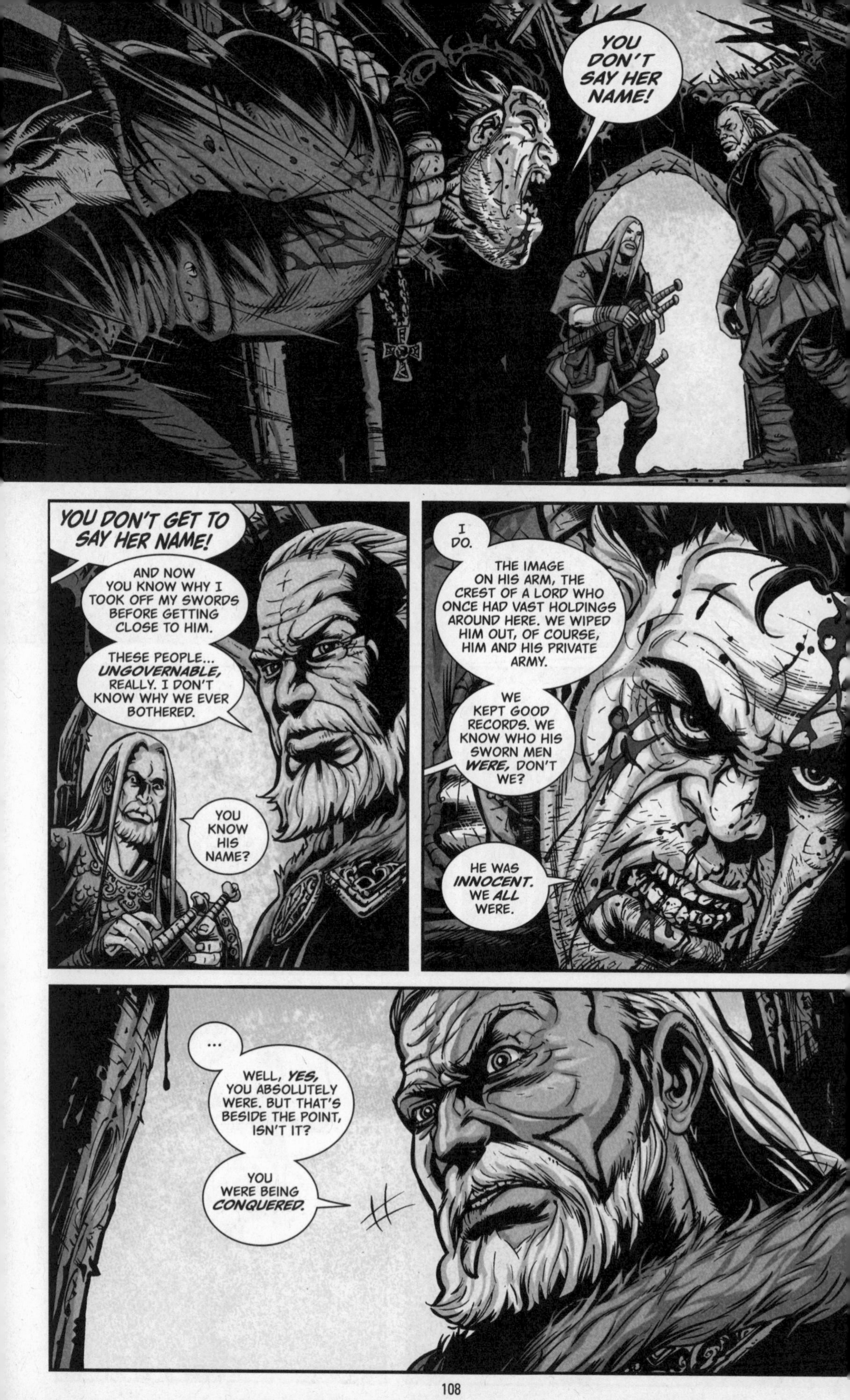
YOU DON'T SAY HER NAME!
YOU DON'T GET TO SAY HER NAME!
AND NOW YOU KNOW WHY I TOOK OFF MY SWORDS BEFORE GETTING CLOSE TO HIM.
THESE PEOPLE... UNGOVERNABLE, REALLY. I DON'T KNOW WHY WE EVER BOTHERED.
YOU KNOW HIS NAME?
I DO.
THE IMAGE ON HIS ARM, THE CREST OF A LORD WHO ONCE HAD VAST HOLDINGS AROUND HERE. WE WIPED HIM OUT, OF COURSE, HIM AND HIS PRIVATE ARMY.
WE KEPT GOOD RECORDS. WE KNOW WHO HIS SWORN MEN WERE, DON'T WE?
HE WAS INNOCENT. WE ALL WERE.
...
WELL, YES, YOU ABSOLUTELY WERE. BUT THAT'S BESIDE THE POINT, ISN'T IT?
YOU WERE BEING CONQUERED.

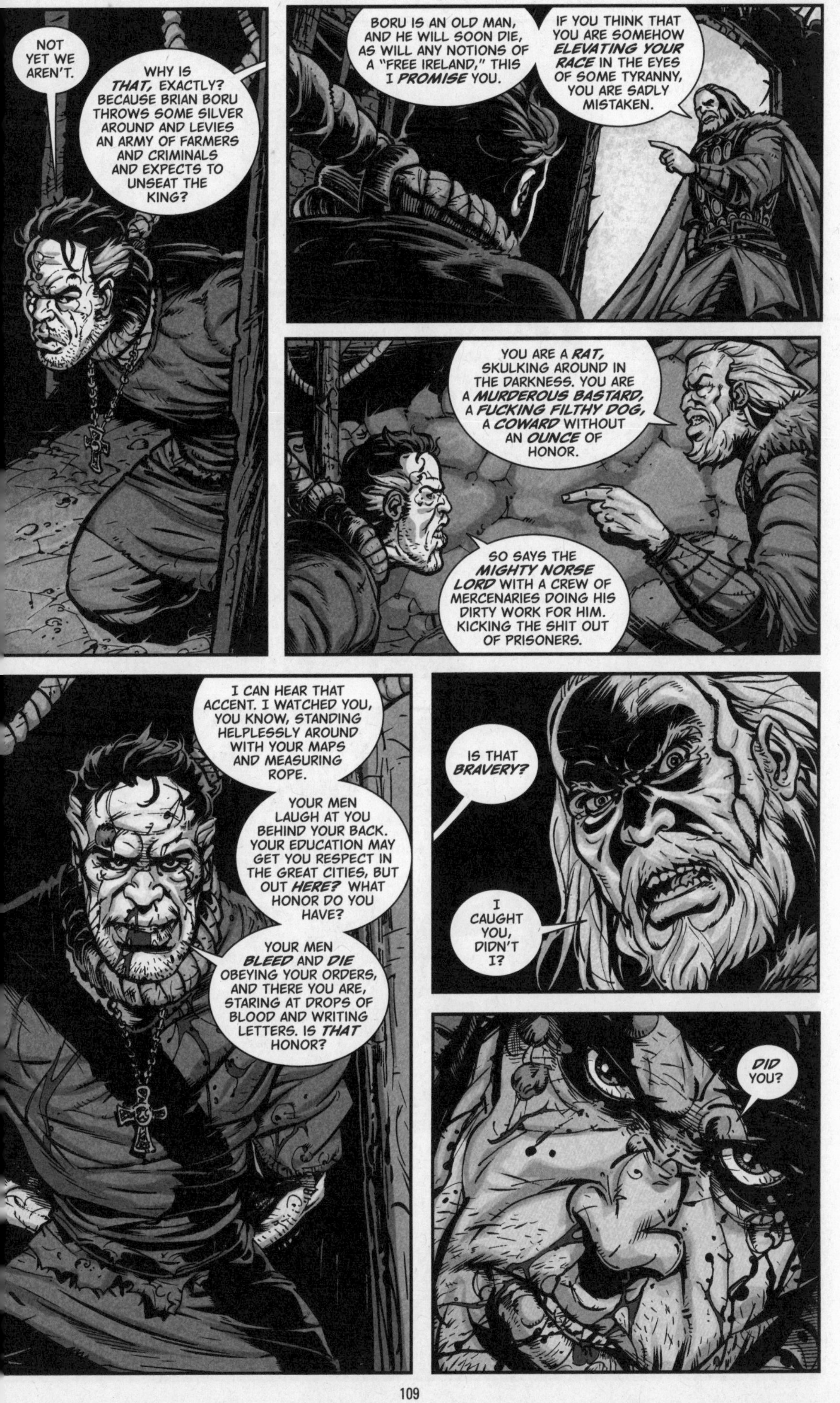
NOT YET WE AREN'T.
WHY IS THAT, EXACTLY? BECAUSE BRIAN BORU THROWS SOME SILVER AROUND AND LEVIES AN ARMY OF FARMERS AND CRIMINALS AND EXPECTS TO UNSEAT THE KING?
BORU IS AN OLD MAN, AND HE WILL SOON DIE, AS WILL ANY NOTIONS OF A "FREE IRELAND," THIS I PROMISE YOU.
IF YOU THINK THAT YOU ARE SOMEHOW ELEVATING YOUR RACE IN THE EYES OF SOME TYRANNY, YOU ARE SADLY MISTAKEN.
YOU ARE A RAT, SKULKING AROUND IN THE DARKNESS. YOU ARE A MURDEROUS BASTARD, A FUCKING FILTHY DOG, A COWARD WITHOUT AN OUNCE OF HONOR.
SO SAYS THE MIGHTY NORSE LORD WITH A CREW OF MERCENARIES DOING HIS DIRTY WORK FOR HIM. KICKING THE SHIT OUT OF PRISONERS.
I CAN HEAR THAT ACCENT. I WATCHED YOU, YOU KNOW, STANDING HELPLESSLY AROUND WITH YOUR MAPS AND MEASURING ROPE.
YOUR MEN LAUGH AT YOU BEHIND YOUR BACK. YOUR EDUCATION MAY GET YOU RESPECT IN THE GREAT CITIES, BUT OUT HERE? WHAT HONOR DO YOU HAVE?
YOUR MEN BLEED AND DIE OBEYING YOUR ORDERS, AND THERE YOU ARE, STARING AT DROPS OF BLOOD AND WRITING LETTERS. IS THAT HONOR?
IS THAT BRAVERY?
I CAUGHT YOU, DIDN'T I?
DID YOU?

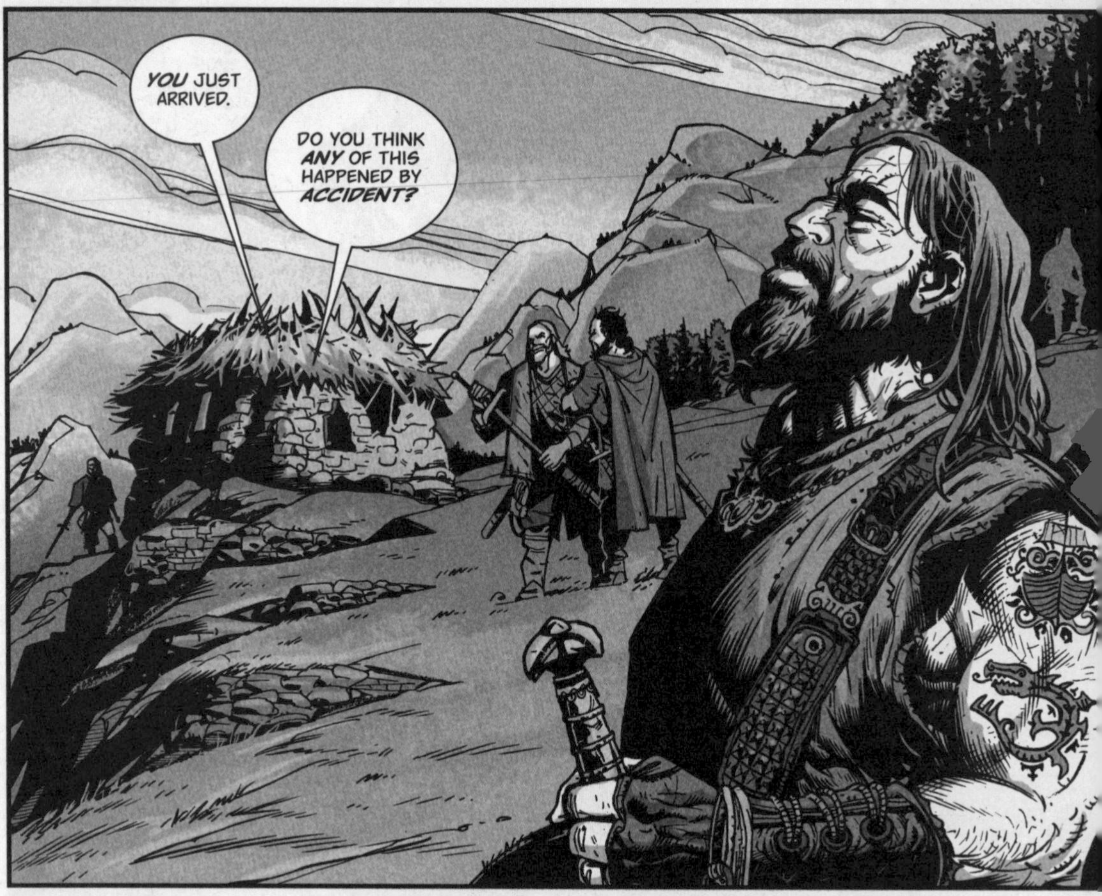
YOU JUST ARRIVED.
DO YOU THINK ANY OF THIS HAPPENED BY ACCIDENT?

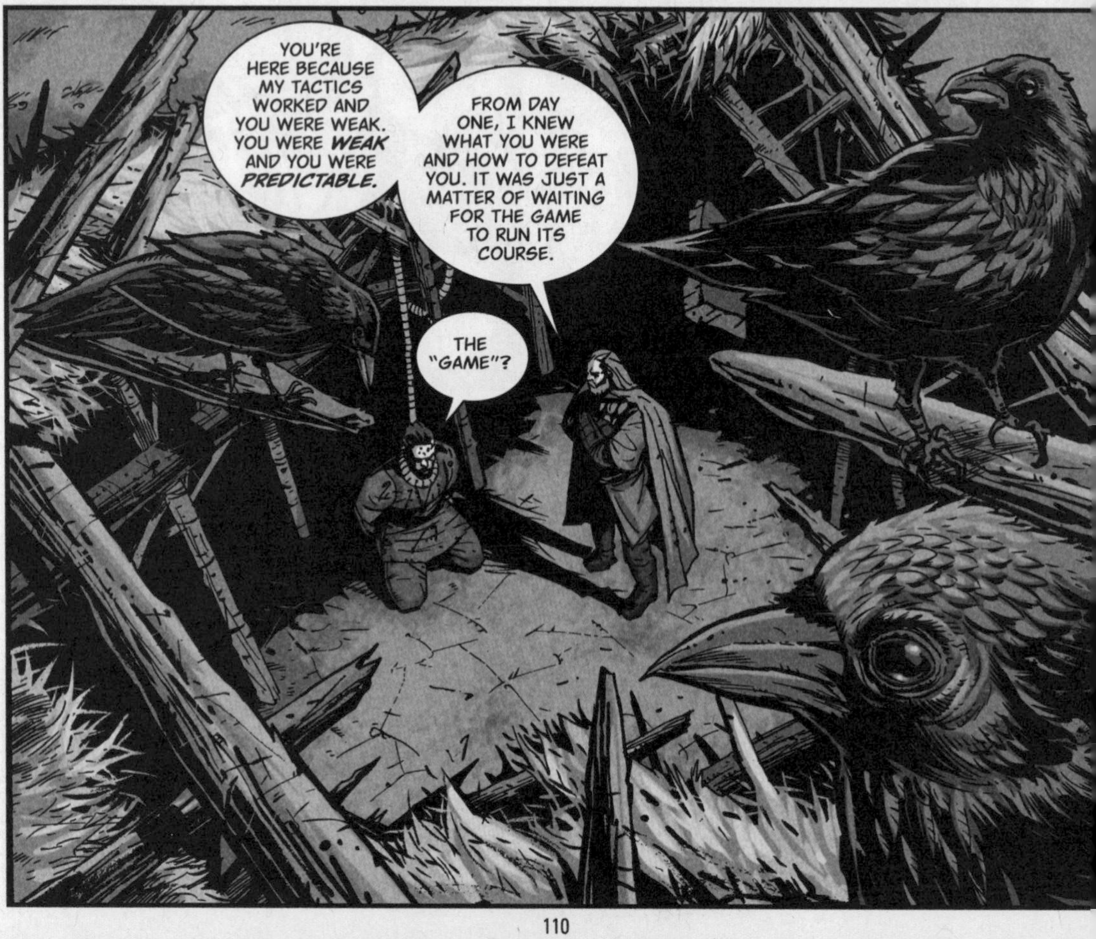
YOU'RE HERE BECAUSE MY TACTICS WORKED AND YOU WERE WEAK. YOU WERE WEAK AND YOU WERE PREDICTABLE.
FROM DAY ONE, I KNEW WHAT YOU WERE AND HOW TO DEFEAT YOU. IT WAS JUST A MATTER OF WAITING FOR THE GAME TO RUN ITS COURSE.
THE "GAME"?

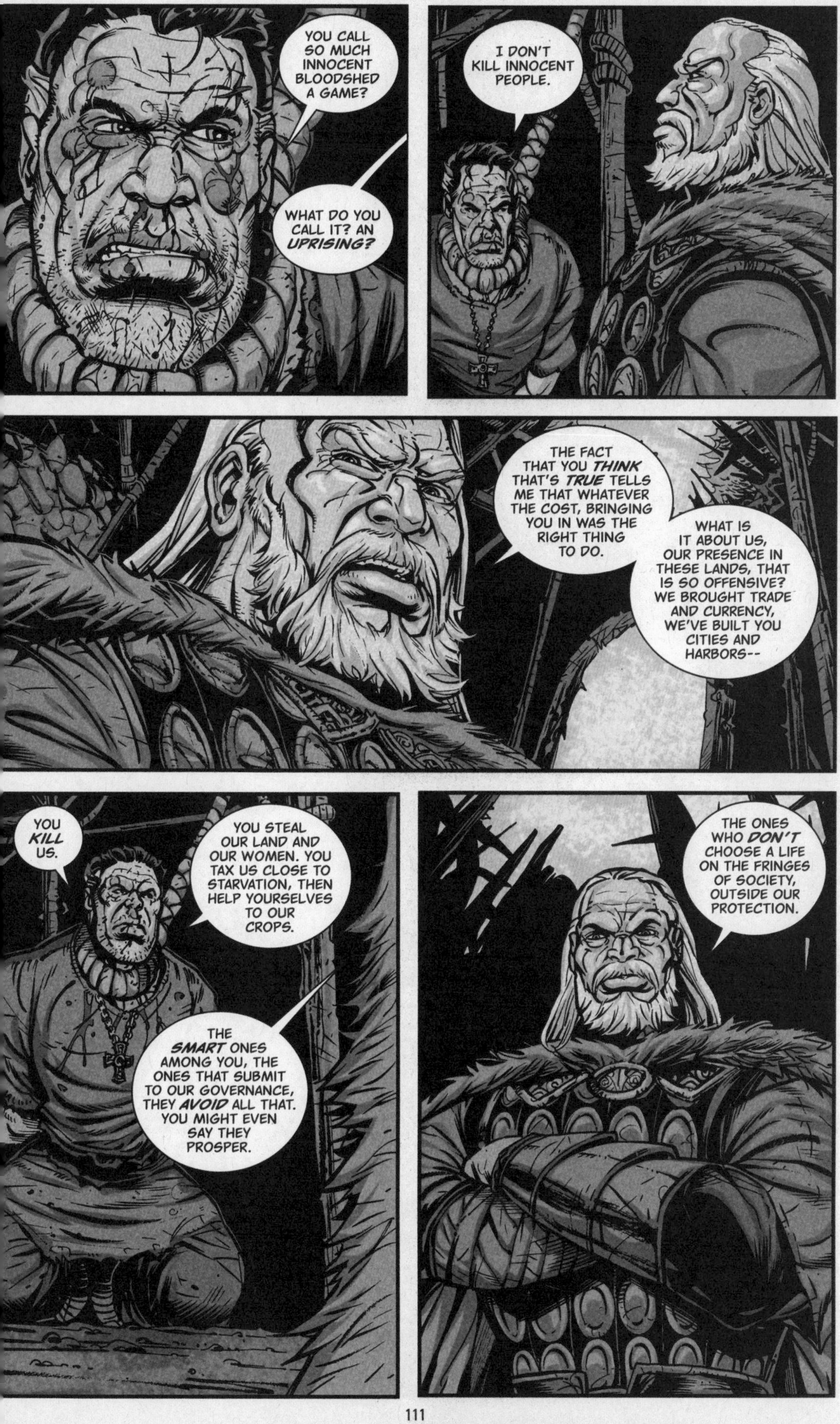
YOU CALL SO MUCH INNOCENT BLOODSHED A GAME?
WHAT DO YOU CALL IT? AN UPRISING?
I DON'T KILL INNOCENT PEOPLE.
THE FACT THAT YOU THINK THAT'S TRUE TELLS ME THAT WHATEVER THE COST, BRINGING YOU IN WAS THE RIGHT THING TO DO.
WHAT IS IT ABOUT US, OUR PRESENCE IN THESE LANDS, THAT IS SO OFFENSIVE? WE BROUGHT TRADE AND CURRENCY, WE'VE BUILT YOU CITIES AND HARBORS--
YOU KILL US.
YOU STEAL OUR LAND AND OUR WOMEN. YOU TAX US CLOSE TO STARVATION, THEN HELP YOURSELVES TO OUR CROPS.
THE SMART ONES AMONG YOU, THE ONES THAT SUBMIT TO OUR GOVERNANCE, THEY AVOID ALL THAT. YOU MIGHT EVEN SAY THEY PROSPER.
THE ONES WHO DON'T CHOOSE A LIFE ON THE FRINGES OF SOCIETY, OUTSIDE OUR PROTECTION.

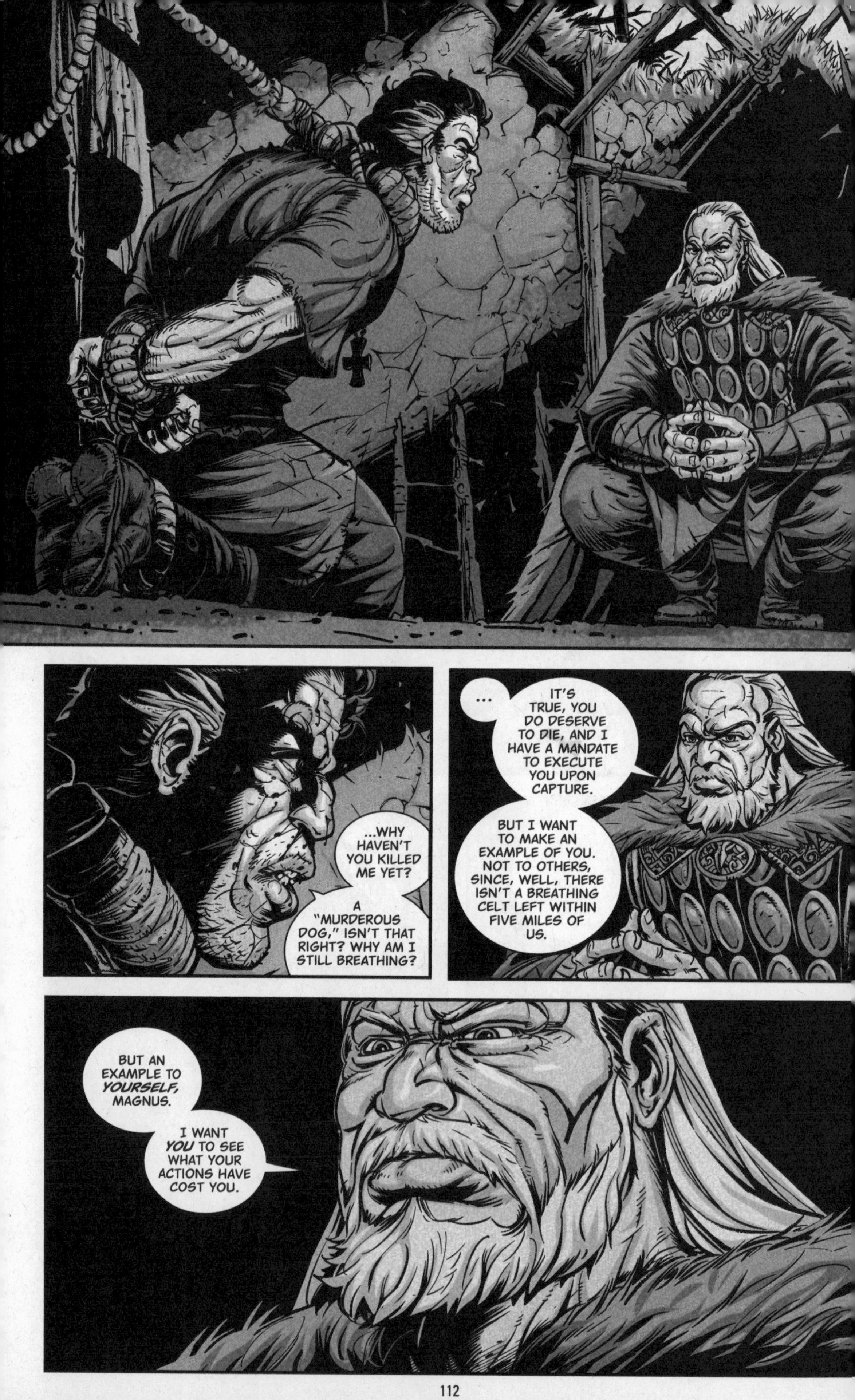
...WHY HAVEN'T YOU KILLED ME YET?
A "MURDEROUS DOG," ISN'T THAT RIGHT? WHY AM I STILL BREATHING?
...
IT'S TRUE, YOU DO DESERVE TO DIE, AND I HAVE A MANDATE TO EXECUTE YOU UPON CAPTURE.
BUT I WANT TO MAKE AN EXAMPLE OF YOU. NOT TO OTHERS, SINCE, WELL, THERE ISN'T A BREATHING CELT LEFT WITHIN FIVE MILES OF US.
BUT AN EXAMPLE TO *YOURSELF,* MAGNUS.
I WANT *YOU* TO SEE WHAT YOUR ACTIONS HAVE COST YOU.

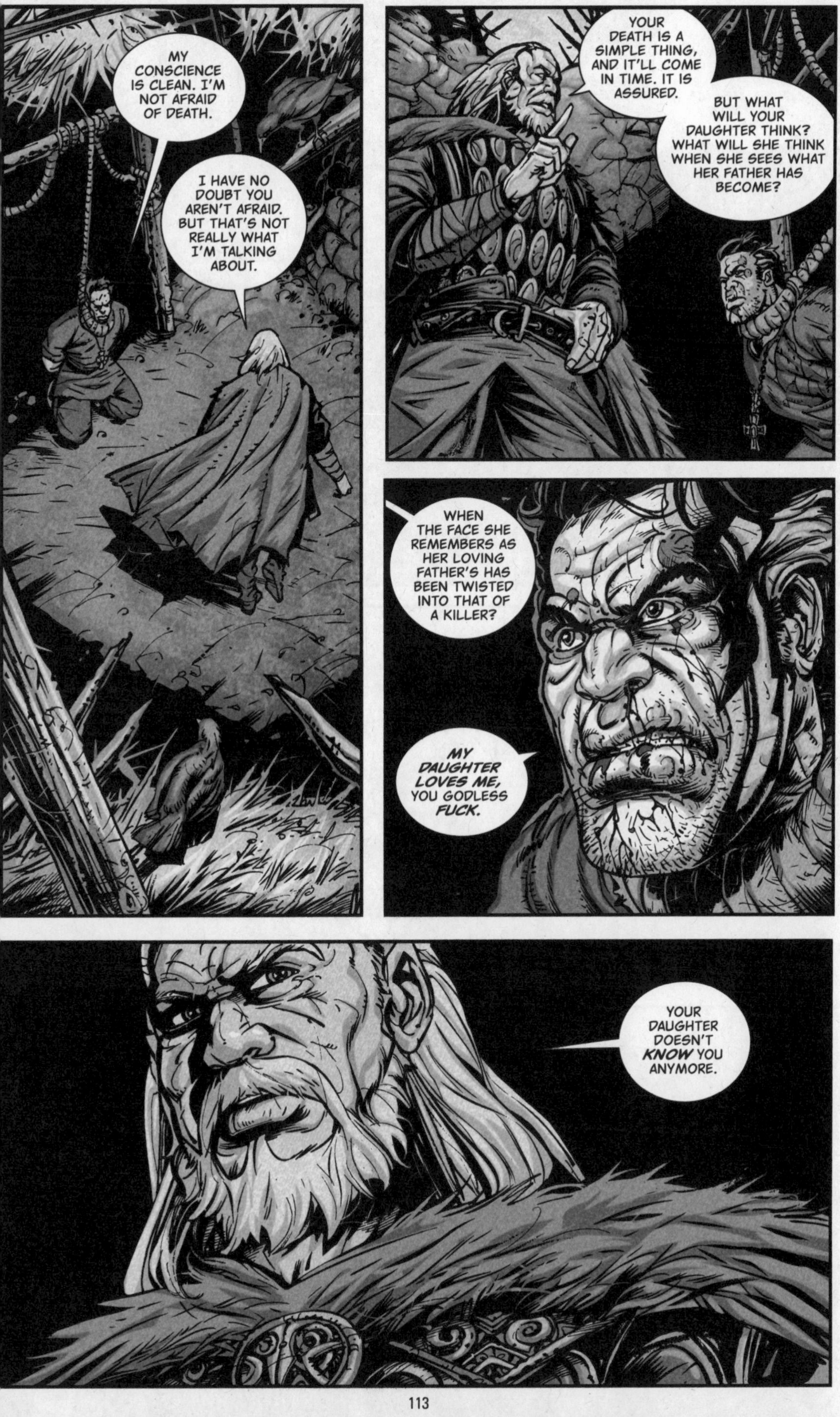
MY CONSCIENCE IS CLEAN. I'M NOT AFRAID OF DEATH.
I HAVE NO DOUBT YOU AREN'T AFRAID. BUT THAT'S NOT REALLY WHAT I'M TALKING ABOUT.
YOUR DEATH IS A SIMPLE THING, AND IT'LL COME IN TIME. IT IS ASSURED.
BUT WHAT WILL YOUR DAUGHTER THINK? WHAT WILL SHE THINK WHEN SHE SEES WHAT HER FATHER HAS BECOME?
WHEN THE FACE SHE REMEMBERS AS HER LOVING FATHER'S HAS BEEN TWISTED INTO THAT OF A KILLER?
MY DAUGHTER LOVES ME, YOU GODLESS *FUCK.*
YOUR DAUGHTER DOESN'T *KNOW* YOU ANYMORE.

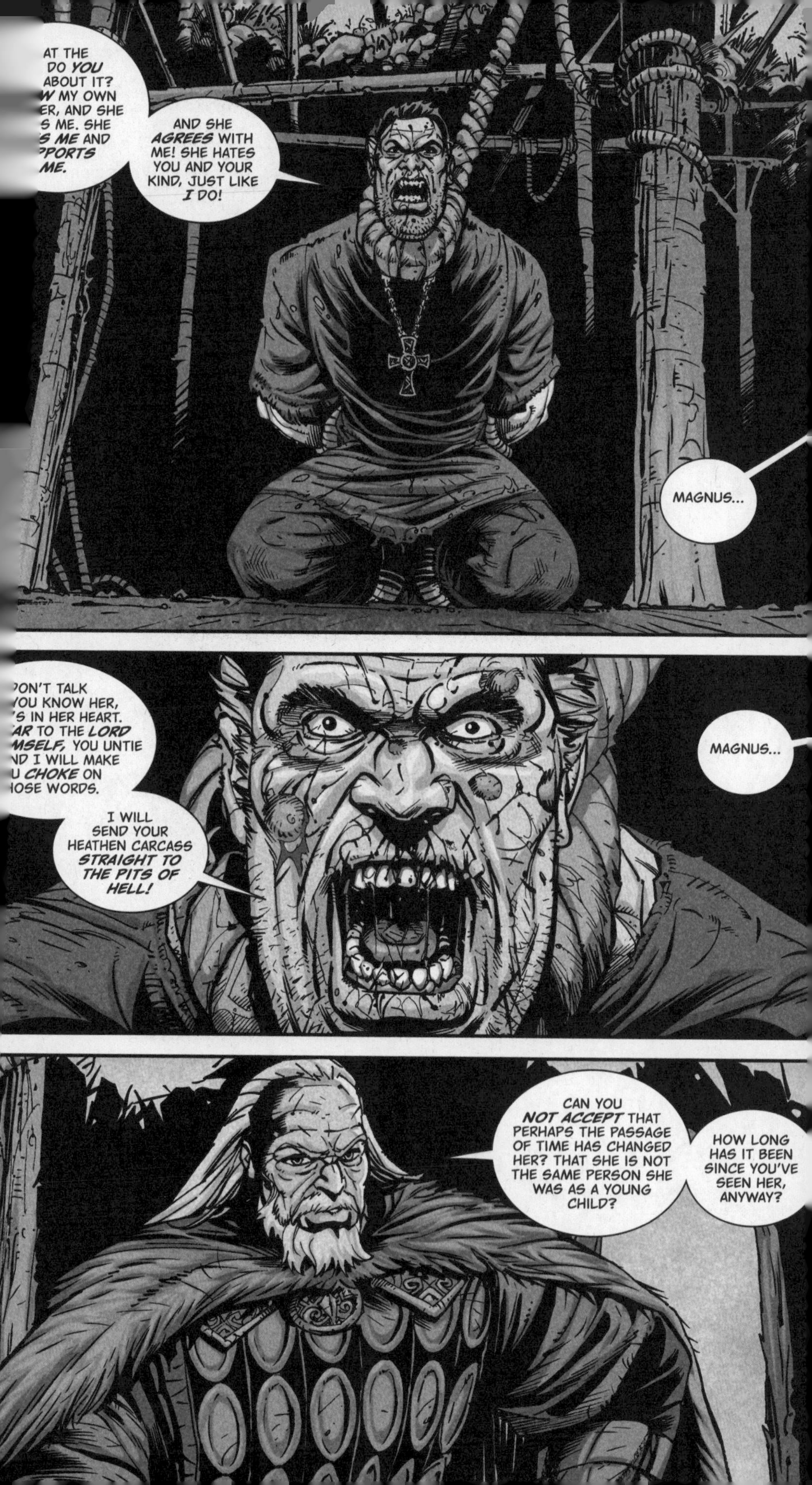
AT THE DO YOU ABOUT IT? W MY OWN ER, AND SHE S ME. SHE S ME AND PPORTS ME.
AND SHE AGREES WITH ME! SHE HATES YOU AND YOUR KIND, JUST LIKE I DO!
MAGNUS...
DON'T TALK YOU KNOW HER, 'S IN HER HEART. AR TO THE LORD MSELF, YOU UNTIE ND I WILL MAKE U CHOKE ON HOSE WORDS.
I WILL SEND YOUR HEATHEN CARCASS STRAIGHT TO THE PITS OF HELL!
MAGNUS...
CAN YOU NOT ACCEPT THAT PERHAPS THE PASSAGE OF TIME HAS CHANGED HER? THAT SHE IS NOT THE SAME PERSON SHE WAS AS A YOUNG CHILD?
HOW LONG HAS IT BEEN SINCE YOU'VE SEEN HER, ANYWAY?

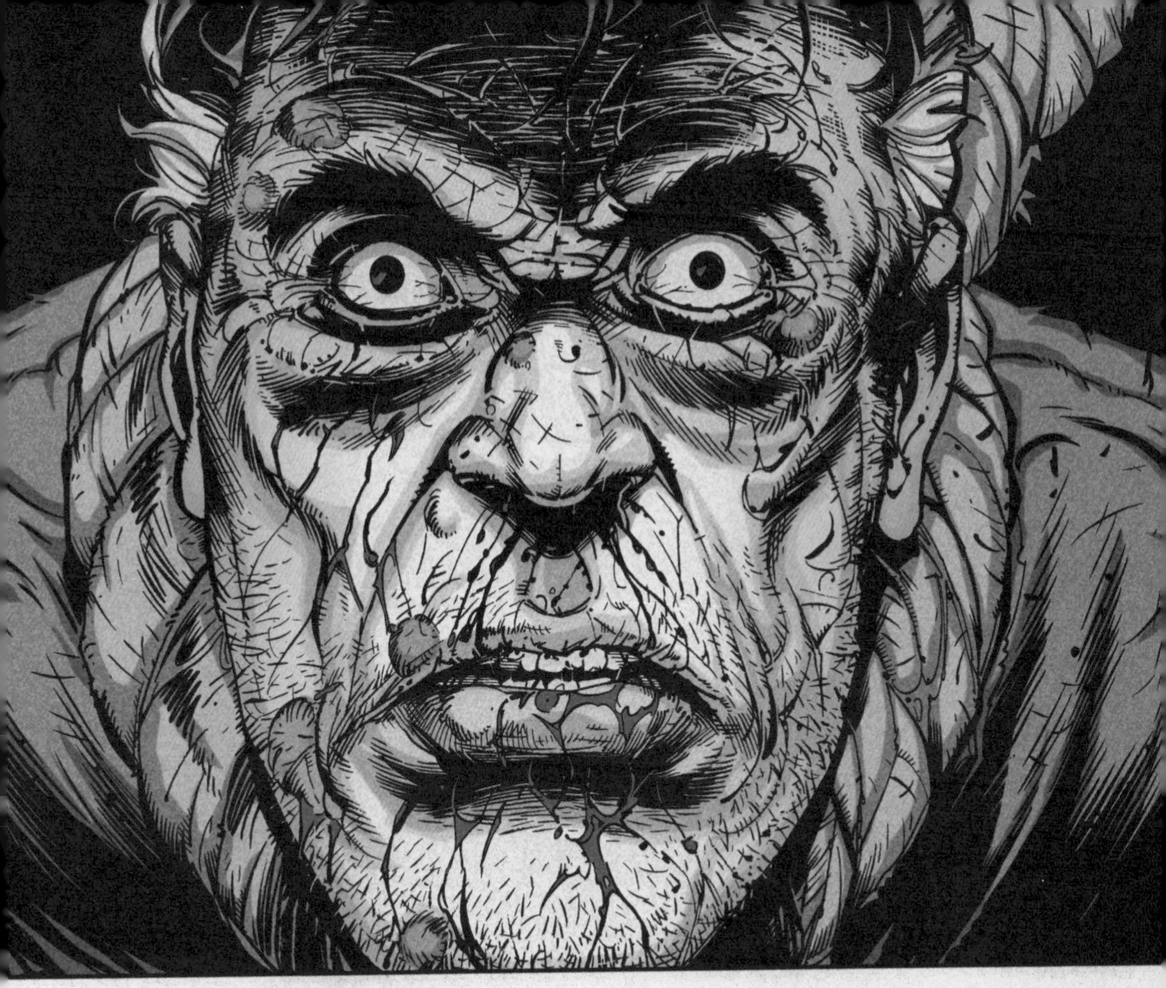

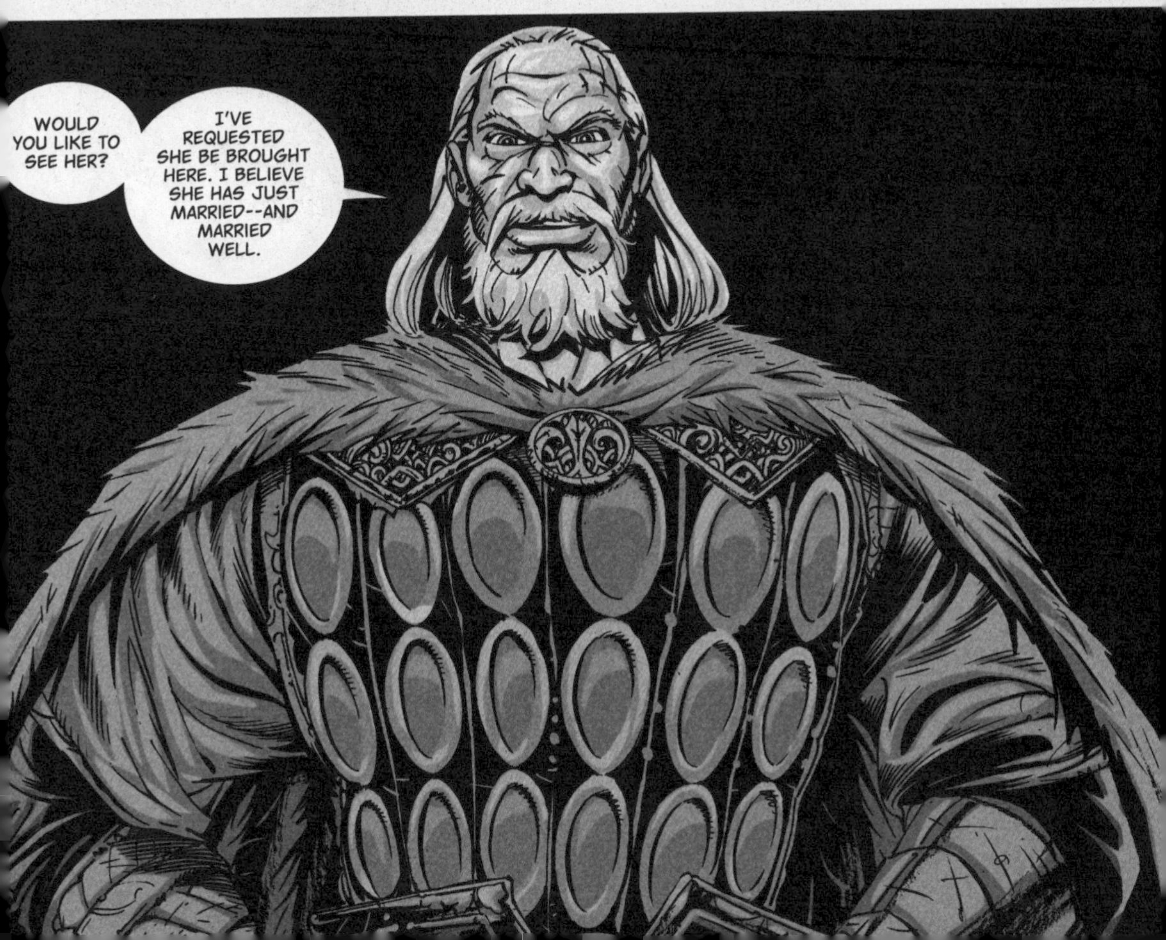
WOULD YOU LIKE TO SEE HER?
I'VE REQUESTED SHE BE BROUGHT HERE. I BELIEVE SHE HAS JUST MARRIED--AND MARRIED WELL.

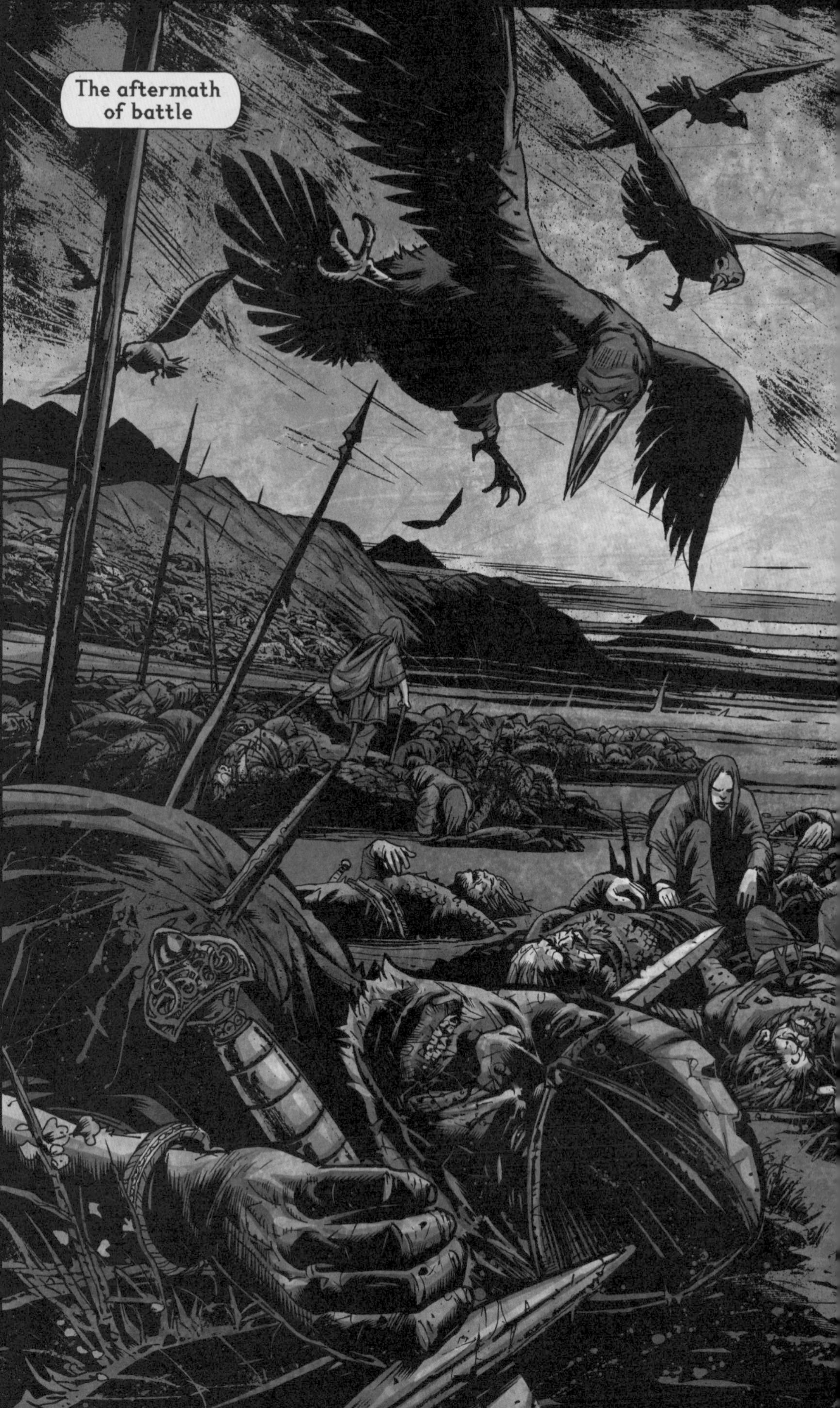
The aftermath of battle

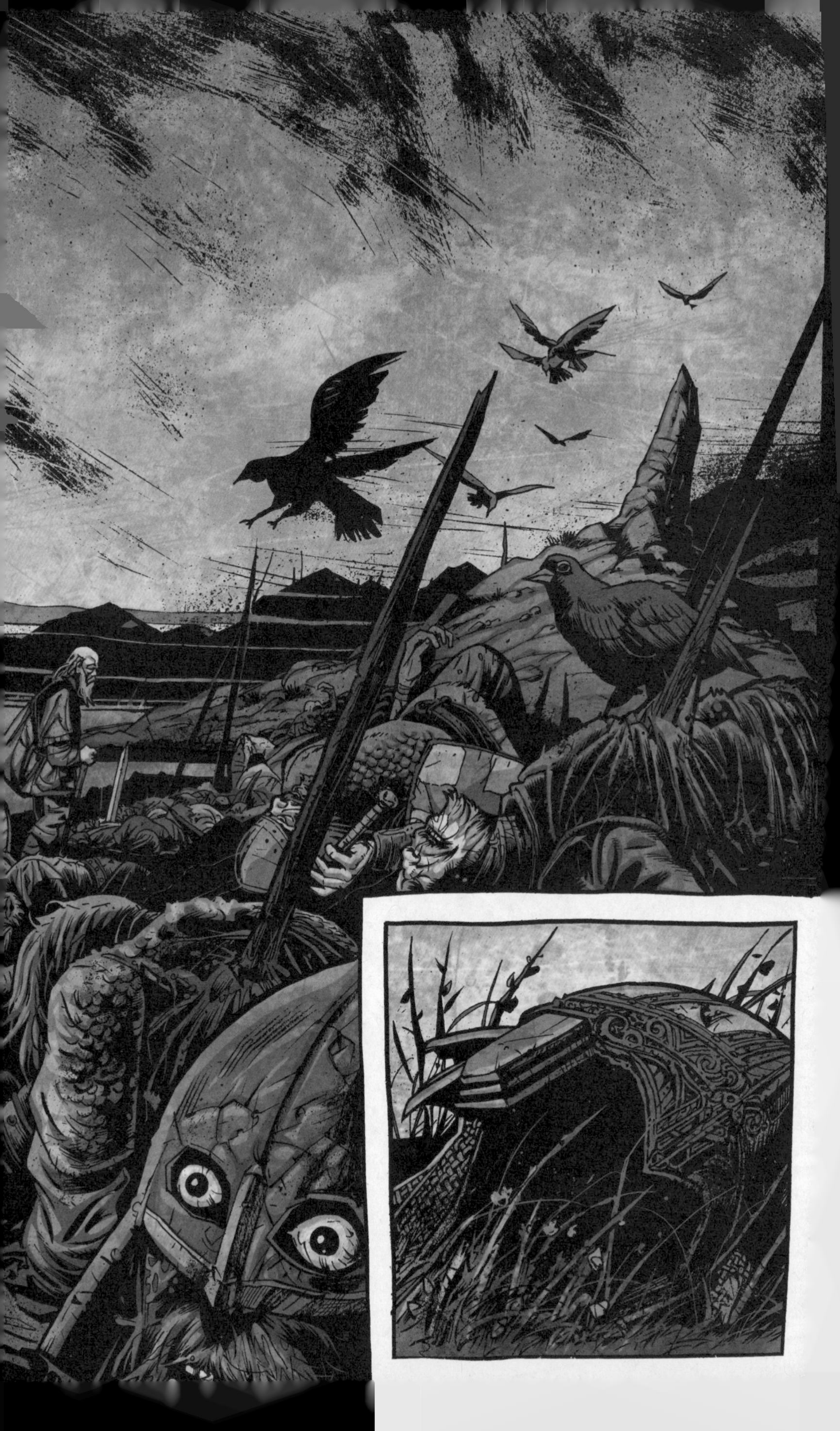

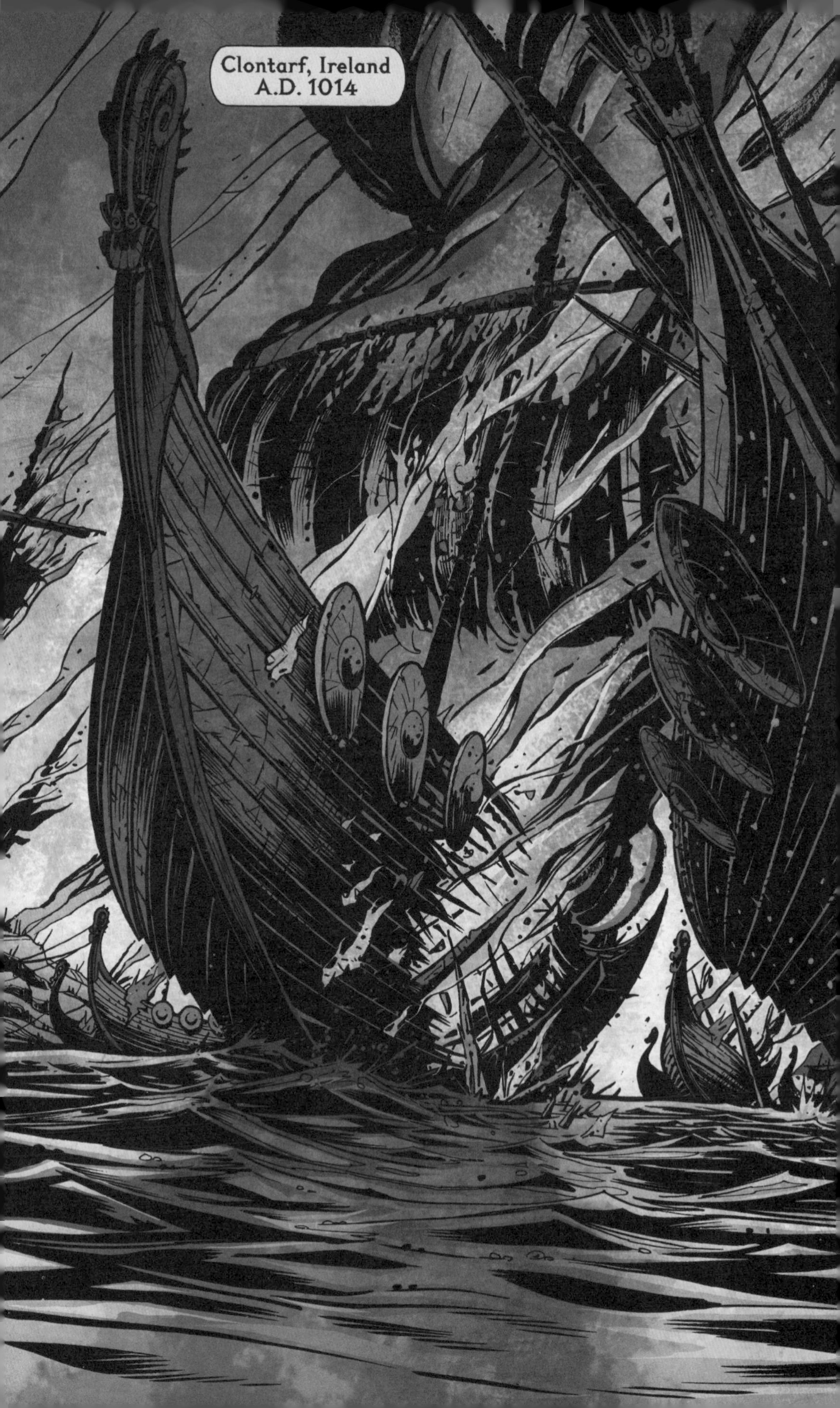
Clontarf, Ireland
A.D. 1014

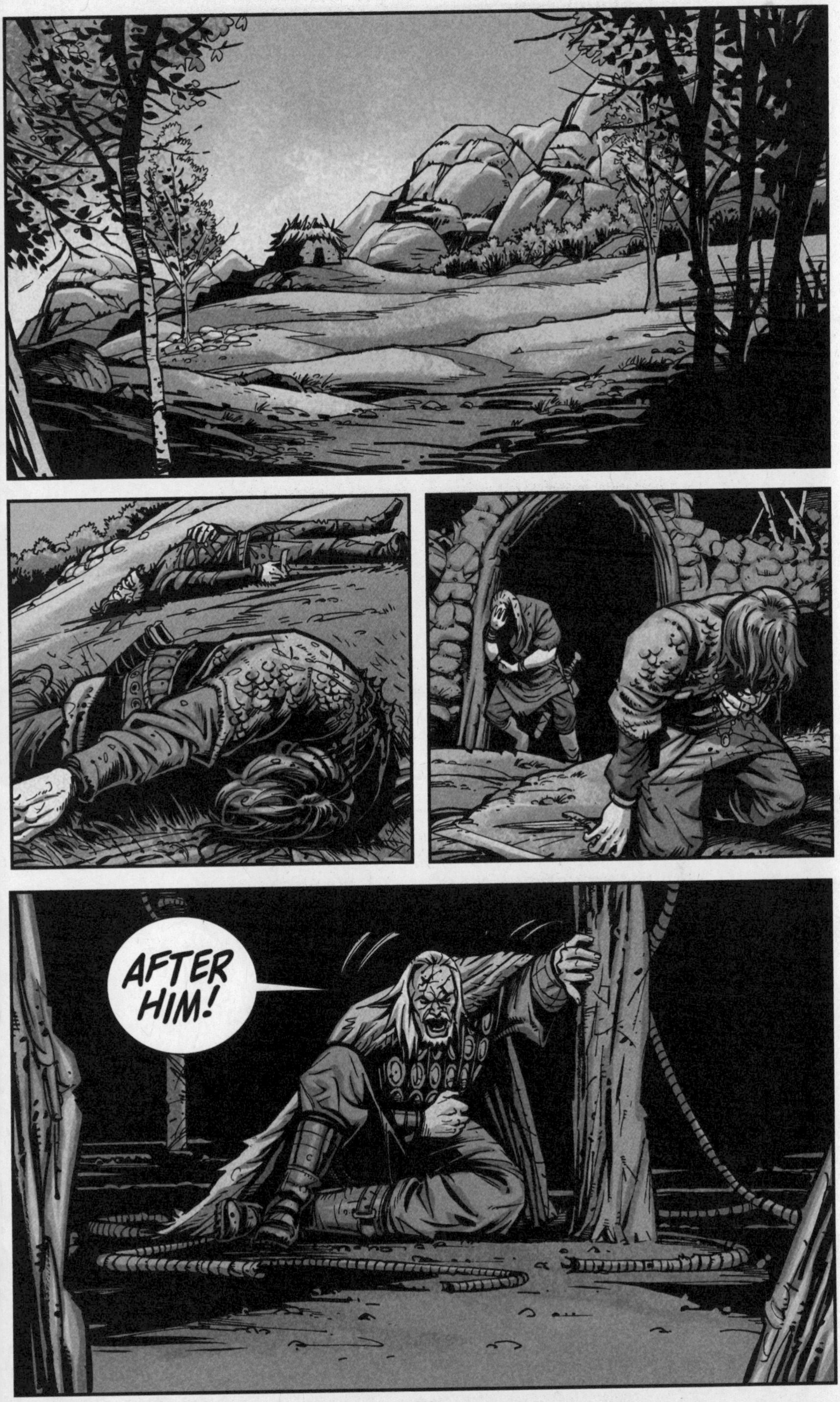
AFTER HIM!

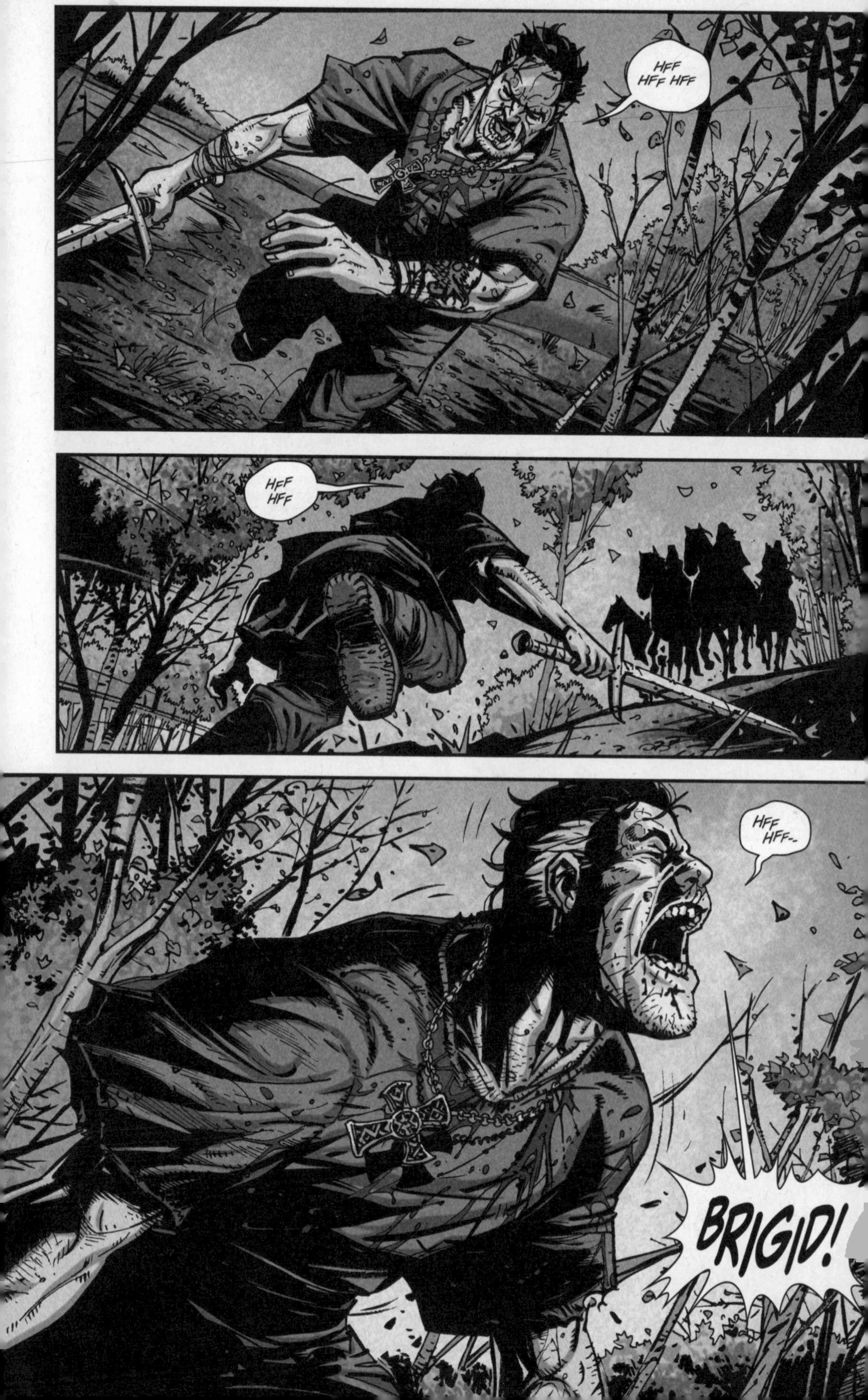
HFF HFF HFF
HFF HFF
HFF HFF--
BRIGID!

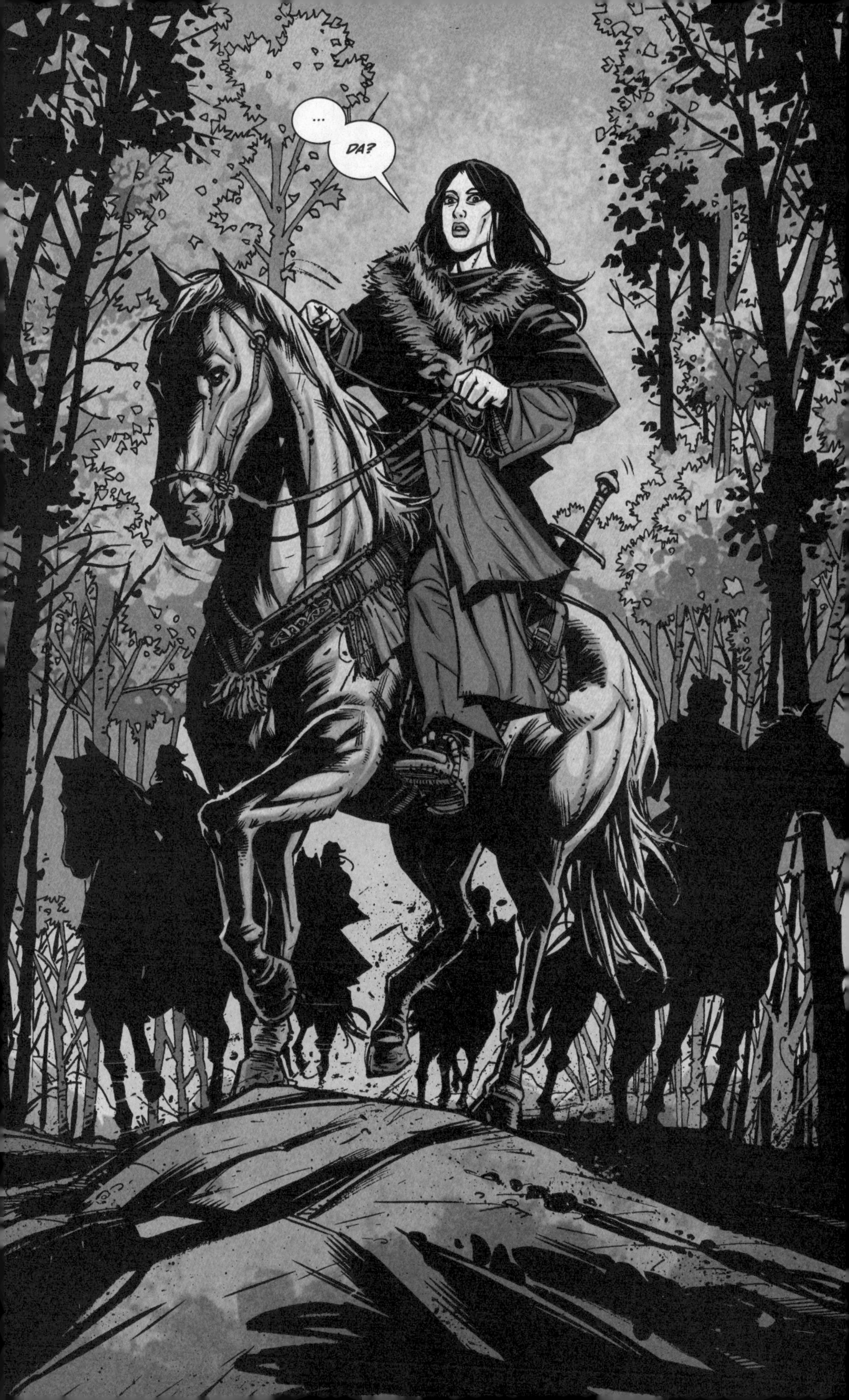
...
DA?

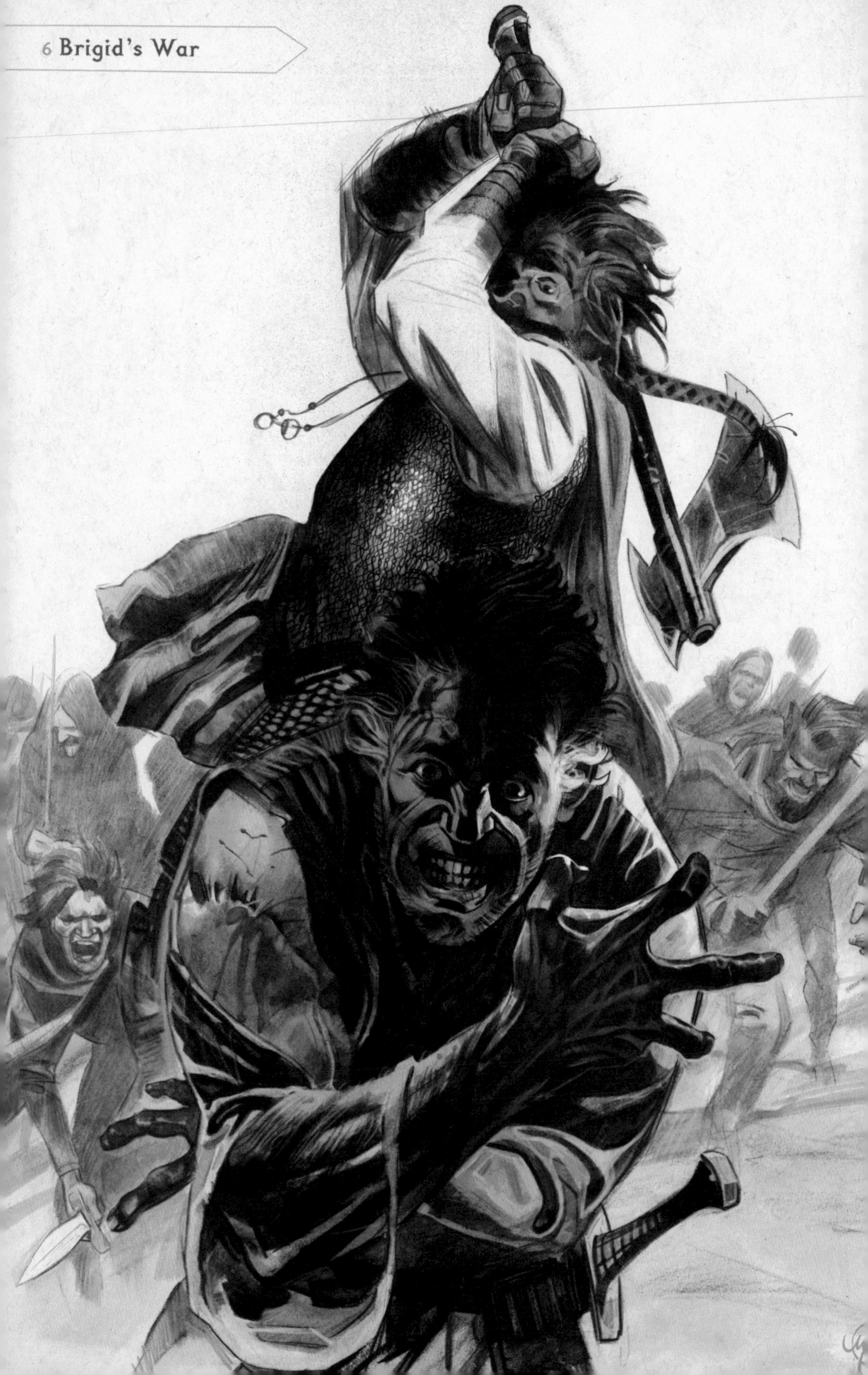

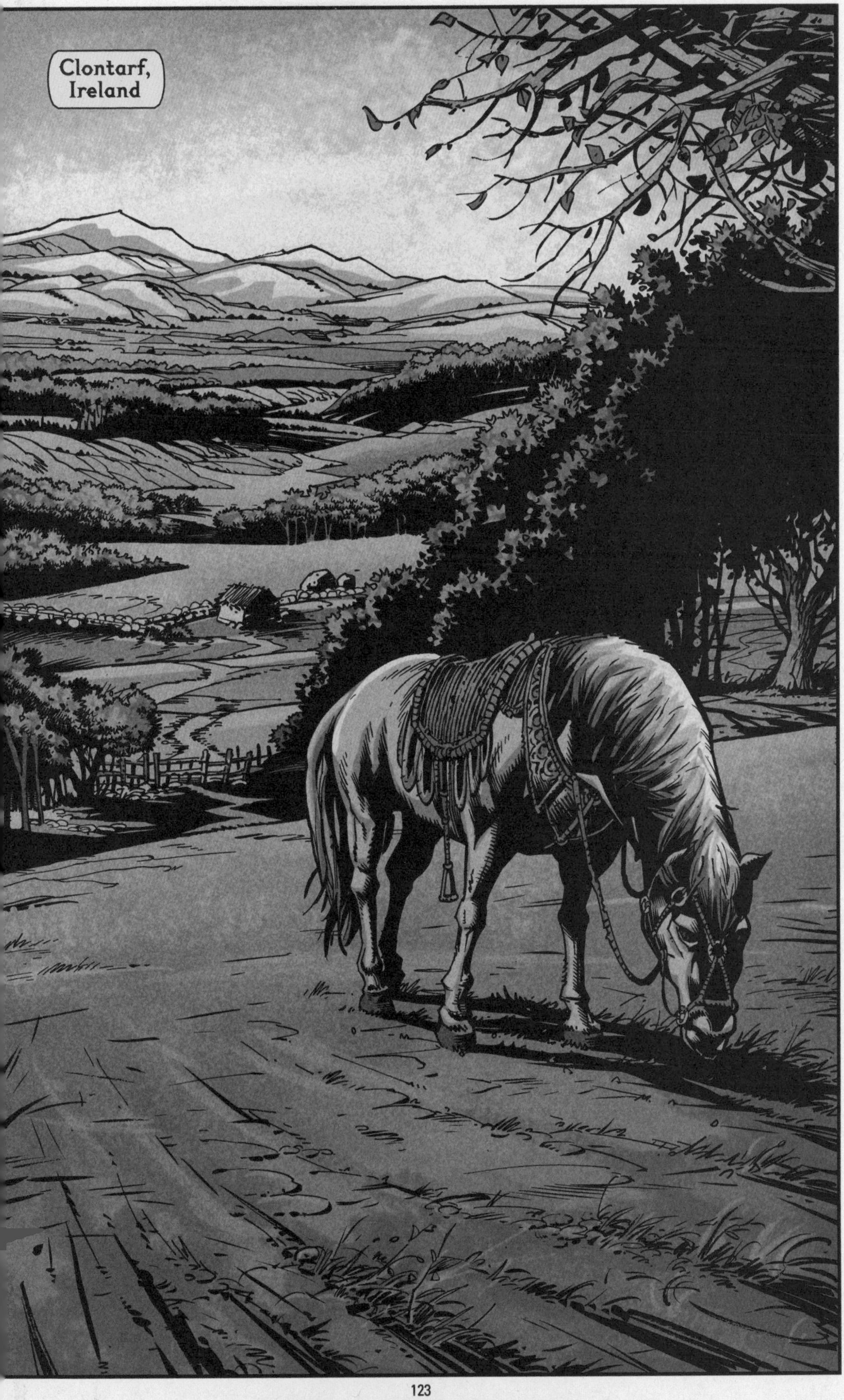
Clontarf, Ireland

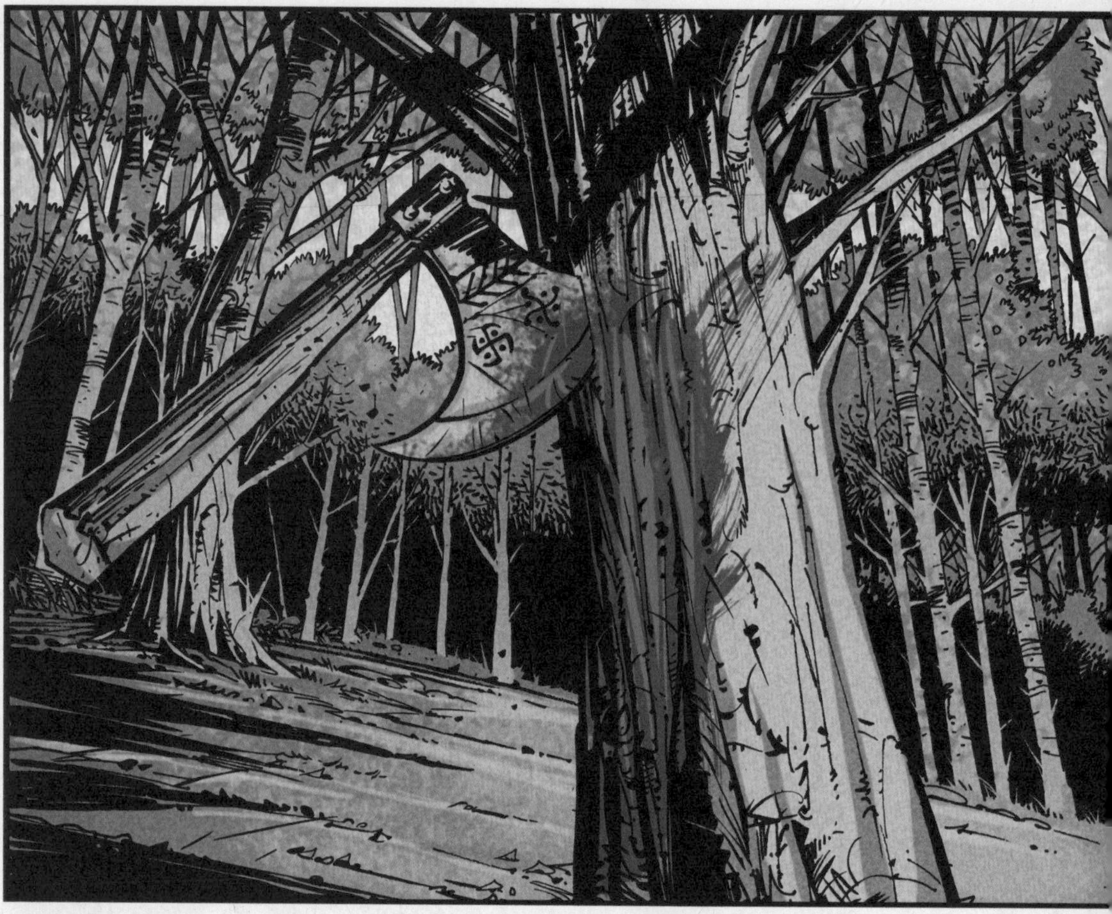

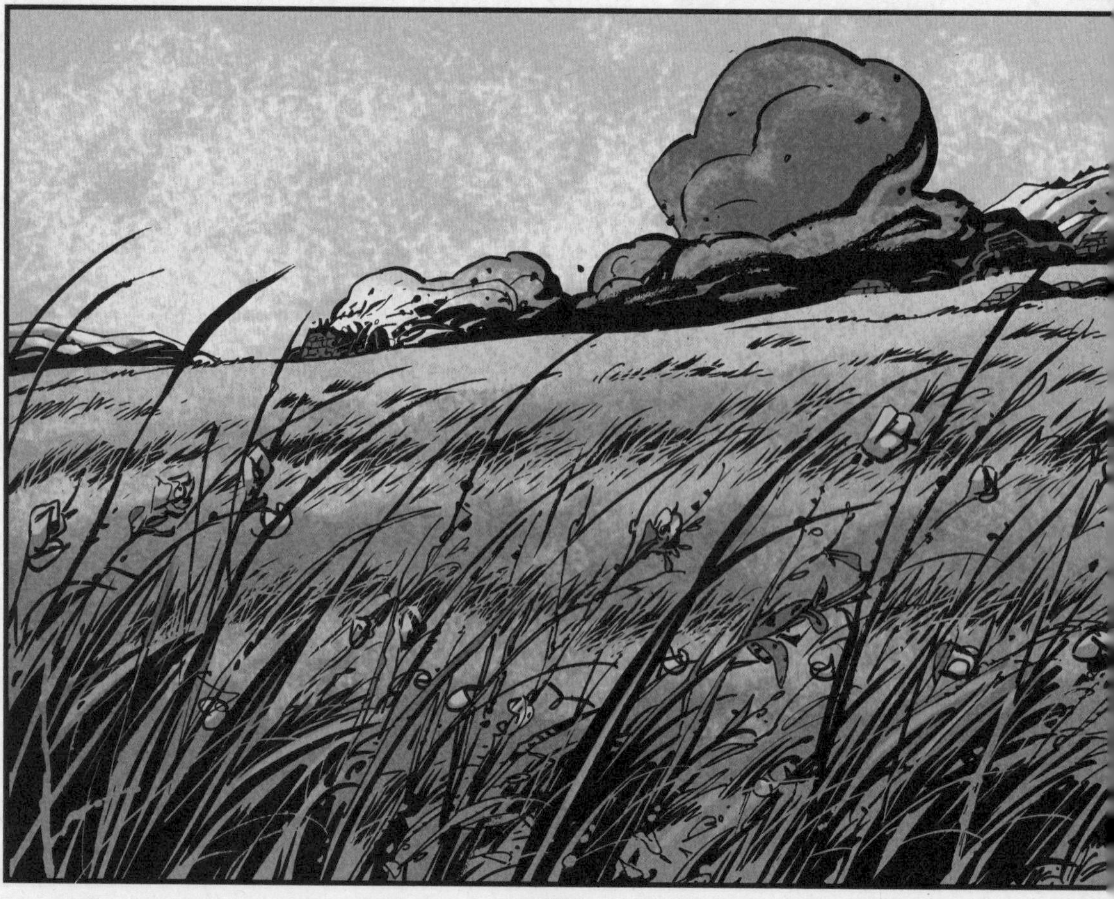

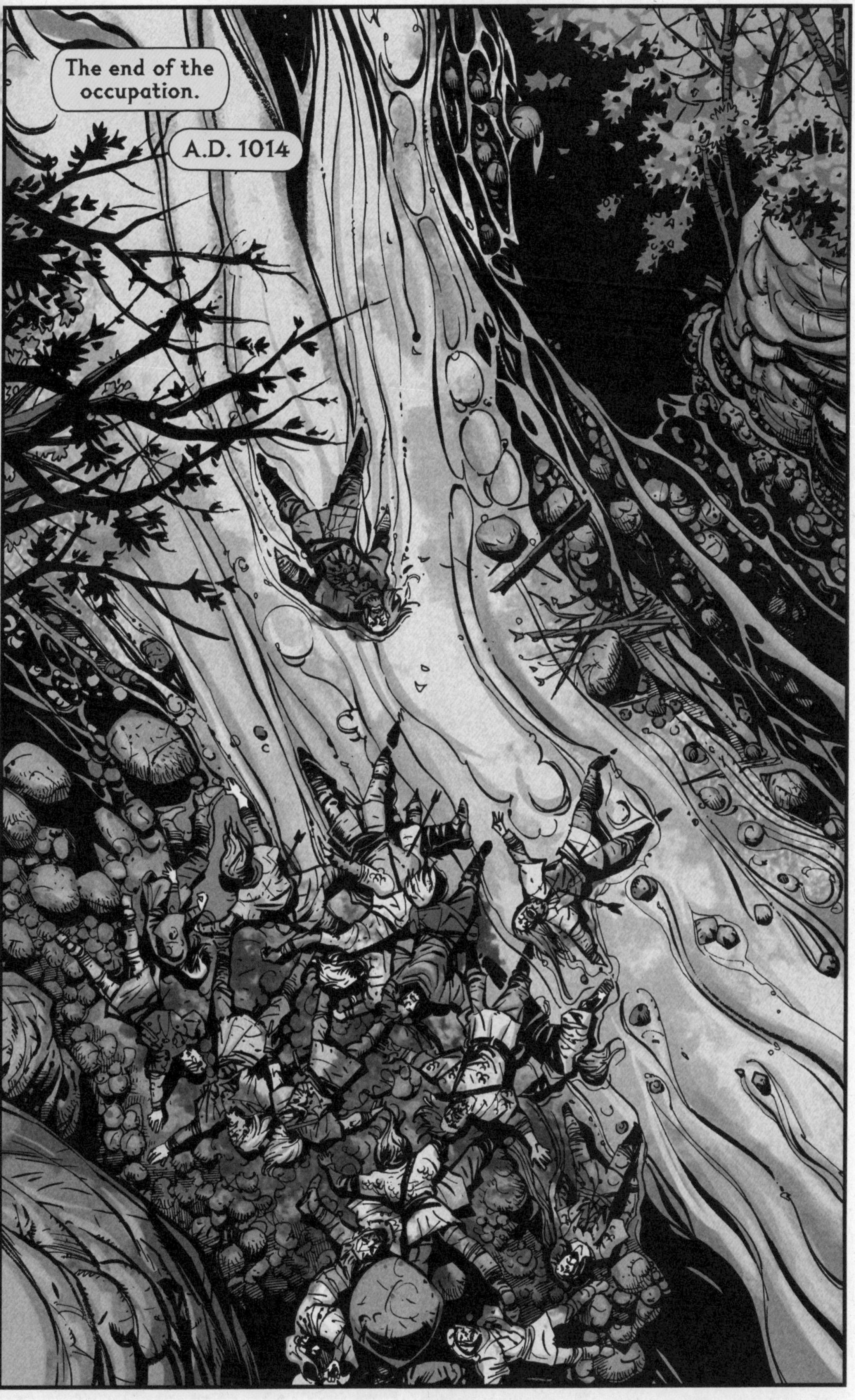
The end of the occupation.
A.D. 1014

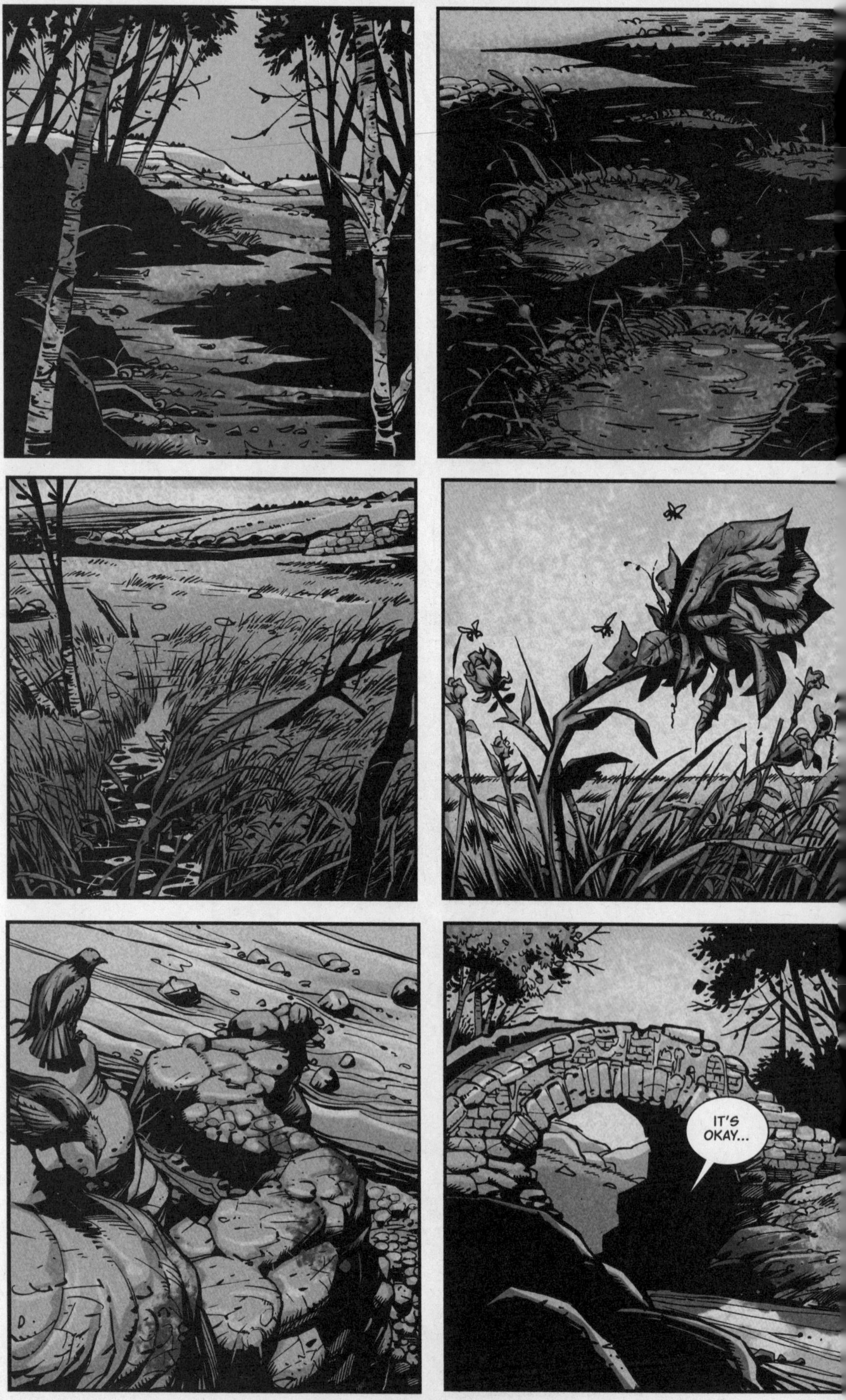
IT'S
OKAY...

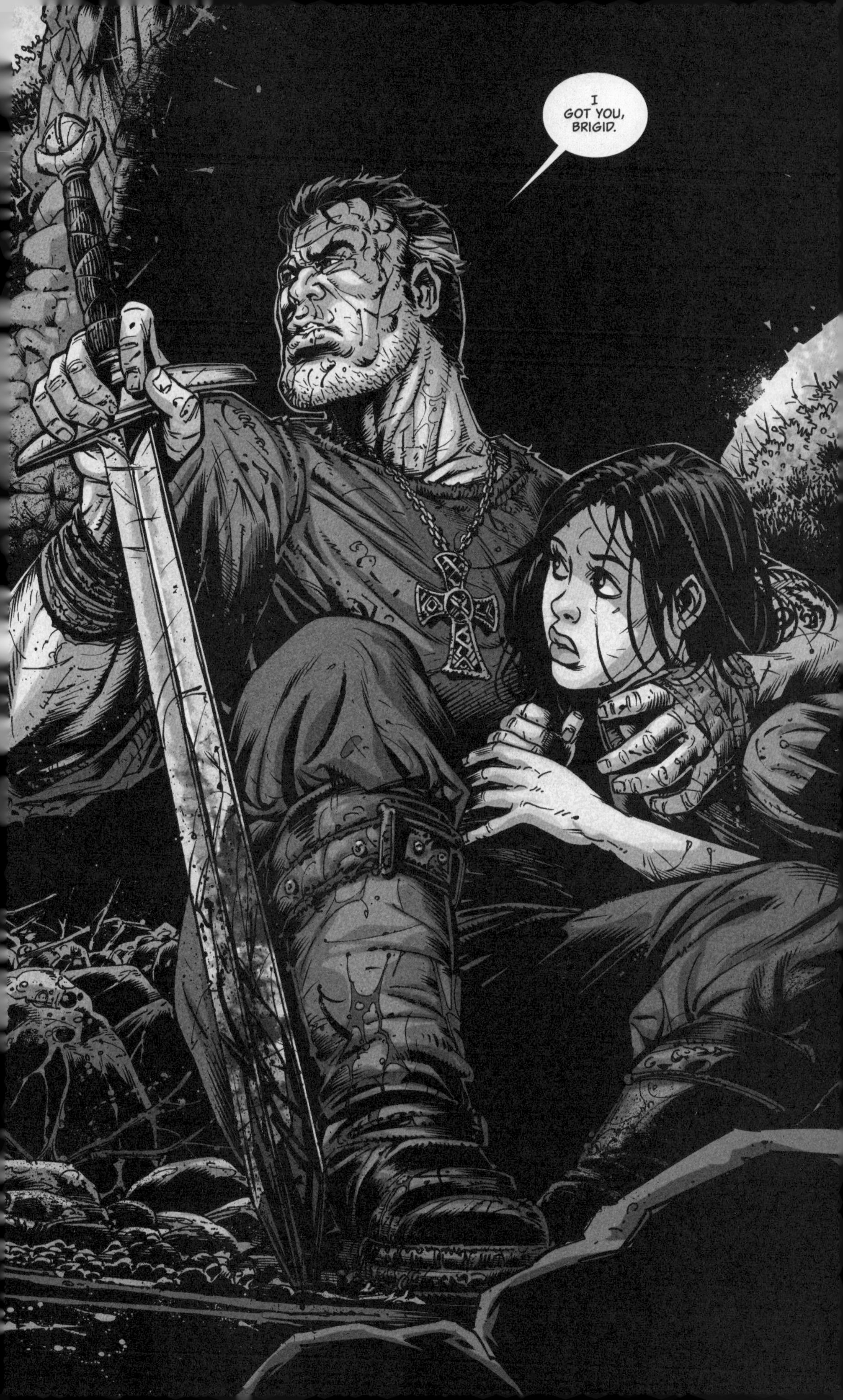
I GOT YOU, BRIGID.

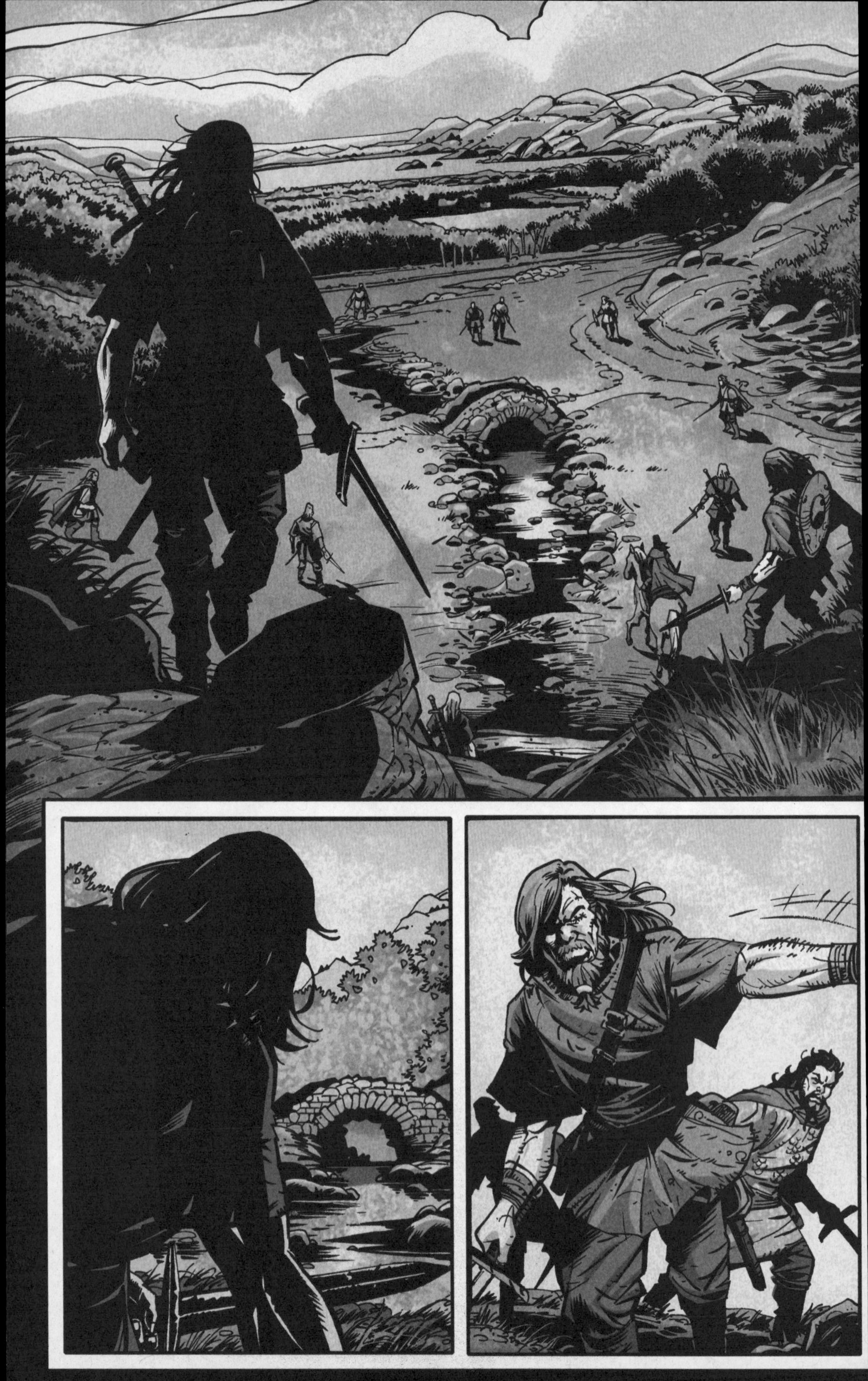

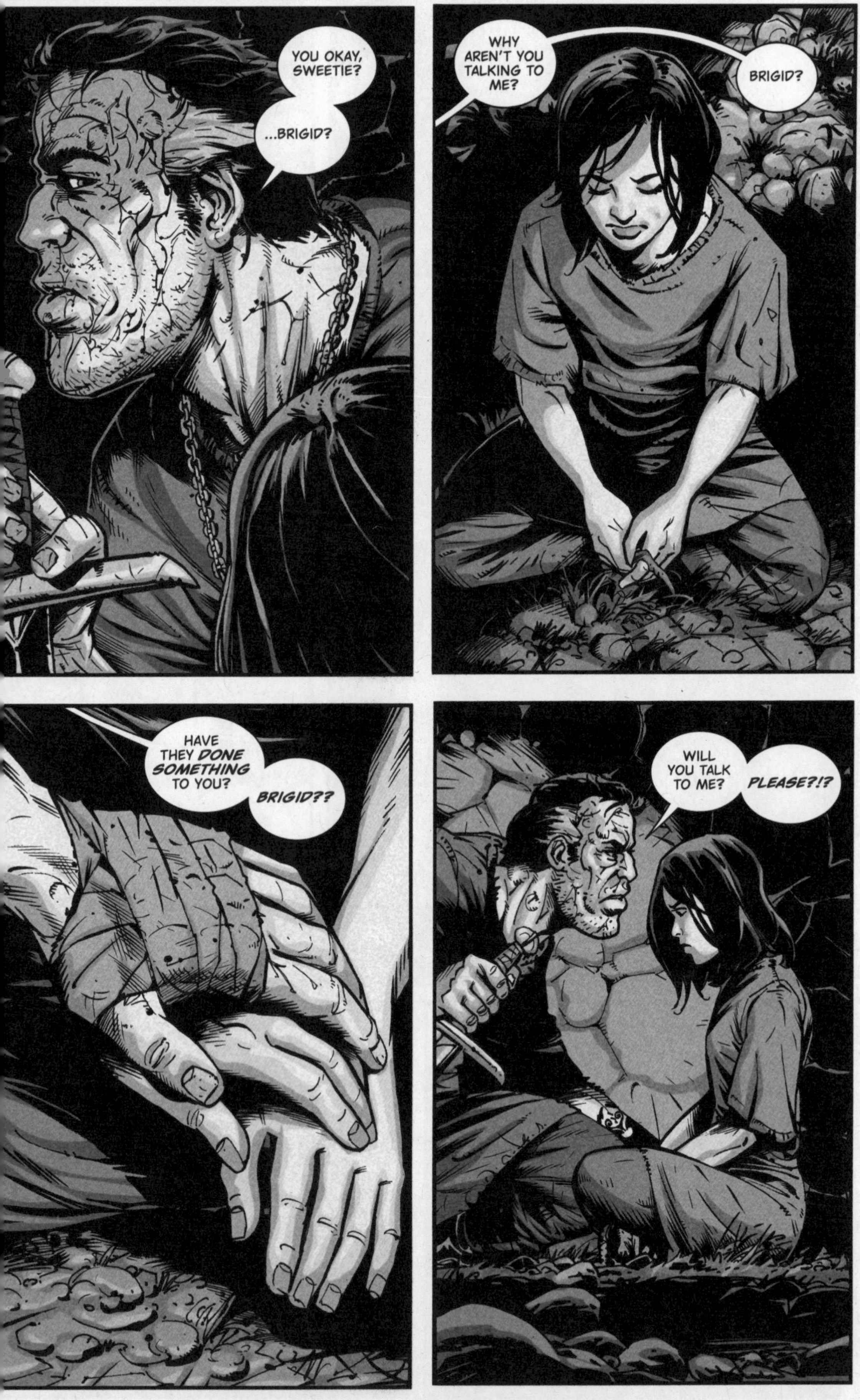
YOU OKAY, SWEETIE?
...BRIGID?
WHY AREN'T YOU TALKING TO ME?
BRIGID?
HAVE THEY *DONE SOMETHING* TO YOU?
BRIGID??
WILL YOU TALK TO ME?
PLEASE?!?

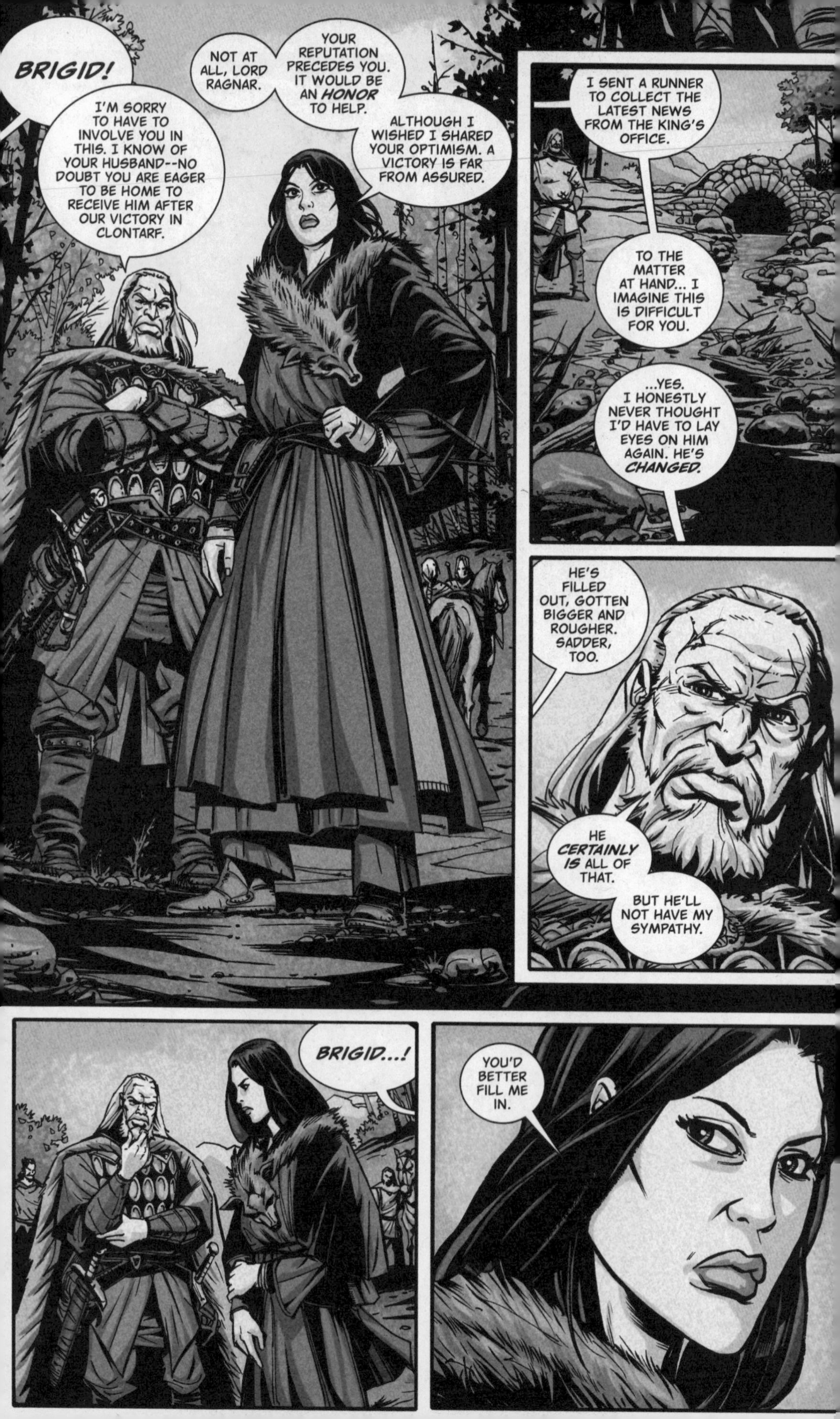
BRIGID!
NOT AT ALL, LORD RAGNAR.
YOUR REPUTATION PRECEDES YOU. IT WOULD BE AN *HONOR* TO HELP.
I'M SORRY TO HAVE TO INVOLVE YOU IN THIS. I KNOW OF YOUR HUSBAND--NO DOUBT YOU ARE EAGER TO BE HOME TO RECEIVE HIM AFTER OUR VICTORY IN CLONTARF.
ALTHOUGH I WISHED I SHARED YOUR OPTIMISM. A VICTORY IS FAR FROM ASSURED.
I SENT A RUNNER TO COLLECT THE LATEST NEWS FROM THE KING'S OFFICE.
TO THE MATTER AT HAND... I IMAGINE THIS IS DIFFICULT FOR YOU.
...YES. I HONESTLY NEVER THOUGHT I'D HAVE TO LAY EYES ON HIM AGAIN. HE'S *CHANGED.*
HE'S FILLED OUT, GOTTEN BIGGER AND ROUGHER. SADDER, TOO.
HE *CERTAINLY IS* ALL OF THAT.
BUT HE'LL NOT HAVE MY SYMPATHY.
BRIGID...!
YOU'D BETTER FILL ME IN.

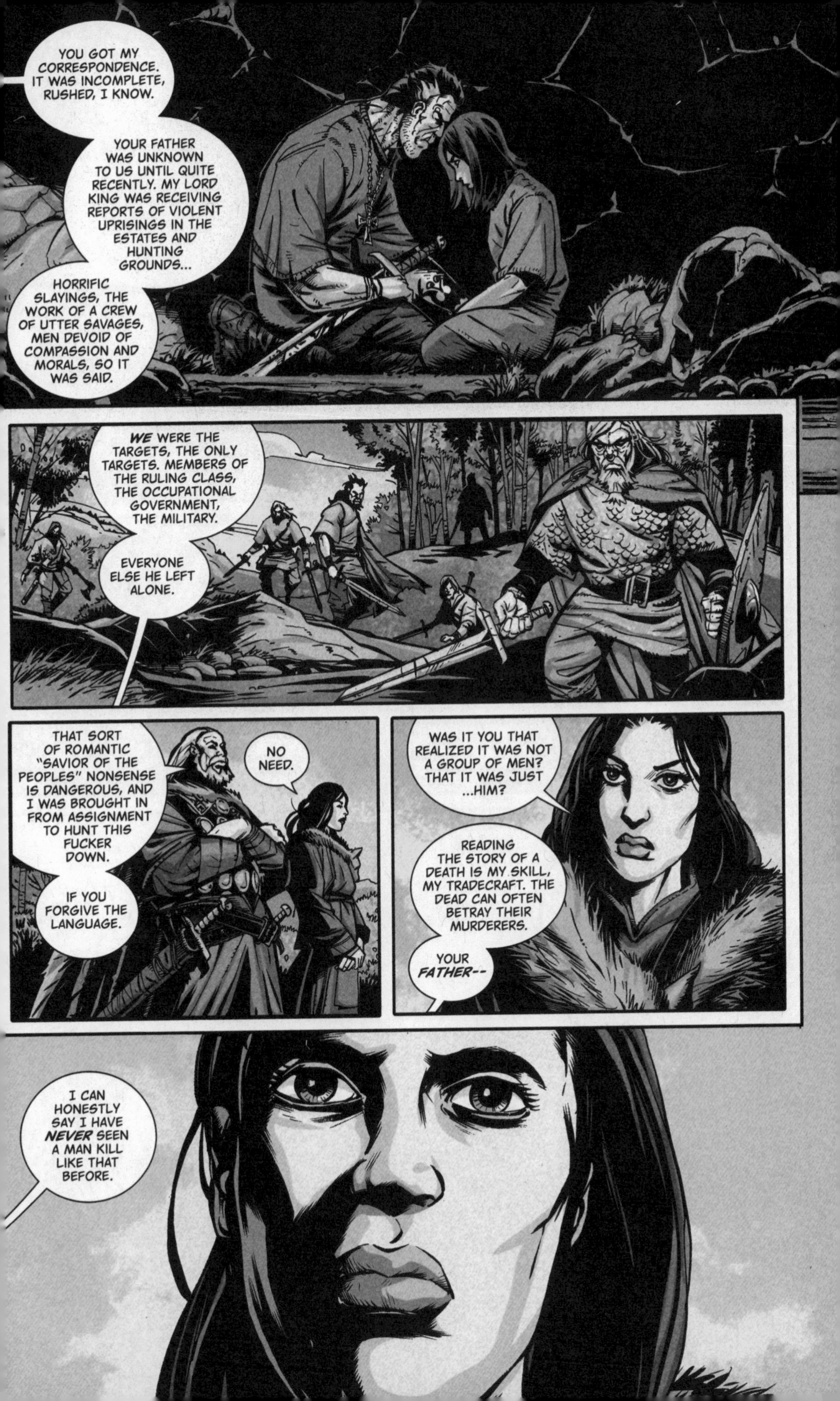

YOU GOT MY CORRESPONDENCE. IT WAS INCOMPLETE, RUSHED, I KNOW.
YOUR FATHER WAS UNKNOWN TO US UNTIL QUITE RECENTLY. MY LORD KING WAS RECEIVING REPORTS OF VIOLENT UPRISINGS IN THE ESTATES AND HUNTING GROUNDS...
HORRIFIC SLAYINGS, THE WORK OF A CREW OF UTTER SAVAGES, MEN DEVOID OF COMPASSION AND MORALS, SO IT WAS SAID.
WE WERE THE TARGETS, THE ONLY TARGETS. MEMBERS OF THE RULING CLASS, THE OCCUPATIONAL GOVERNMENT, THE MILITARY.
EVERYONE ELSE HE LEFT ALONE.
THAT SORT OF ROMANTIC "SAVIOR OF THE PEOPLES" NONSENSE IS DANGEROUS, AND I WAS BROUGHT IN FROM ASSIGNMENT TO HUNT THIS FUCKER DOWN.
IF YOU FORGIVE THE LANGUAGE.
NO NEED.
WAS IT YOU THAT REALIZED IT WAS NOT A GROUP OF MEN? THAT IT WAS JUST ...HIM?
READING THE STORY OF A DEATH IS MY SKILL, MY TRADECRAFT. THE DEAD CAN OFTEN BETRAY THEIR MURDERERS.
YOUR FATHER--
I CAN HONESTLY SAY I HAVE NEVER SEEN A MAN KILL LIKE THAT BEFORE.

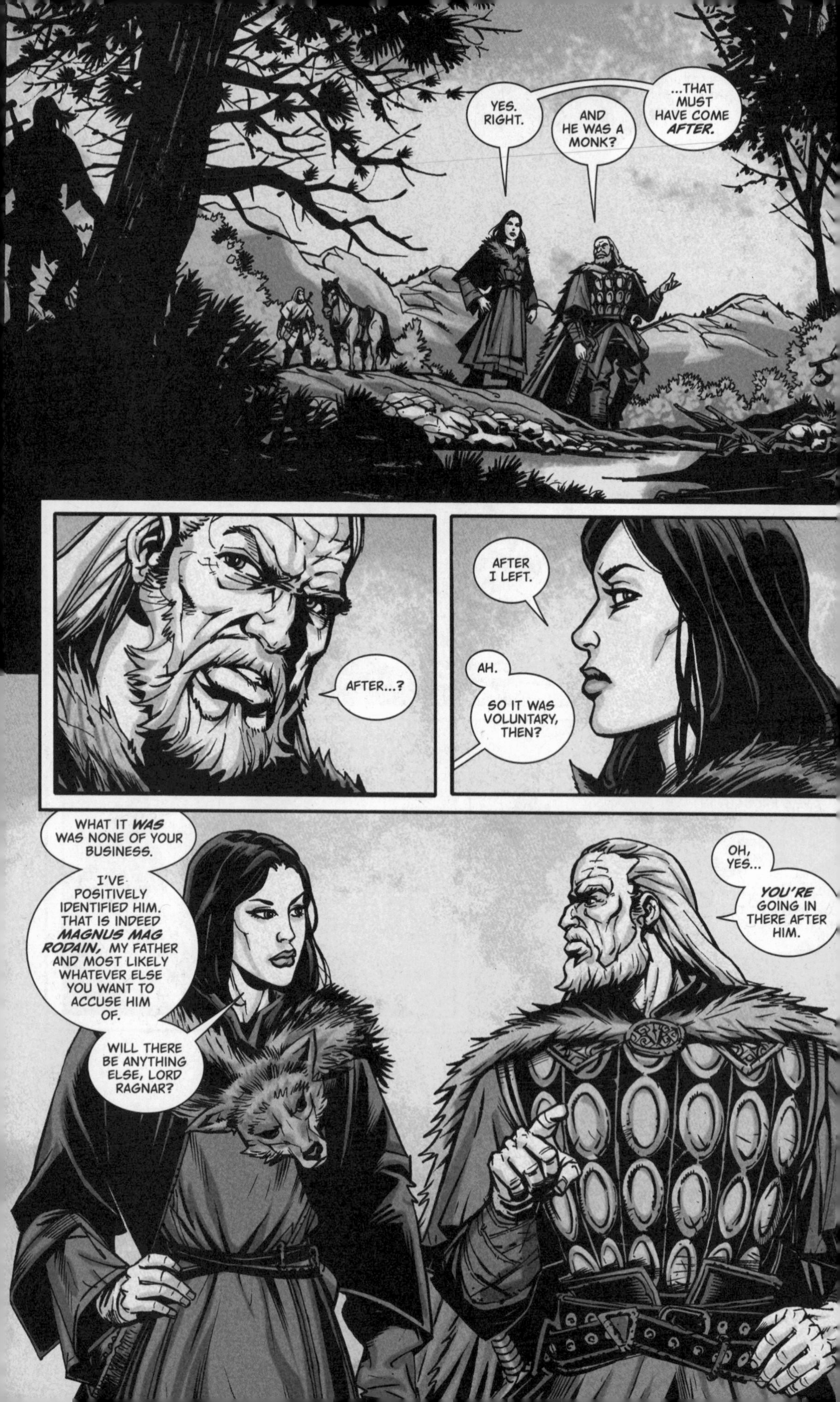
YES. RIGHT.
AND HE WAS A MONK?
...THAT MUST HAVE COME AFTER.
AFTER...?
AFTER I LEFT.
AH.
SO IT WAS VOLUNTARY, THEN?
WHAT IT WAS WAS NONE OF YOUR BUSINESS.
I'VE POSITIVELY IDENTIFIED HIM. THAT IS INDEED MAGNUS MAG RODAIN, MY FATHER AND MOST LIKELY WHATEVER ELSE YOU WANT TO ACCUSE HIM OF.
WILL THERE BE ANYTHING ELSE, LORD RAGNAR?
OH, YES...
YOU'RE GOING IN THERE AFTER HIM.

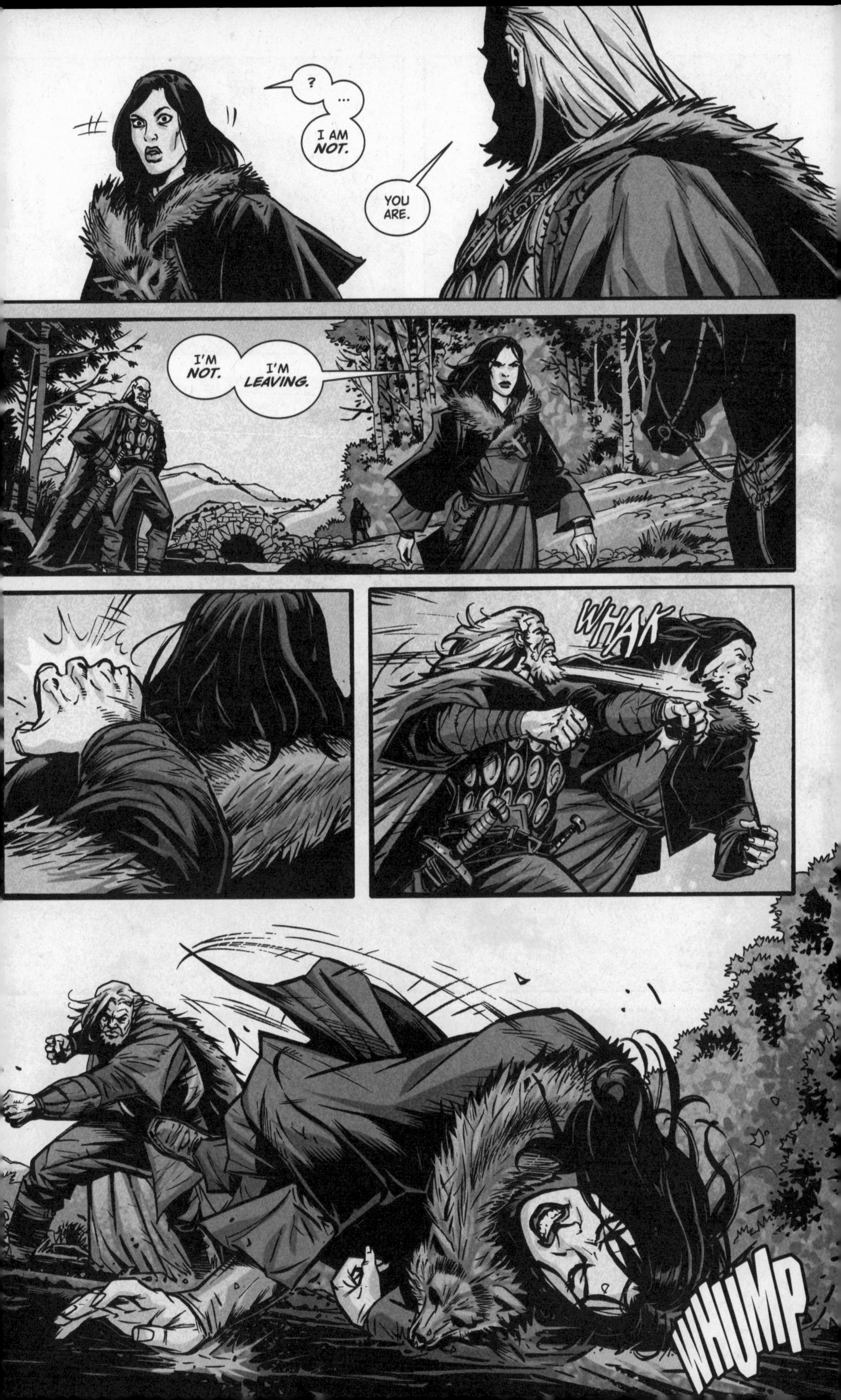

?
...
I AM NOT.
YOU ARE.
I'M NOT.
I'M LEAVING.
WHAK
WHUMP

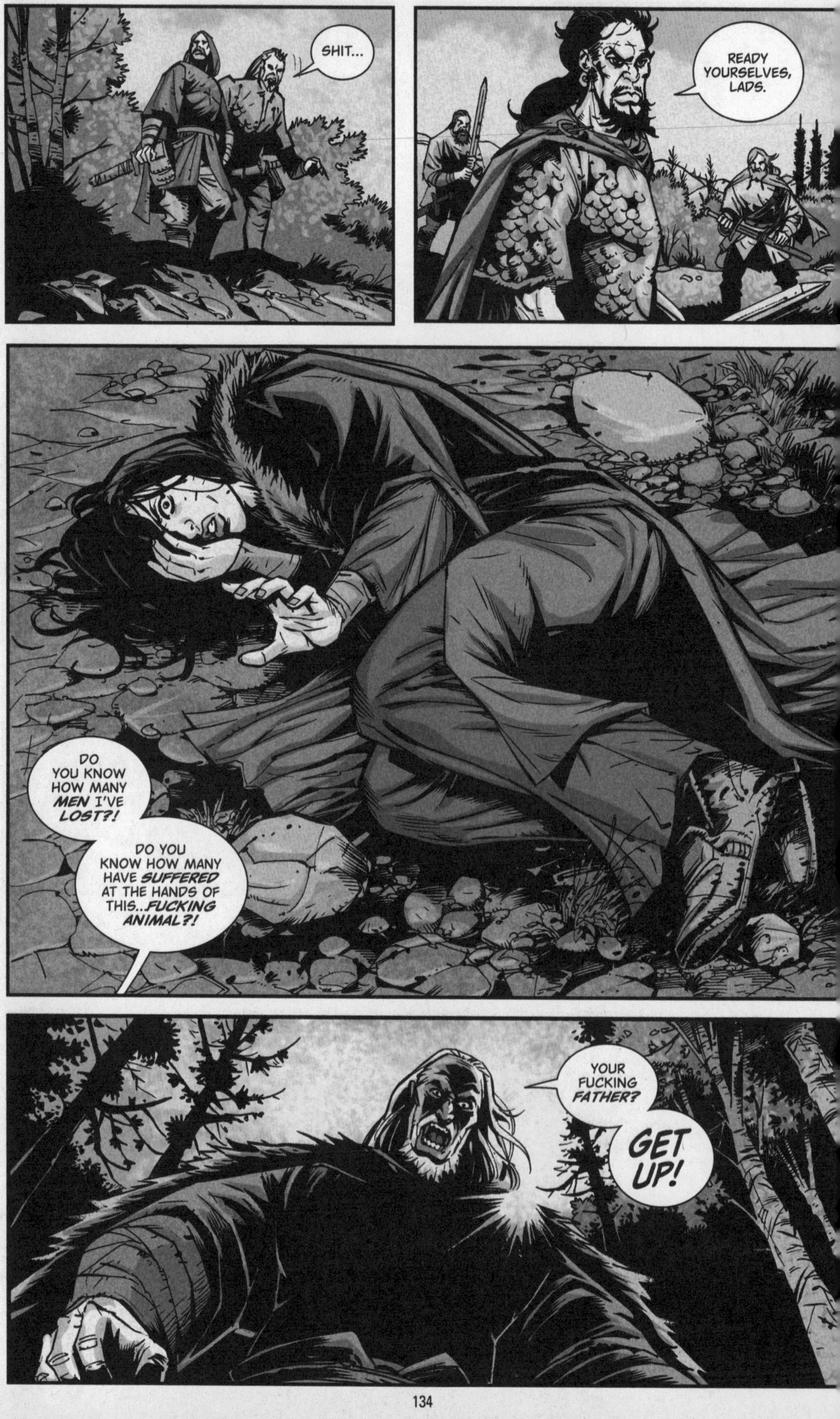
SHIT...
READY YOURSELVES, LADS.
DO YOU KNOW HOW MANY MEN I'VE LOST?!
DO YOU KNOW HOW MANY HAVE SUFFERED AT THE HANDS OF THIS...FUCKING ANIMAL?!
YOUR FUCKING FATHER?
GET UP!

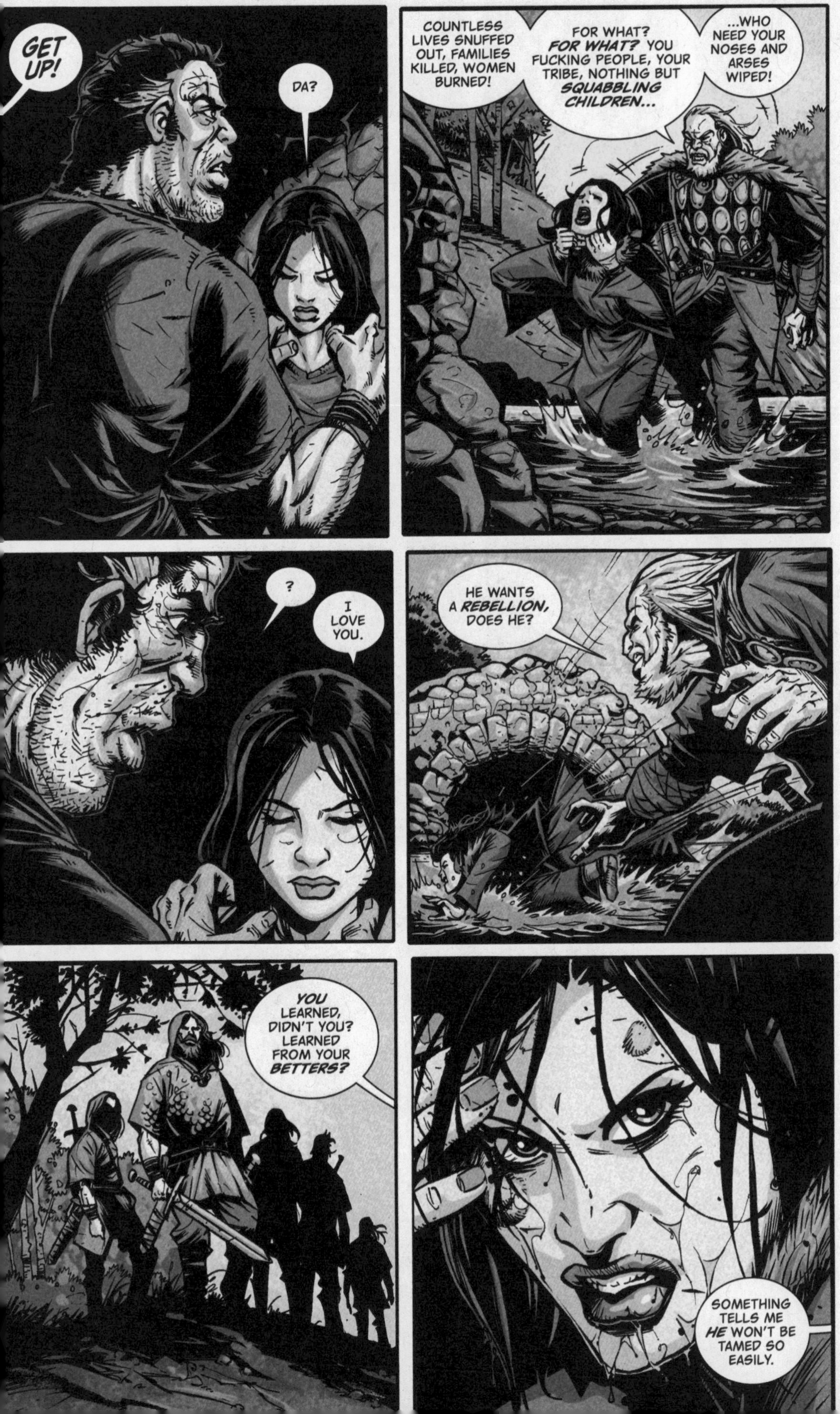
GET UP!
DA?
COUNTLESS LIVES SNUFFED OUT, FAMILIES KILLED, WOMEN BURNED!
FOR WHAT? *FOR WHAT?* YOU FUCKING PEOPLE, YOUR TRIBE, NOTHING BUT *SQUABBLING CHILDREN...*
...WHO NEED YOUR NOSES AND ARSES WIPED!
?
I LOVE YOU.
HE WANTS A *REBELLION,* DOES HE?
YOU LEARNED, DIDN'T YOU? LEARNED FROM YOUR *BETTERS?*
SOMETHING TELLS ME *HE* WON'T BE TAMED SO EASILY.

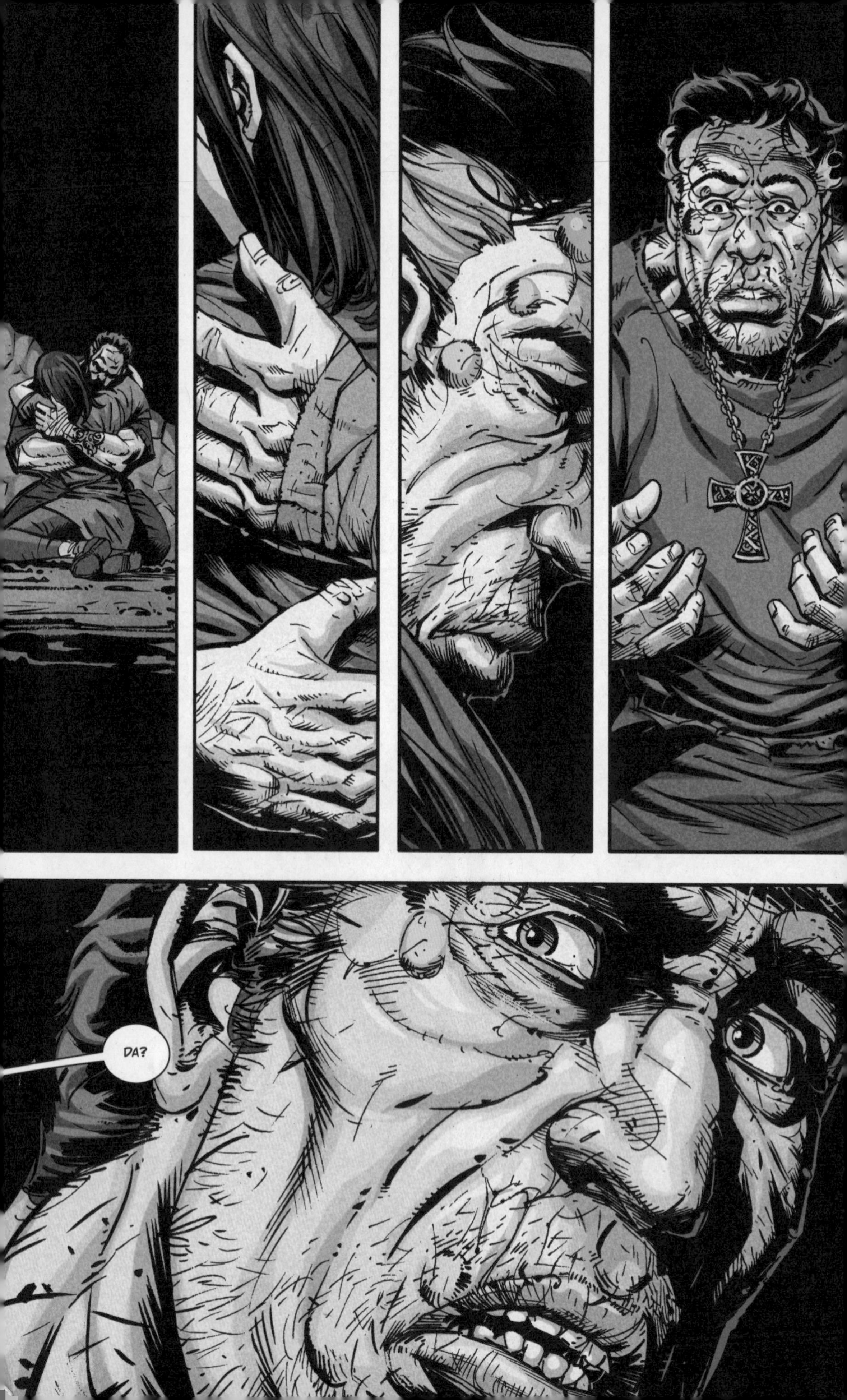
DA?

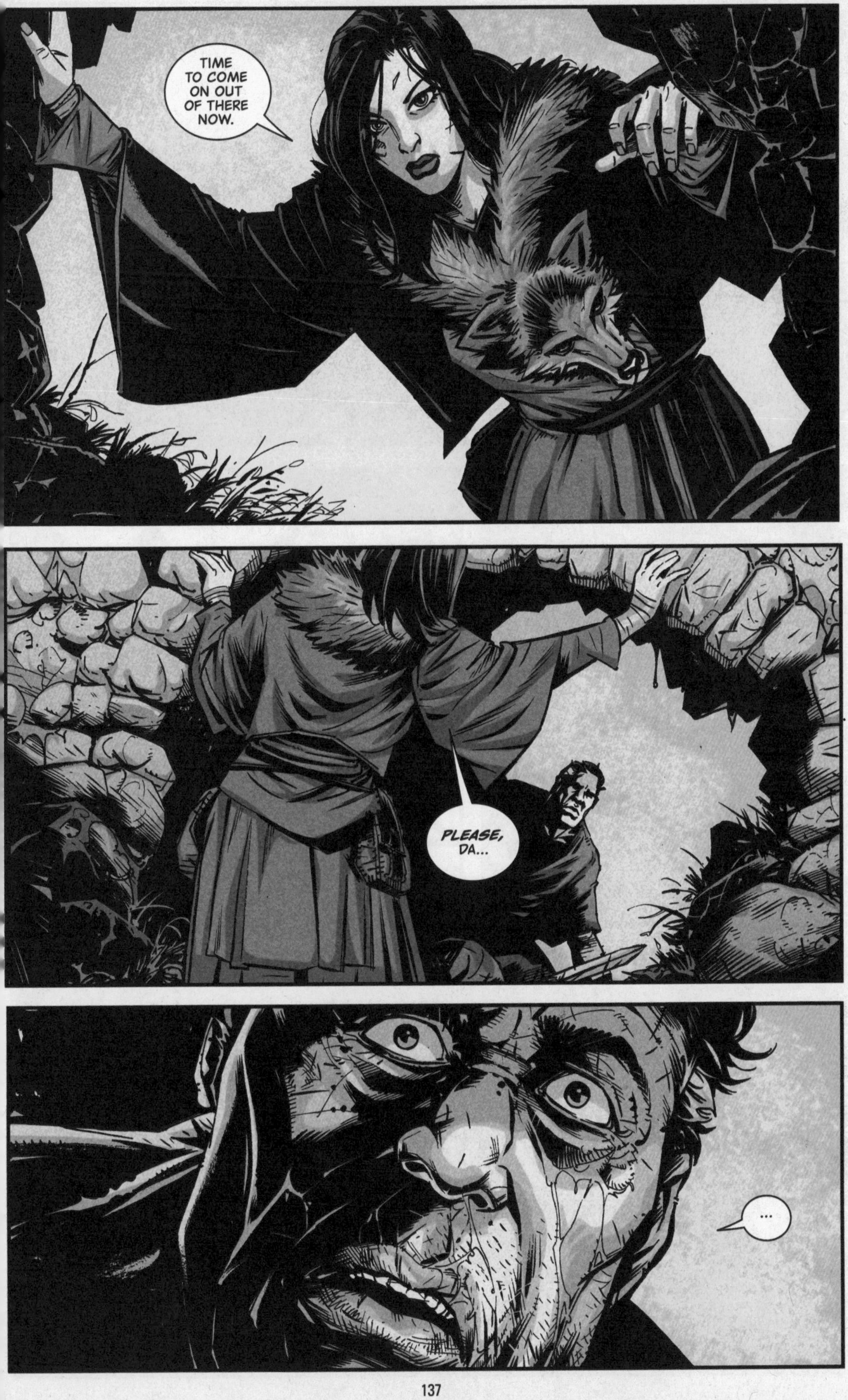
TIME TO COME ON OUT OF THERE NOW.
PLEASE, DA...
...

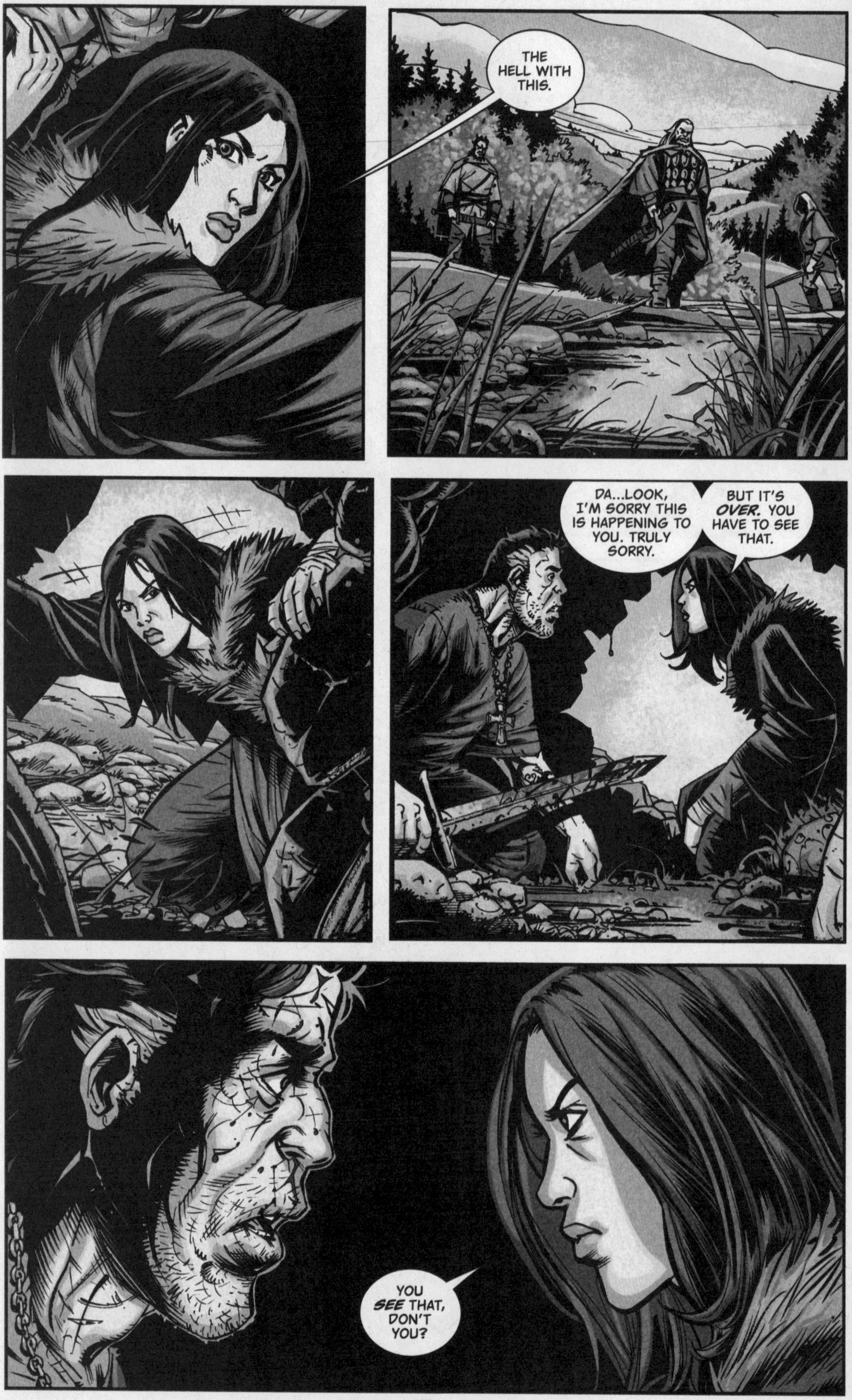
THE HELL WITH THIS.
DA...LOOK, I'M SORRY THIS IS HAPPENING TO YOU. TRULY SORRY.
BUT IT'S *OVER.* YOU HAVE TO SEE THAT.
YOU *SEE* THAT, DON'T YOU?

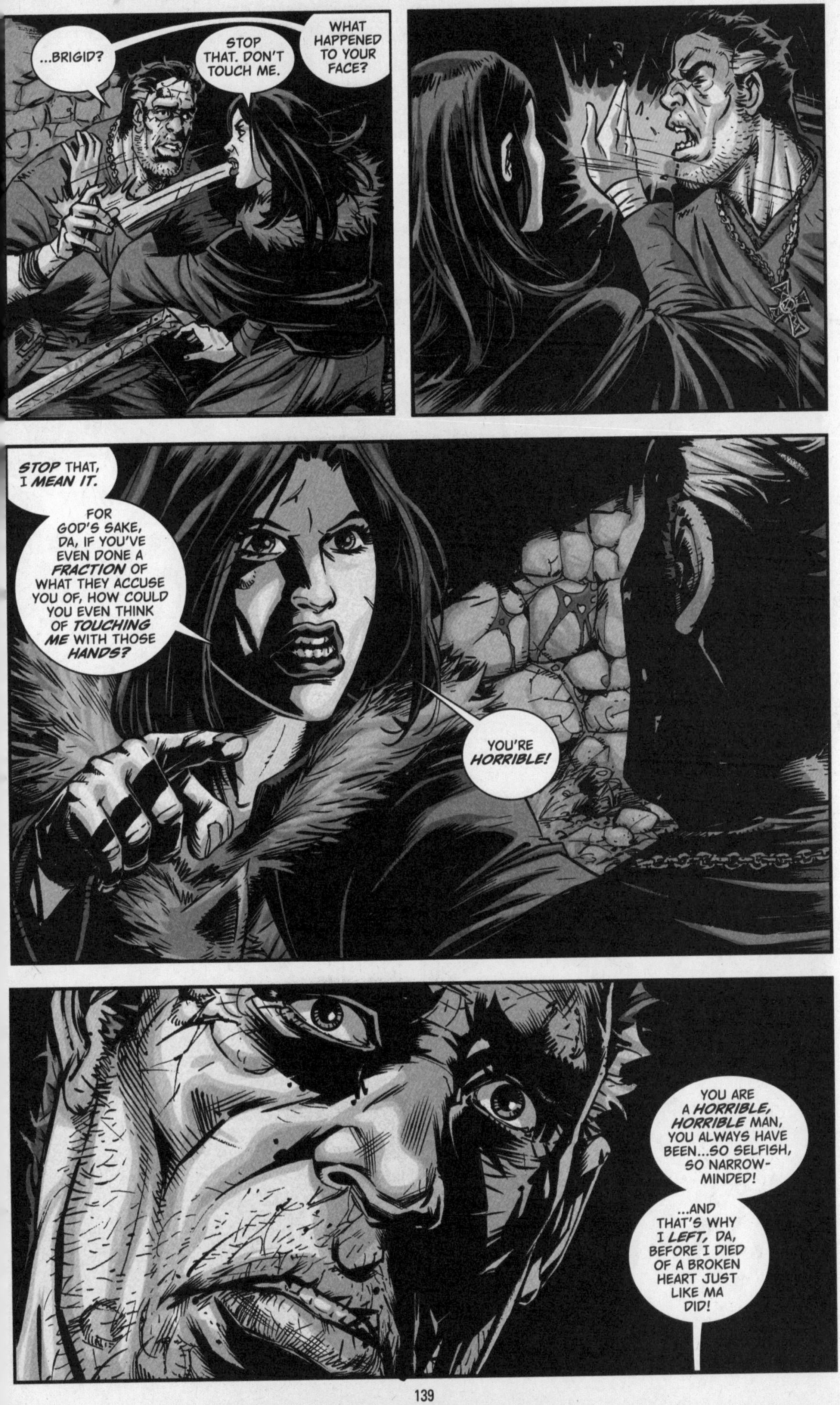
...BRIGID?
WHAT HAPPENED TO YOUR FACE?
STOP THAT. DON'T TOUCH ME.
STOP THAT, I MEAN IT.
FOR GOD'S SAKE, DA, IF YOU'VE EVEN DONE A FRACTION OF WHAT THEY ACCUSE YOU OF, HOW COULD YOU EVEN THINK OF TOUCHING ME WITH THOSE HANDS?
YOU'RE HORRIBLE!
YOU ARE A HORRIBLE, HORRIBLE MAN, YOU ALWAYS HAVE BEEN...SO SELFISH, SO NARROW-MINDED!
...AND THAT'S WHY I LEFT, DA, BEFORE I DIED OF A BROKEN HEART JUST LIKE MA DID!

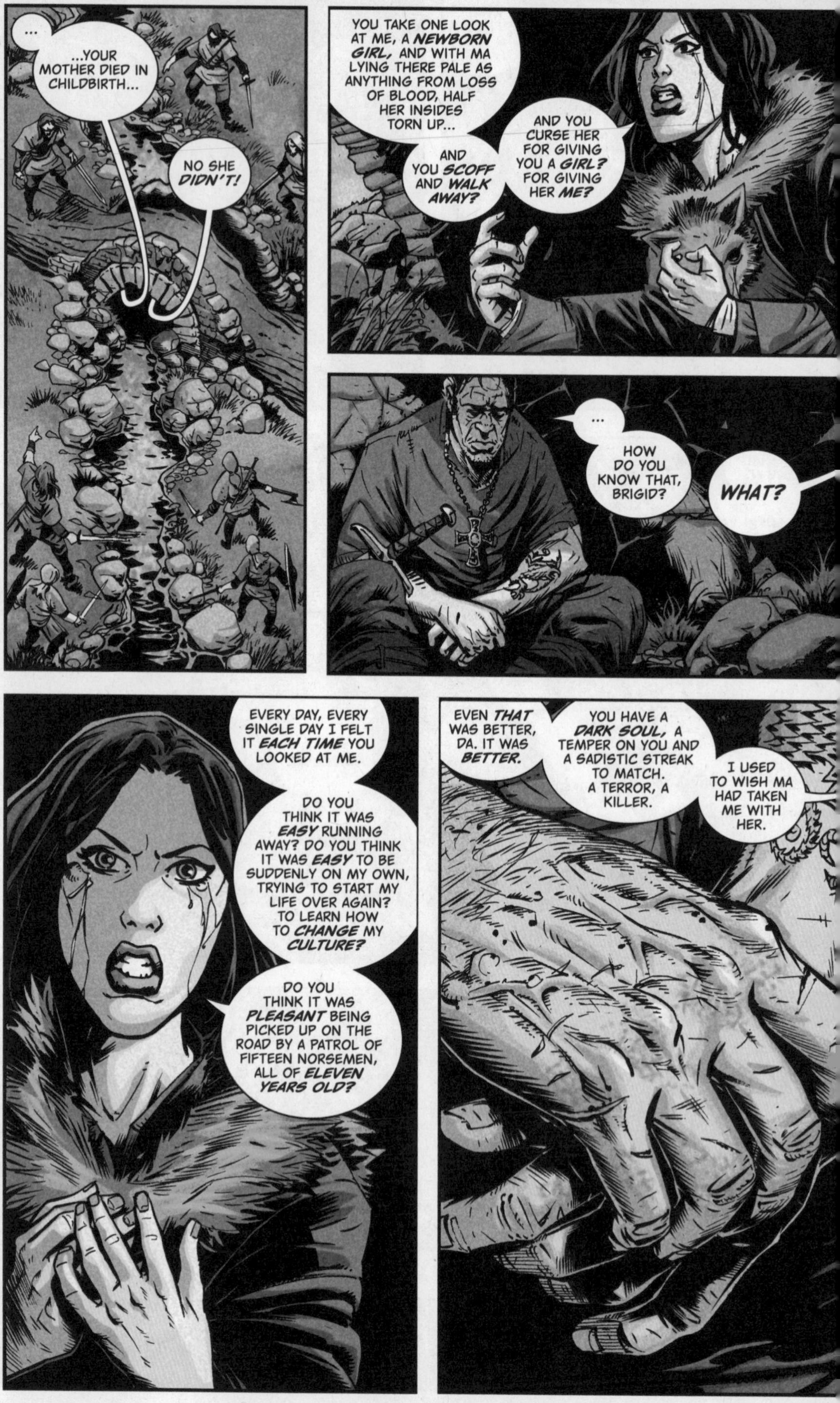
...
...YOUR MOTHER DIED IN CHILDBIRTH...
NO SHE DIDN'T!
YOU TAKE ONE LOOK AT ME, A NEWBORN GIRL, AND WITH MA LYING THERE PALE AS ANYTHING FROM LOSS OF BLOOD, HALF HER INSIDES TORN UP...
AND YOU SCOFF AND WALK AWAY?
AND YOU CURSE HER FOR GIVING YOU A GIRL? FOR GIVING HER ME?
...
HOW DO YOU KNOW THAT, BRIGID?
WHAT?
EVERY DAY, EVERY SINGLE DAY I FELT IT EACH TIME YOU LOOKED AT ME.
DO YOU THINK IT WAS EASY RUNNING AWAY? DO YOU THINK IT WAS EASY TO BE SUDDENLY ON MY OWN, TRYING TO START MY LIFE OVER AGAIN? TO LEARN HOW TO CHANGE MY CULTURE?
DO YOU THINK IT WAS PLEASANT BEING PICKED UP ON THE ROAD BY A PATROL OF FIFTEEN NORSEMEN, ALL OF ELEVEN YEARS OLD?
EVEN THAT WAS BETTER, DA. IT WAS BETTER.
YOU HAVE A DARK SOUL, A TEMPER ON YOU AND A SADISTIC STREAK TO MATCH. A TERROR, A KILLER.
I USED TO WISH MA HAD TAKEN ME WITH HER.

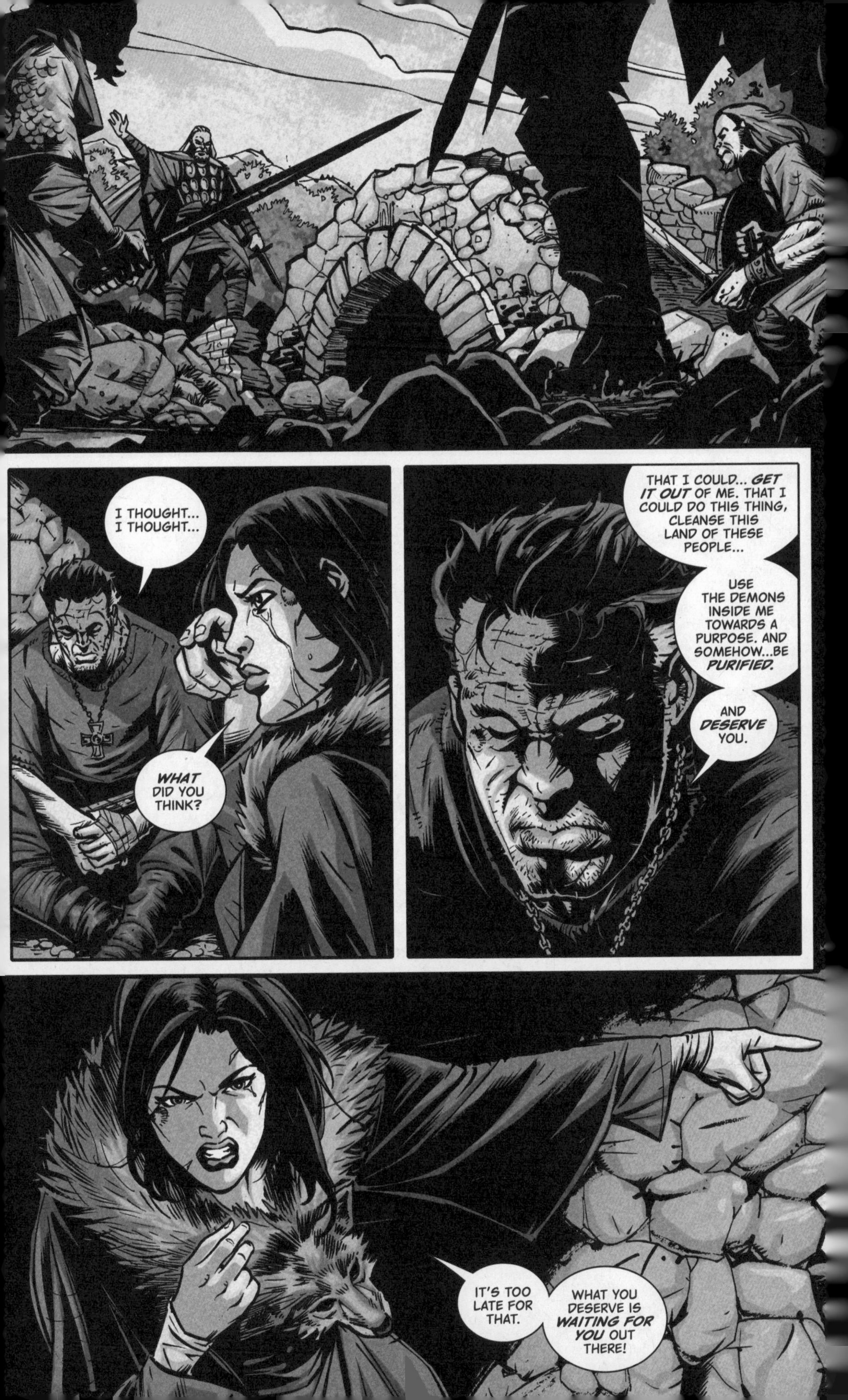
I THOUGHT... I THOUGHT...
WHAT DID YOU THINK?
THAT I COULD... GET IT OUT OF ME. THAT I COULD DO THIS THING, CLEANSE THIS LAND OF THESE PEOPLE...
USE THE DEMONS INSIDE ME TOWARDS A PURPOSE. AND SOMEHOW...BE PURIFIED.
AND DESERVE YOU.
IT'S TOO LATE FOR THAT.
WHAT YOU DESERVE IS WAITING FOR YOU OUT THERE!

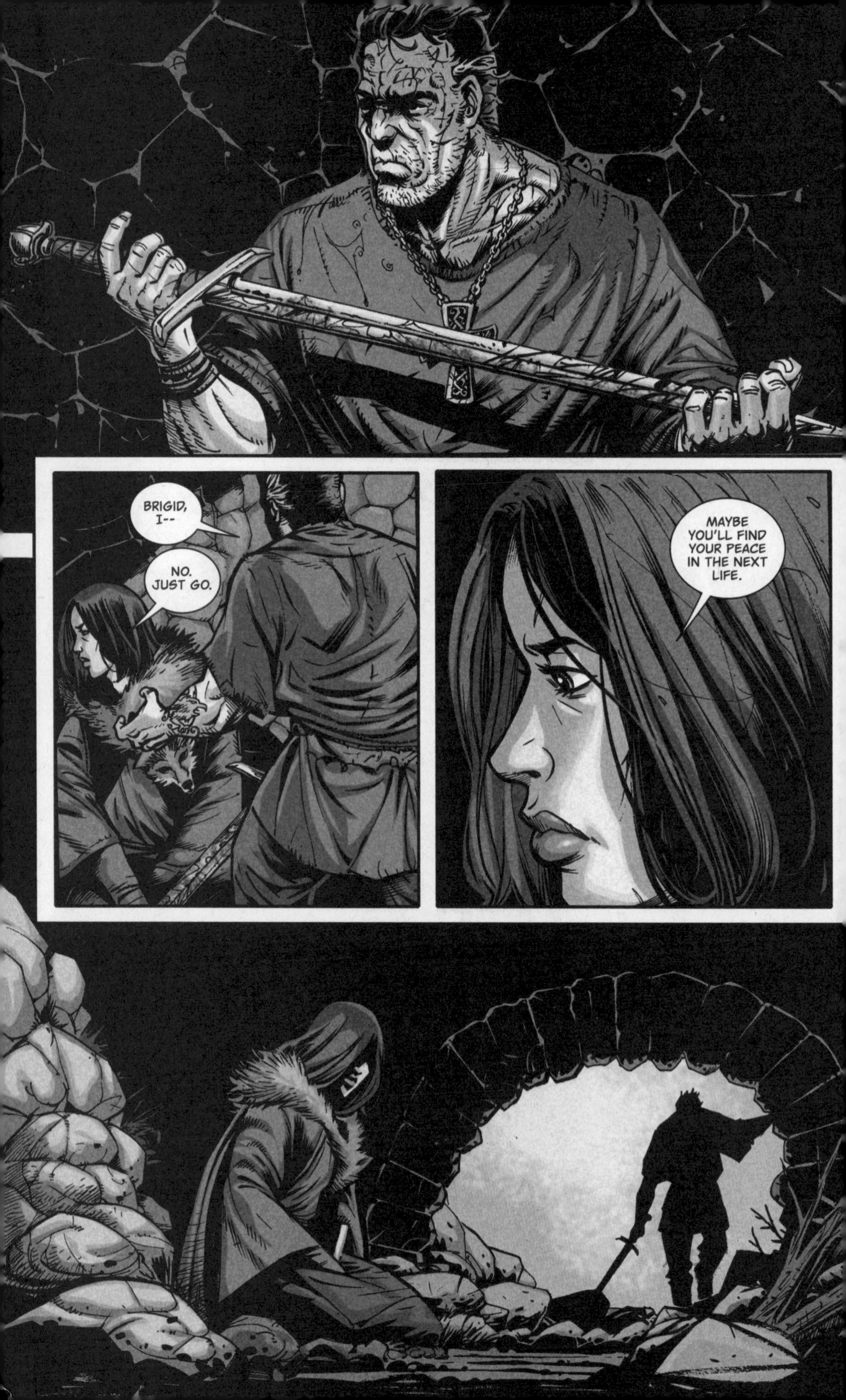
BRIGID, I--
NO. JUST GO.
MAYBE YOU'LL FIND YOUR PEACE IN THE NEXT LIFE.

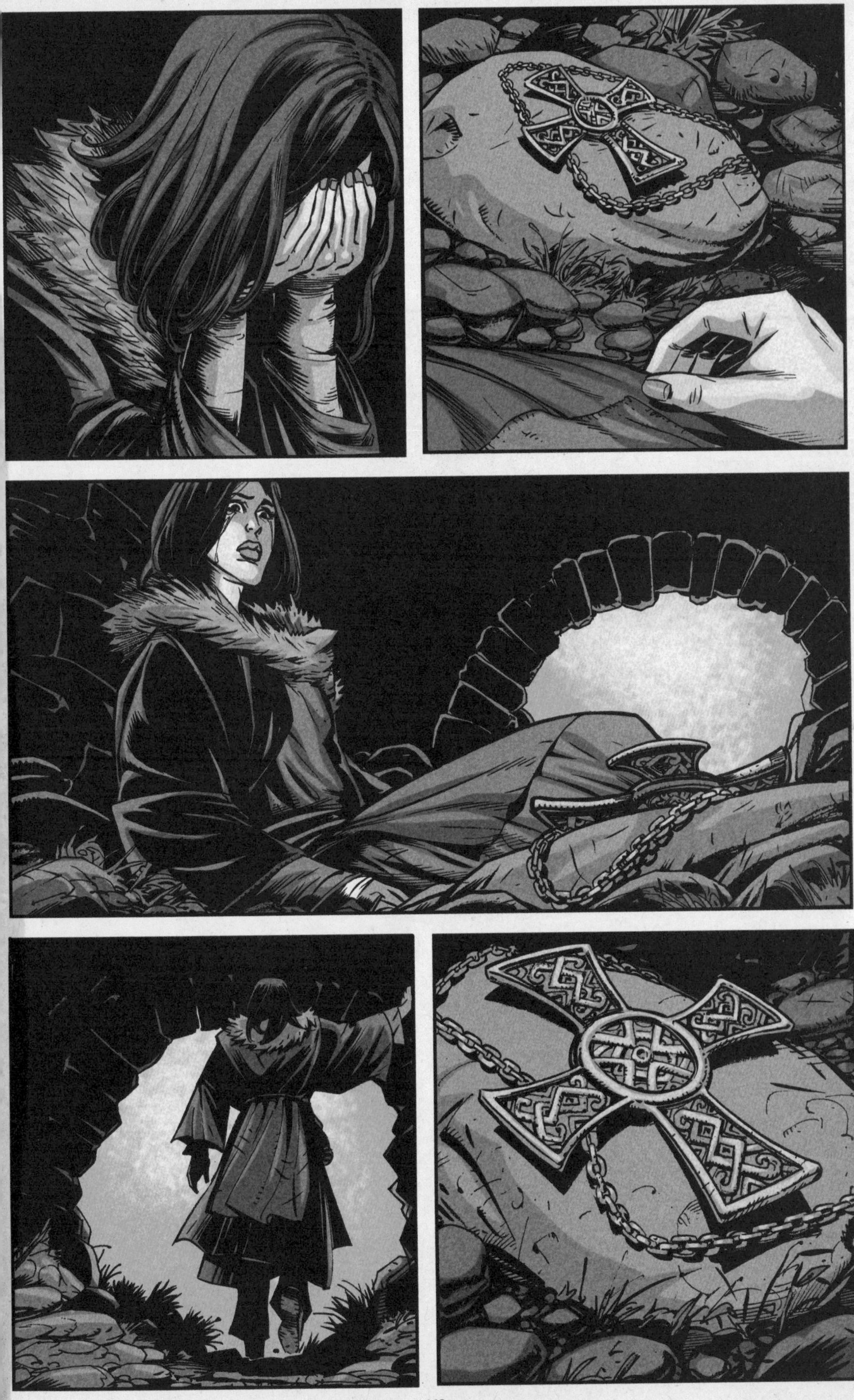

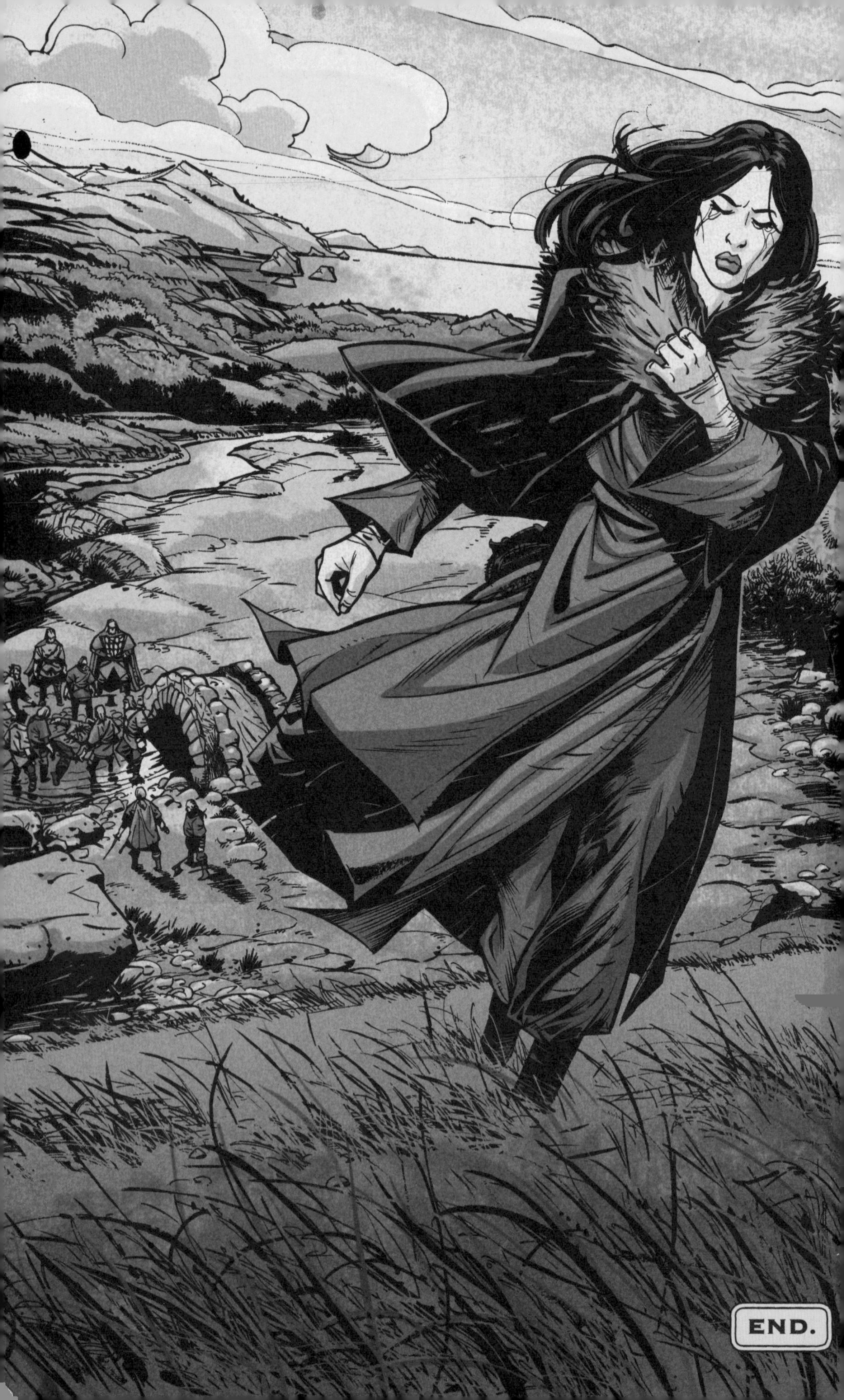
END.